"An unremittingly honest yet admiring account of Donald J. Trump. Incandescent intelligence and uplifting prose and vocabulary escort the reader on Trump's journey from hard-charging businessman to equally robust president. Deeply informative about things not well known or not reported, the book is a luminous account of our fascinating and always interesting chief."
　　　—William Bennett, bestselling author and former United States Secretary of Education

"Conrad Black's new book on Donald Trump is a brilliant analysis of the remarkable talents and unusual foibles that brought Trump to the presidency of the United States. Black knows Mr. Trump and—with his uncommon knowledge of American history—is able to place him in a fascinating context. Readers will be delighted with Black's skills as a writer—his scholarship, sense of humor, and irony are on prominent display. A must-read at this seminal juncture in American history."
　　　—The Right Honourable Brian Mulroney, former Prime Minister of Canada

DONALD J. TRUMP

Donald J. Trump

Trump

A PRESIDENT LIKE NO OTHER

CONRAD BLACK

REGNERY
PUBLISHING
A Division of Salem Media Group

Regnery® is a registered trademark of Salem Communications Holding Corporation

Cataloging-in-Publication data on file with the Library of Congress

ISBN 978-1-62157-787-4
e-book ISBN 978-1-62157-788-1

Published in the United States by
Regnery Publishing
A Division of Salem Media Group
300 New Jersey Ave NW
Washington, DC 20001
www.Regnery.com

Manufactured in the United States of America

10 9 8 7 6 5 4 3 2 1

Books are available in quantity for promotional or premium use. For information on discounts and terms, please visit our website: www.Regnery.com.

To the presidents of the United States whom it has been my privilege to know and admire: Lyndon B. Johnson, Richard M. Nixon, Gerald R. Ford, Ronald Reagan, George H. W. Bush, William J. Clinton, and Donald J. Trump.

CONTENTS

Foreword by Victor Davis Hanson   xi

Chapter 1
The Trumps in America   1

Chapter 2
Donald Trump's Financial Crisis and Recovery   23

Chapter 3
Politics Beckons   37

Chapter 4
Rebranding for Profit and Elections   47

Chapter 5
Preparing to Seek the Grand Prize   59

Chapter 6
Storming Babylon   73

Chapter 7
The Republican Nominee   91

Chapter 8
Race to the Wire   109

Chapter 9
President-Elect   129

Chapter 10
President at Last   149

Chapter 11
A Honeymoon of Hand-to-Hand Combat   167

Chapter 12
Gaining the Upper Hand   193

Acknowledgments   215
Notes   217
Index   221

FOREWORD

BY VICTOR DAVIS HANSON

Conrad Black's erudite biography of Donald J. Trump is different from the usual *in mediis rebus* accounts of first-year presidents. He avoids the Bob Woodward fly-on-the-wall unattributed anecdote, and "they say" gossip mongering. Nor is the book a rush-to-publish product from former insiders of the Trump campaign or administration. Instead, Black, a prolific and insightful historian, adopts the annalistic method in carefully tracing Trump's earliest years in business through his various commercial misadventures, financial recoveries, and sometimes wild antics. Black's aim is to illustrate how much of what Trump has done since announcing his presidential candidacy in summer 2015 is hardly mysterious. Instead, Trump's methods are fully explicable by what he has always done in the past—in the sometimes troubling, but more often reassuring, sense.

Black is neither a hagiographer nor an ankle-biter. He seeks to understand Trump within the three prominent landscapes in which Americans had come to know their new president: politics, the celebrity world, and the cannibalistic arena of high-stakes Manhattan real estate and finance. Of the three, Black is most jaded about the anti-Trump hysteria within the first two, not because the real estate business is inherently a nobler profession, but because it more often lacks the moral preening and hypocrisies of both the beltway and tabloids. The result is an argument that the first president to have neither prior political nor military service nevertheless has his own demonstrable skill sets that are making his presidency far more dynamic than either his critics or supporters quite imagined. Black's unspoken assumption is that it is more difficult to build a skyscraper in Manhattan than to be a career politician or an evening news reader.

In Trump's rise and fall and rise as a billionaire, Black never white-washes his ruthlessness, his fast and loose relationship with the truth (e.g., "He is not so much a cynic as a methodological agnostic, not a liar as much as a disbeliever in absolute secular truths"), and his occasionally tawdry P. T. Barnum hawking.

As he guides the reader through Trump's various land deals, casino crashes, name merchandising, risky hotel gambits, and golf course developments, Black offers unusual insight into how Trump, or for that matter anyone else, could survive such a rollercoaster of catastrophe and great fortune. While most of Trump's rivals share his same carnivorous ethos, very few succeeded as did Trump.

What made Trump different from his competitors? Likely, his cunning, his almost Thucydidean reading of human nature, and his sixth sense about timing and salesmanship. In Plutarchian fashion, Black focuses on Trump's physicality, especially his boundless energy and his impatience with nuance and self-doubt ("desperate cunning, unflagging determination, unshakeable self-confidence, ruthless Darwinian instincts of survival, and a sublime assurance that celebrity will heal all wounds"). Of course, the media and politicians were not ready for the naked applicability of these traits to the White House. But, as Black notes, the proverbial people after decades of misgovernance were—as if to let loose Trump on their country as both avenger and deliverer.

How many times did critics recoil in shock at Trump's coarse epithets such as "Little Marco," "Low-Energy Jeb," "Lying Ted Cruz," and "Crooked Hillary"—only to note that such appellations kept reverberating in their critics' heads, both appropriate and humorous if often cruelly so? Whose careerist agendas fared better after provoking the counter-punching Trump? For Black, Trump became president because he out-worked and outhustled his competitors, because he saw that most seasoned politicians were split-the-difference 51 percent hedgers—and that the country by 2016 desperately wanted some sort of Samson to tear down the pillars of a complacent if not corrupt establishment, even if they and their deliverer might sometimes be injured in the rubble.

Black instinctively captures the essence of the Trump paradox: how did someone supposedly so crude, so mercantile, and so insensitive display a sensitivity to the forgotten people that was lost both on his Republican competitors and Hillary Clinton? Certainly, no one on stage at any of the debates worried much about 40 percent of the country written off as John McCain's "crazies," Hillary Clinton's "deplorables" and "irre-deemables," and Barack Obama's "clingers," who were judged wanting for not capitalizing on the bicoastal dividends of American-led globalism.

Black notes the Trump-hinterland synergy. The country was looking for a third alternative to both free-market economics and neo-socialism, and yet again to both political correctness and the Republican often groveling surrender to it. Or as Black puts it, "Trump's rise was an expression of sub-revolutionary anger by a wide swath of dissatisfied and mainly not overly prosperous or influential people." But he adds that Trump was no third-party Ross Perot "charlatan" (or for that matter a Quixotic Ralph Nader), who came off quirky and without a workable agenda. Trump took a path that was far different from third-party would-be revolutionaries, in seeking to appropriate rather than to run against the apparatus of one of the two major political parties.

Most experts discounted Trump's "make American great again" visions as anachronistic in the age of Silicon Valley cool, "peak oil," the "knowledge-based" economy, and the "information age." Trump dou-bled down and became even louder about free but fair trade, legal, diverse, and meritocratic immigration, "drill, baby, drill" oil policy, lower taxes and smaller government, an end to identity politics and political correctness, and a Jacksonian deterrent foreign policy that avoided both optional nation-building and the "blame America first" apologetics of Barack Obama's lead from behind internationalism. Only half the country was ready for the Trump message (and perhaps less than that for the messenger)—but it was the more electorally important half in the key swing states of Florida, Michigan, North Carolina, Ohio, Pennsylvania, and Wisconsin. Trump assumed that even in the age of high techies and billionaire financiers, one can still not build a tower without the muscular labor of welders, cement layers, and glass installers.

Black's final third of the book is magisterial, as he recites nascent Trump achievements—tax reform, deregulation, the end of the Affordable Care Act individual mandate, superb judicial appointments, curbs on illegal immigration, expanded oil and gas production, a restoration of deterrence abroad—against a backdrop of nonstop venom and vituperation from the so-called "Resistance." He is certainly unsparing of the Left's desperate resort to discard the Electoral College, sue under the emoluments clause, invoke the Twenty-Fifth Amendment, introduce articles of impeachment, and embrace a sick assassination chic of threats to Trump's person and family. Some element of such hysteria is due to Trump's ostensible Republican credentials (the Left had devoured even their once beloved John McCain, as well as the gentlemanly and judicious Mitt Romney), but more is due to Trump's far more conservative agenda and his take-no-prisoners style.

Trump's friends and critics assure us that his incessant twittering and carnival rally-barking are suicidal. Black is too insightful to settle for such a one-dimensional critique (while often lamenting that Trump's bluster and rhetorical excess are hurting full appreciation of his otherwise solid accomplishments). Instead, Black sees much of Trump's targeting as comeuppance and long overdue—given a sanctimonious, corrupt media, and a gate-keeping political class that weakened the country over the last two decades of fiscal, social, cultural, and military irresponsibility.

Three final themes make Black's book different. One, he writes at times from firsthand experience as one who has known—and liked—Trump as an acquaintance rather than as a partner or adversary. His citation of Trump's past displays of loyalty to friends and genuine concern for the middling classes may be illustrated in Trump's most un-Republican use of the first-person plural possessive, as in "our" miners, "our" farmers, "our" vets, and "our" workers.

Second, Black knows what it is like to be targeted by an overzealous prosecutor, and how the criminal justice system can be warped well before the advent of a formal trial. For Black the yearlong and heretofore mostly empty pursuit of Trump the supposed colluder, then Trump the purported obstructer, is in some sad sense the logical trajectory of the American criminal justice system that gives federal prosecutors unchecked power, especially when driven by political agendas amplified by the tabloid press. Few of us have ever had a Robert Mueller hounding us 24/7, with partisan lawyers, opportune leaks, and false news fueling his inquisition.

Finally, Black is a singular prose stylist of what in the ancient world would be called the Asiatic, or florid and decorative, style—multisyllabic and sometimes near archaic vocabulary, ornate imagery, melodic prose rhythms, diverse syntax, and classical tropes of deliberate understatement, juxtapositions of Latinate and Anglo-Saxon words, and plentiful metaphors and similes. In the modern world, few in English write (or can write) any more like Edward Gibbon or Winston Churchill, but Black does so effortlessly and with precision. So it is often a treat to read an Isocrates or Cicero in modern English.

Most readers, like myself, have never met either Conrad Black nor Donald J. Trump. But after reading this engaging biography, those of any political persuasion would wish to do both.

CHAPTER 1

The Trumps in America

The traits that elevated Donald Trump to the White House are the traits of America. It was not a country of a culture and language of its own; but a land of dreams and discovery, of aspiration and mystery, with its carefully devised mythos of freedom and opportunity. The legend was the future and not the past. America's rise to greatness has been a mélange of toil, fortune, and heroism, but with a touch of the gimcrack and of the illusory: where dream and sham sometimes conjoin. Many great American personalities combined these elements to some degree in their own personalities. Jefferson was partially a poseur; Hamilton an impetuous adventurer; Aaron Burr a scoundrel; Fremont, MacArthur, Halsey, and Patton were swashbuckling egotists and to a degree mythmakers. FDR was in part a political trickster of extraordinary virtuosity. The Kennedys, LBJ, Nixon, Reagan (a genuine man but full of Hollywood tinsel too), even the Clintons, and Donald Trump all have admirable qualities and have rendered great service, but none has been an altogether straight arrow. Many of the most hallowed events in American history were neither inevitable nor as nobly intended as they have been presented. It has rarely been George Washington and the cherry tree or Honest Abe splitting rails, and when it goes wrong, as with Aaron Burr, or Nixon in his second term, it can go badly wrong.

Like the country he represents, Donald Trump possesses the optimism to persevere and succeed, the confidence to affront tradition and convention, a genius for spectacle, and a firm belief in common sense and the common man.

His rise, like America's, has been vertiginous. His proclamation of making America great again echoes a longstanding American belief that this nation's greatness was predestined and would be ever-expanding. That greatness has been put at risk on many occasions, and in the last twenty years, Americans have been prone to ever greater self-doubt about America's virtues and prospects. Nothing has done more to divide Americans than the Left's rejection of the traditional melting pot in favor of identity politics, magnifying the grievances of atomized "minority groups," delegitimizing American history, and casting doubt on the entire American enterprise, though always in the name of perfecting it. For a long time, this insidious trend has been largely unopposed—until Donald Trump gave voice to those tens of millions of Americans who opposed it and thought they were losing their country and were largely ignored or forgotten.

Donald Trump's nature has always been to believe that almost anything can be achieved—that almost any obstacle and challenge can be overcome—through very hard work and cunning. It is also his nature, honed by the rough and tumble of his career, including observing his father's business, to believe that no competitive activity beyond the playing field (if that) is quite as pristine as represented. He is not so much a cynic as a methodological agnostic, not a liar as much as a disbeliever in absolute secular truths. He sees most political correctness as peddled by the media and the establishment, as sham and hypocrisy.

Trump is untroubled by what he calls his "truthful hyperbole" and "alternate facts" that are "essentially true." Trump rarely tells outright lies, such as the media endlessly impute to him, and a political leader who fudges facts is hardly unprecedented. For Trump, establishing the facts of a matter is as much a competition as anything else.

Trump is widely, and correctly, seen as leading a populist movement, meaning an expression of middle- and working-class and agrarian discontent, and remedies of the non-revolutionary Left, or as in this case, of pragmatic and humane conservatism. Though the United States has, historically, been fertile populist ground, it has never in America been escalated into revolution. Even the struggle for independence was preeminently an act of secession, challenging remote British rule and establishing local self-government. It did not overturn the socioeconomic organization of the country. Likewise, the Civil War was not so much a revolution as a second war of secession, seeking the retention of slaveholding and with the Confederate Constitution modeled on the United States Constitution. While populist and apparently shoot-from-the-hip in its spontaneity and boosterism ("It will be huge!"), the Trump campaign of 2016 was very carefully calibrated and rather conservative, but not at all extreme.

Just as Mrs. Clinton kept the party of Roosevelt and his successors out of the hands of the wild-eyed Left led by the loopy Democratic Marxist senator Bernie Sanders, Trump threw out the bathwater of the indistinct, post-Reagan Republican establishment without fumbling the gurgling infant, the GOP itself, into the hands of the often agile paleoconservative smoothie, Senator Ted Cruz. Trump's election program was really moderate conservatism, which he successfully sold to centrists and Reagan Democrats as a mighty improvement on Obaman quasi-socialist declinism, and with polemical pyrotechnics about illegal immigration and law enforcement, to right-wing and Tea Party elements as radical change. In the brilliant American tradition of political hucksterism that has almost always attended even the noblest official American causes, Donald Trump sold the same political agenda, dressed in different packaging, to the Center and to the Right.

Donald Trump has never suffered from a lack of confidence, and while he climbed the rickety ladder of American celebrity, he always suspected that the highest political office could be achieved by an unorthodox route. He believed he understood the American people; he had sold them his wares and himself at every socioeconomic echelon, and had long been consistent on some key political subjects: a strong military and law enforcement, education reform, and America-first priorities on trade and immigration. He considered himself a political realist, doubting that most of his presidential predecessors were as impeccably selfless as posterity has portrayed them. Many of these attitudes and beliefs come directly from his personal experience and family history.

■ ■ ■

The first Trump in America was Donald's grandfather, Friedrich Drumpf (it is not clear exactly when the family name was changed, perhaps on arrival in America), who came from Germany in 1885 aged sixteen. He made his way west, first to Seattle and then to the Canadian Yukon. He operated restaurants, bars, and hotels catering to prospectors, and the other adventurers of the area. Most accounts allege that he was in fact operating whorehouses and clip joints, sometimes with no lease or title to the land.[1] Friedrich moved to the Bronx after marrying his German childhood sweetheart, Elizabeth Christ, and bringing her to America. He built up some small real estate holdings, including five vacant lots in New York's outer boroughs. It was enough to build on. Friedrich died in the great influenza epidemic of 1918, aged only forty-nine. Elizabeth, however, lived on into the 1960s, to the age of eighty-five, working for her son, Donald Trump's father, Fred, collecting the coins from automatic vending and laundry machines in Trump properties.

Donald Trump's father lived in Queens. One of his early successes was building government-subsidized housing, especially for armed servicemen returning from World War II. He later became a successful builder of middle-class homes in New York's outer suburbs. He married Mary McLeod, who had emigrated from the sparse and remote Scottish Outer Hebrides island of Lewis, in 1930, when she was eighteen. She worked as a nanny and domestic servant, and met Fred Trump by chance at a party in 1935. It was love at first sight and they were married at a Madison Avenue Presbyterian church on January 11, 1936.

Donald John Trump, the fourth child of Fred and Mary Trump, was born in New York City on June 14, 1946. His sister Maryanne was nine years older, his brother Fred Jr. was seven years older, his sister Elizabeth was four, and another brother, Robert, was born in 1948. He grew up in a commodious Queens twenty-three-room home that crowded its double-lot. His father was always working, and on weekends and holidays sometimes took his children to inspect projects. He was chauffeured everywhere in two Cadillac limousines, license plates FT 1 and FT 2. (These were the first sprouts of a public egotism that in the next fifty years would emblazon the whole world.)

Where Fred was reserved and unsociable (he took a Dale Carnegie course at one point to lighten up a bit),[2] Mary was affable and outgoing. The Presbyterian Trumps were churchgoers, lived frugally, worked hard, and were strict enough as parents that when they learned that Donald—an alert, confident, and mischievous child—had been playing with a switchblade, they resolved to send him to New York Military Academy, a Spartan boarding school. Donald adapted quickly, being naturally punctual, organized, hard-working, proud of appearances, and a good athlete. He did well in school and graduated with distinction in 1964.

In the summers, he worked for his father, chauffeuring, running errands, and working in a machine shop. He was thorough and diligent; he became adept at many of the building trades and got along well with his colleagues, despite being the son of the boss.[3] He attended Fordham University, and after two years transferred to the Wharton School of Business Administration of the University of Pennsylvania, which had a course in real estate development. He graduated in 1968 and went to work for his father. He had a prodigious work ethic and mastered every aspect of his father's business, down to cleaning boilers, costing carpeting, and mixing anti-cockroach insecticide himself to avoid the expense of exterminators.

The industrious Trump earned his father's confidence and in 1972 was named president of The Trump Organization. (His father became chairman.) Donald was only twenty-six, and he moved to a modest midtown, mid-level Manhattan apartment, making a reverse commute every day to the Trump office on Avenue Z in Brooklyn.

One of their first major challenges was rebutting Justice Department accusations that they had discriminated against African American tenants. Donald hired controversial lawyer Roy Cohn whose cut-throat strategy was: never surrender, counterattack at once, and claim victory no matter what really happened. Cohn advised the Trumps to countersue the U.S. government, which they did. The result was a settlement in which the Trumps admitted no wrongdoing, and in a technique that would become familiar to America and the world, claimed victory (which was neither altogether true nor entirely false).

Roy Cohn had become famous as counsel to red-baiting Senator Joseph R. McCarthy in the Communist scare of the early fifties, and advised many prominent conservatives, including Richard Nixon, Ronald Reagan, and Francis J. Cardinal Spellman. This was one of Donald's introductions to politics. In what would become a fateful and even historic relationship, Cohn also introduced Rupert Murdoch to Donald Trump in 1973.

If Trump had not been noticeably politically active before, he was certainly interested in politics now. He knew many Vietnam War veterans, particularly among his fellow alumni of the New York Military Academy, and he supported Richard Nixon's successful appeal to the "Silent Majority" to support his "Vietnamization" of the war that gradually withdrew American forces and replaced them with South Vietnamese, trained, supplied, and heavily supported from the air by the United States.

The Watergate debacle, partly due to Nixon's mismanagement, caused the evaporation of executive authority and led to the immolation of one of the most successful presidencies in American history. The Democrats in the Congress seized the opportunity to cut off all assistance to South Vietnam and doomed Indochina to the murderous attention of the Viet Minh, Viet Cong, Khmer Rouge, and Pathet Lao, and millions perished. As Trump watched the assault on Nixon, the disorderly rout in Vietnam as the Democrats undid Nixon's "peace with honor," and the irresolution of the Carter administration, he believed he saw the failure of the self-proclaimed best and brightest, the Eastern Establishment, the Ivy League, and the career State Department. The national media, academia, and the Democratic political establishment celebrated the defeat in Vietnam and the Watergate putsch as triumphs of American integrity, but the thirtyish Donald Trump strongly suspected that this was self-serving claptrap thinly masking a series of largely self-induced national disasters. Though under very different circumstances, Trump would become intimately familiar with the shameless guerrilla tactics of the same media, academic, and political elites who had bloodlessly assassinated Nixon. He was forewarned.

■ ■ ■

In the mid-1970s, New York City was almost bankrupt, a fact that the young Trump saw as an opportunity to pick up property cheaply, never doubting that New York would recover swiftly, and he was assiduous in building political relationships, including with Abraham Beame, a friend of his father's and soon to become mayor, and Brooklyn Congressman Hugh Carey, who was about to become the Democratic governor of New York, after four terms of Republican Nelson Rockefeller (who became vice president of the United States in 1974).

Donald Trump's first great real estate score resulted from intensive negotiation and maneuvering over several years after the bankruptcy of the ramshackle and dysfunctional merger of the Northeast's two largest railroads into Penn Central. Trump made clever and opportunistic sidedeals with lawyers for angry shareholders and other interested parties in the terribly complex court proceedings, and emerged with court authorization in 1975 to develop the railway yards along the Manhattan side of the Hudson River, 120 acres from 34th to 60th Streets. In the end, the deal, after unimaginably complicated negotiations, did not proceed, because Trump could not find investors on terms which made him confident of an adequate profit, but it gave him immense publicity, due to his frequent press conferences, extravagant claims, and endless presentation of ambitious architectural renderings. He did ultimately collect on his option, as the City eventually determined to build the Jacob K. Javits Convention Center at the southern end of the yards. As a plausible Manhattan property developer, he had arrived.

Donald did crack the New York market with the acquisition and renovation of the Commodore Hotel and its metamorphosis into the glass-sheathed and completely modernized Park Hyatt. The hotel and the city were so desperate that Trump risked little money and recruited the Hyatt chain owned by Chicago's Pritzker family; his timing was exemplary.

The area around Grand Central Station had deteriorated; the Commodore was between the railway terminal and the fabled Chrysler Building. Texaco had departed the Chrysler Building, which fell into receivership, and crime was rampant. Business was fleeing to the suburbs, and commuters were coming by car or subway more than trains. Trump was gambling on an immediate revival of a very decrepit area. But he didn't gamble much. He told Penn Central he had a firm deal with Hyatt before he did, called a press conference in May 1975 to announce that he had signed a deal with the railway to buy the hotel (named after the founder of the New York Central, Commodore Cornelius Vanderbilt), and he had, but the railway had not yet signed and Trump had not paid the $250,000 option fee, but that did not deter Trump from unveiling elaborate plans for the Commodore, by an architect his father had commissioned. Trump used what looked like a finalized agreement with Penn Central, but wasn't, to satisfy the city of his bona fides, and the New York municipal legal department, as Trump surmised would be the case, did not scrutinize the agreement diligently enough to realize what it was.

The city, pressed by alleged deadlines and not wishing the deal to lapse and to be blamed for it and hounded by Trump, approved the project, whereupon Hyatt came aboard and Penn Central signed and returned Trump's offer which he had led the press to believe at his press conference was already an enforceable contract. Even at this point, Trump had no financial backing to carry out the project, and his calls on the banking system for a construction loan were not successful. But he managed to persuade the almost dormant Urban Development Corporation to spare him and Hyatt $400 million of taxes over forty years by a sale-leaseback arrangement, although there was vehement agitation by other hoteliers against such a giveaway, and they claimed that they could do a better deal. Trump bluffed them down before he had the arrangement with Penn Central, and then saw them off after his tax deal with the UDC and the transaction was rushed through. It was a brilliant coup, though practical and commercial challenges remained.

The reconstruction was complicated as the Commodore had deteriorated more seriously than Trump had realized; homeless men squatted in the boiler rooms and rats were so large and numerous they drove out an inadequate number of cats that Trump's builders had inserted to exterminate them: human and feline reinforcements were deployed.[4] Once the project was in hand, the participants had to see it through. It was renovated as a luxury hotel and reopened in 1980 to great fanfare with five hundred fewer bedrooms, but still fourteen hundred, and seventy thousand square feet of retail space. It was a huge success and Trump turned (and deserved) a very fine profit, in several stages. The renovated hotel contributed importantly to the revival of the area. Trump sold his interest to Hyatt in 1996 for $142 million. Given what he managed to conceive and reap in profit on such a small initial stake, by creativity, bravura, and relentless persistence, it is little wonder that he came to believe that he could achieve almost any goal he sought if he understood the components of the challenge.

Donald Trump met Ivana Zelnickova Winklmayr a fugitive from Czech communism, in 1976, in either Montreal or New York, depending on the vintage of the account from Donald or Ivana. Winklmayr was a marriage of convenience to get her through the Iron Curtain and to Canada, and the marriage was virtually dissolved on arrival. There was initially a Trump-propagated myth that she was on the Czech Olympic ski team; she seems to have been a model, though not the "super model" Donald intermittently torqued himself up to allege. Trump was now thirty and with his parents' fine marriage as an example, he fancied taking a loyal wife for "support at home, not someone who's always griping and bitching."[5]

Ivana seemed to fit that bill and she found him "just a nice all-American kid, tall and smart, lots of energy: very bright and very good-looking." She claimed not to have noticed that he was also "famous" or "fabulously wealthy." Their courtship, replete with arguments over a prenuptial agreement, was played out in the gossip columns of New York and the blessed event was an on-again-off-again affair for months as Roy Cohn conducted the financial negotiations. Ivana balked at having to return gifts from Donald if the marriage broke down. Trump conceded that point and agreed to a $100,000 "rainy day fund" that was essentially a checking account set aside for her that she could begin using after one month of wedded bliss. They were married by Norman Vincent Peale, whom Fred and Donald Trump admired and supported for his "Power of Positive Thinking," at Peale's Marble Collegiate Church, which they had often attended. It was just before Easter 1977. The reception was at the 21 Club, and was attended by about two hundred people, including the mayor of New York, Abraham Beame. Donald and Ivana would have two sons, Donald Jr. (born 1977) and Eric (born 1984), and a daughter, Ivanka (born 1981).

If Donald was rising, his older brother, Fred Trump Jr., was falling. Fred, a former airline pilot, had left the Trump Organization and moved to Florida, where he failed to find success, and then moved back to New York and worked as a maintenance man. He died of chronic alcoholism in September 1981, aged forty-two. It was a great sadness and Donald mourned him, mourns him yet, and redoubled his own determination never to drink.

Trump's most famous project, which started to germinate in 1978, is now one of the most famous buildings in America—Trump Tower at Fifth Avenue and 56th Street, seven hundred feet tall, a splendid glass and brass multi-faceted sawtooth façade with a large atrium. It is one of the largest buildings in the country with a poured concrete, rather than structural steel, skeleton, and a champion of mixed use: retail, office, and residential. Even in the eyes of his critics, it was a splendid building. It was also the first skyscraper in the world whose construction was supervised by a woman, an exceptionally talented engineer, Barbara Res. She and other senior Trump women executives are routinely overlooked by those who delight in accusing Trump of sexism and misogyny. Donald Trump took a three-story, fifty-three-room penthouse of extraordinary opulence for himself and Ivana and Donald Junior.

Throughout this period, Trump was constantly on the move, in his chauffeur-driven car, looking for building sites. He singled out the Bonwit Teller site on Fifth Avenue, found out who owned the lease (the Genesco Corporation), and secured an option to buy out the lease for $25 million. This gave him a blocking position, but he couldn't do anything without the land, owned by Equitable Life, and the air rights, which were owned by Tiffany and Company, the world-famous jeweler next door. After his success at the Commodore, Trump got from Chase Manhattan a loan to buy Tiffany's rights and a hundred-million-dollar construction loan, and got the land from Equitable, which had had a happy experience with Trump at the Commodore, in exchange for a half interest in the Trump Tower project.

His radical plan was widely praised, with one exception. He initially said he would keep two friezes and a bronze grill above the door at Bonwit's, and give them to the Metropolitan Museum in exchange for a generous tax treatment of the gift. In the event, Trump had his crew destroy the objects, claiming they had no value and would have cost more than $30,000 to transport. It was a crude and clumsy move that changed his public relations status in New York and was widely presented as a know-nothing, brutal, destructive act: philistinism as well as bad faith. The *New York Times* called it "aesthetic vandalism." He has never explained why he didn't scoop up the goodwill with the tax deduction. This avoidable blunder and others like it have dogged his career ever since.

The Bonwit building was too tightly enclosed to be reducible with wrecking balls and had to be deconstructed by special work crews. Polish workers were imported without working visas and worked double shifts, seven days a week at below the minimum wage under a threat of deportation. They were agile craftsmen but not a happy workforce. Many resided at the site and there were constant squabbles about back pay. As the job wound up in 1983, The House Wreckers Union sued Trump for deliberately employing undocumented workers under illegal conditions. He denied knowing they were in the country illegally, and the lawsuit was settled confidentially in 1999. The incident reveals Trump to be a tight-fisted, devious employer, a very tenacious litigant, and an efficient and imaginative developer. It was somewhat piquant when, presumably contemplating politics, more than twenty years later, he called illegal immigration "a wrecker's ball aimed at U.S. taxpayers."[6]

There was further controversy over the alleged facts that there were no work-stoppages at Trump Tower, even when there was a city-wide strike in the building trades in 1982. The girlfriend of the local head of the Teamsters' Union, which controlled the cement trucks, had an apparently free condo in the complex, just below the floors Trump himself occupied. This whole tawdry but comical episode was dragged out in court and the woman in question resorted to hilarious explanations of how she lived so opulently with no income. When the union boss, John Cody, was imprisoned for a racketeering conviction, Trump evicted his girlfriend for non-payment of maintenance fees, and the condo was seized by her creditors and resold. (When asked under oath why her unit was almost unfurnished, she explained that the contents were stored, but she couldn't remember where: "In America, Brooklyn, who knows where these things go?") When Cody died in 2001, Trump called the convicted racketeer "a psychopathic crazy bastard...real scum."[7]

Trump also built, almost simultaneously, a fine East Side co-op called Trump Plaza, and a complex at Columbus Circle which he called Trump Parc, after a battle with tenants in an elegant limestone building that he wished to fold into the development. Many of the tenants were well-to-do and fiercely resisted Trump's antics to move them out, such as reducing lighting in the halls and taking lounge chairs out of the lobby, and "offering" to house the homeless, in practice usually hallucinating schizophrenics and drug abusers, in unoccupied units in the complex. These and other controversies, as well as Donald's (and his critics') ever more publicized forays into hyperbole (one critic called his Trump Tower penthouse "Louis XIV on LSD" and Donald himself compared his painted ceiling there to Michelangelo's Sistine Chapel), caused Donald's fame to soar but the nature of his publicity in the New York media to turn sharply negative. Garry Trudeau's *Doonesbury* cartoons depicted Trump in a gigantic yacht cutting a path through small boats, a reference to Trump's acquisition of a 282-foot yacht formerly owned by Saudi arms dealer Adnan Khashoggi. Donald renamed it the *Trump Princess* and docked it at Atlantic City as a special domain for high rollers at the casinos he would soon buy there. (He doesn't like boats very much.) The yacht cost $29 million and eight million more in renovations. The *New York Times*, which had earlier profiled him as a Robert Redford figure whose chief fault was speaking too rapidly, now wrote he would be "a shoo-in for a stupendous unpopularity prize."[8]

None of this negative press reduced his ability to command astounding prices for residential units, especially at Trump Tower. While he was regarded by many as a vulgar and garish egomaniac, it *was* New York, and he was also much admired as an aggressive businessman, a quality developer, and a man with a common touch who bore as a badge of honor the disparagements of the rich and tony of the Upper East Side, Upper West Side, and Gramercy Park. (His early exposure and partial immunization to harsh media treatment would serve him well later in his career.)

Before Trump, most of New York's great landlords and developers tried to avoid personal publicity, but Trump believed he was developing not only buildings but a mighty brand that could be translated into widespread success. He wasn't interested in, as he called it, just "collecting rent." He had bigger dreams than that. (He also had personal experience of collecting rent. As a summer job, he once collected rent for his father. He learned, he told me, not to stand in front of the tenant's door, because a summons for rent could be met by gunfire.)

Trump reasoned that all publicity was good publicity and that even the negative media attention revealed him as a formidable, if ruthless and not entirely ethical, operator. The Tower was an instant success and all units were pre-sold for $277 million, retiring all debt before the building opened. It continues to be a much-admired building. The early unit buyers included Steven Spielberg, Michael Jackson, and Johnny Carson, and the retail space was taken up by high-end luxury tenants like Mondi, Harry Winston, and Asprey.

In 1983, Trump paid $9 million for the New Jersey Generals, a team in the United States Football league, which was a second tier to the National Football League, and played in the spring and early summer to avoid direct competition with it. But Trump immediately began raiding the NFL for players, called for direct competition with the NFL, and had Roy Cohn sue the NFL for $1.32 billion for monopolistic practices. Trump testified effectively at the trial, but, although jurors agreed that the NFL was a monopoly, they failed to find any harm or damage, and awarded one dollar to the plaintiff. As was his practice, Donald claimed a moral victory, but soon abandoned being a football team owner, having apparently lost around $20 million in the process. He had considered it part of the enabling costs to build a splendid, multi-sport, all-weather stadium for the New York area, but that did not happen. None of the metropolitan area's nine major league franchises in baseball, football, basketball, or hockey could be enticed.

■ ■ ■

His next commercial foray was into the casino business. Trump discovered that the Hilton chain of 150 hotels made more than a third of its profits from two large hotels in Las Vegas. When New Jersey voted to legalize gambling, he hoped New York would do the same. Politics, however, made that unlikely, especially after the Abscam scandal,[9] so he made further reconnaissance trips to Atlantic City. Trump selected a site, bought out the previous owners, and gained a license (giving Norman Vincent Peale as a character reference).

To finance it, he set up a partnership with Holiday Inn. Together they built the Trump Plaza in 1984, with sixty thousand feet of casino floor space, making it one of the biggest casinos in the world. When, two years later, Hilton's casino license application was denied, Trump bought that property, with Manufacturers Hanover Bank providing $320 million of financing for what became the Trump Castle.

Holiday Inn, however, was less than enchanted by Trump's acquisition, putting their partner in direct competition a couple of miles away. After a merciless media war between Trump and Holiday Inn, Holiday Inn cut and ran, and Trump became New Jersey's leading casino owner; the Trump Plaza became the Trump Palace; and Trump reaped an enormous profit on his greenmail stock-trading, even after subtracting related legal expenses (including a settlement with the Federal Trade Commission in which he, typically, admitted no guilt but paid a fine. If it had been a strong case, he would have faced the SEC rather than the FCC).

In December 1985, Donald Trump bought the formidable Mar-a-Lago estate of Post Cereals heiress Marjorie Merriweather Post in Palm Beach, Florida. He paid only $8 million for the sumptuous house, less than its original cost to build, and turned it into a club and a money-spinning property, as well as, eventually, a presidential winter residence. Across the Inland Waterway from Mar-a-Lago, he also bought a distressed condominium project, for just two thirds of the value of the mortgage on it, and renamed it the Trump Plaza of the Palm Beaches. It, however, was a less successful investment.

The bonanza in Atlantic City coincided with a rise in New York real estate values and in 1986 *Forbes Magazine* rated Donald Trump, just forty, the fiftieth wealthiest man in America, with a net worth of $700 million, and that was not counting any of his father's $200 million or more.

Trump's addiction to the casino industry after his initial successes was almost fatal. Presumably intoxicated with his impressive gains and vindicated intuition, in 1988 he paid $365 million, almost all of it borrowed, to buy routes and aircraft from Eastern Airlines and to run a shuttle service between Washington, New York, and Boston. Almost simultaneously, he borrowed $407 million to buy the illustrious Plaza Hotel. And then he reached for his third casino in Atlantic City, the gigantic, half-completed Taj Mahal. It was being constructed by Resorts International, when the controlling shareholder of that company, James Crosby, died and the company lost its way. Trump bought stock from some of Crosby's heirs. While Trump's entourage was cautious, he thought that with the Trump Palace and Trump Castle, he would dominate gambling on the East Coast. In 1986, however, because of intense competition and indifferent management, Atlantic City's casinos generated $2.5 billion in revenue but only $74 million in profit; it was not a high-margin business and needed rationalization. In February 1988, Trump assured the Casino Control Commission of New Jersey that he could easily finance the completion of the Taj, a planned one-thousand-room hotel with immense and opulent gambling facilities, without resorting to junk bonds.

But Trump's marriage and his casino ventures were both beginning to fail. His wife, Ivana, was in charge of the Trump Castle Casino, and the property had gone into loss. His casino group manager, the astute Stephen Hyde, and Ivana did not get on. Ivana worked hard and had some aptitude for the business, but Donald decided to pack her off to run the Plaza Hotel, hoping for better results. He was also having an affair with Marla Maples, a startlingly attractive woman, almost a Marilyn Monroe look-alike, and a former homecoming queen and second-level model from Dalton, Georgia, "the carpet capital of America." It didn't splash into public view until 1989, but there was considerable strain on both the marital and business relationship of the Trumps. At her parting ceremony from the Trump Castle Casino, Ivana became emotional and wept. it was the occasion for one of Donald's more déclassé performances. He told the gathered employees: "Look at this. I had to buy a $350 million hotel just to get her out of here and look at how she's crying. Now that's why I'm sending her back to New York. I don't need this, some woman crying. I need somebody strong in here."[10]

Trump got his way with the commission, but his privatization bid for Resorts International was challenged by television star and producer Merv Griffin, who put up a 245-million-dollar competing offer. They compromised, with Griffin taking Resorts International's existing casinos in

Atlantic City and Trump getting the Taj Mahal as part of the deal. Banks were not conspicuously enthused, and Trump had to cut both the costs of his hotel and stoop to the issuance of $675 million of the junk bonds he had promised to avoid, at a scorching yield of 14 percent.

By acquiring airlines, the Plaza Hotel, and the Taj Mahal, Trump was rolling the dice like his casino patrons, and the odds were not appreciably better.

That didn't stop him from placing more bets on a continuation of the Reagan economic boom. In January 1985, Trump had bought the Penn Central yards from 34th Street to 60th Street along the Hudson riverside, on which he had negotiated an option ten years before. He proposed a fantastically vast project, Television City, including the world's tallest building, 1,910 feet high, a row of seven other buildings of approximately eighty stories, and an immense new studio for NBC, which had proclaimed that it had grown too large for Rockefeller Center and needed to move.

In the spring of 1986, to dramatize his competence to undertake this great project, he engaged in an acerbic public exchange with the combative mayor of New York, Ed Koch, over the city's inability to get the Wollman ice rink in Central Park back into active use. It had been idle for more than three years and the renovation was $7 million over allotted cost. He offered to get the rink working in four months and at cost and Koch accepted in very sarcastic and skeptical terms. Trump recruited a team that had just built the new arena for Montreal's frequently world champion hockey team Les Canadiens. Trump outdid himself in holding press conferences for every stage of the proceedings—laying pipe, pouring cement, and so forth—and delivered the rink in functioning order two months early and $750,000 under budget. It was a tremendous public relations success, but not a wise tactic for recruiting the mayor's support of Television City, without which, the project could not proceed.

Koch finally approved Trump's application for the Television City project but under tax terms that gave it no prospect for economic success, even after it was pared down significantly from Trump's original extraordinary plan. Trump pulled out and blamed NBC also (it had opted to stay in enlarged premises at Rockefeller Center). He and Koch were worthy adversaries as verbal jousters. Koch had denounced those who voted for other candidates in the Democratic primary for governor of New York in 1982, as rubes living amongst "cows and pigs, and forests," not a great vote winner upstate. In this case, Trump called Koch a "moron" and said he should be impeached for involvement in the customary financial skullduggery of New York municipal officials. Koch responded with high amusement that Trump was "squealing like a stuck pig," and warmed to the theme, accusing him of greed and repeating: "Piggy, piggy, piggy." Trump rode the mayor for a while, offering to speed up the renovation of Central Park Zoo and taking out full-page advertisements in the New York newspapers attacking Koch's softness and placatory statements when a young woman was brutally raped and nearly killed in Central Park.

A few weeks later he began what would prove a very successful side-career as a promoter of championship prize fights, starting in Atlantic City with a bout between Michael Spinks and Gary Cooney. It was in Atlantic City also, that he developed his interest in beauty pageants, where he would become a great impresario.

At the same time as the corporate tussle with Merv Griffin over Resorts International, Trump's marital and romantic pressures finally surged into the public domain and became a serious distraction. In February 1990, after rumors had been intense but unpublished for months, Ivana gave the story to Liz Smith, veteran columnist of the *New York Daily News*, while Donald was in Japan trying to sell the Plaza Hotel and watching a Mike Tyson prizefight. With the *News* story out, the *New York Post*—which had had the story but had been restrained from publishing by its owner, Peter Kalikow, who was a friend of Trump's—leapt into the fray and the two newspapers competed for which would give the most column inches to the Trump affair. Marla's and Ivana's photos and statistics were published and compared, as if they were two prizefighters before a championship bout. The *News* divided celebrities according to which side they were allegedly on: Cher,

Elton John, and Frank Sinatra sided with Donald and Marla; Calvin Klein, Oprah Winfrey, and Princess Diana sided with Ivana; President and Mrs. Bush were undecided. (Almost all of this was rank fabrication.) The *Post* came back with an alleged remark of Marla's about Donald: "Best sex I've ever had." The controversy was stoked up by a semi-public confrontation between Ivana and Marla at a café on Aspen Mountain in early 1990. When rumors swirled that their relationship was falling apart, Trump, pretending to be his publicist rather than himself, responded to a call from a *Post* reporter and said that Trump had split with Marla but had lots of possible replacements, including Carla Bruni (future first lady of France) and Madonna. Not only did Trump glory in all the vulgar tabloid attention, but it apparently boosted his brand. All the publicity coincided with increased revenues at his casinos and at the Plaza Hotel.

Donald and Marla eventually married at the Plaza in December 1993, with a thousand guests in attendance. Howard Stern, the opinionated and outrageous radio personality, said he thought the marriage would last "four months." Retired football star O. J. Simpson said that if this marriage lasted, "anyone's relationship can work." (He was accused of murdering his ex-wife six months later, but was acquitted.) The *Times*' acid comment on the wedding was that there "wasn't a wet eye in the house." Trump announced that the caviar at the reception had cost him $690,000. It was far from a fairy-tale match. The newlyweds' daughter, Tiffany, Donald Trump's fourth child, was born two months before, and the marriage continued for six years, though there was never any suggestion of perfect marital bliss, and there were always rumors of alleged infidelities.[11] It must be said that Ivana's next marriage took place at Mar-a-Lago and that both Ivana and Marla, as ex-wives, have always spoken well of Donald Trump, and he has had nothing but praise for them.

In the autumn of 1987, Trump published his first book, *The Art of the Deal*, which established him as a bestselling author in that prototypical American genre of self-help success books. Coauthored with Tony Schwartz of *New York Magazine*, who had been very critical of

Trump at times, the book was released in a splashy ceremony at Trump Tower. Gwenda Blair, an unsympathetic biographer of Trump, wrote that the book was a celebration of "one of the most showy, self-involved, and seductive voices of the era."[12] (She hadn't seen anything yet.) Throughout the late '80s, Trump appeared on television interview programs like *Larry King Live*, and *Oprah Winfrey*, and as a critic of the country's incumbents, began laying out the foundation of what would eventually become his presidential platform. As if to prove the point, Trump let it be known that he might have presidential ambitions. At the time, his presidential ambitions were preposterous and seemed like rank hucksterism. It need hardly be added that they proved not to be entirely risible.

He had offered, several years before, to serve as an armaments negotiator opposite the Soviet Union. He was evidently oblivious to the fact that this required considerable technical military and scientific background, and wasn't like foreclosing buildings, maneuvering for building permits, and accommodating or defeating recalcitrant union leaders in the New York building trades.

In the lead-up to the 1988 elections, Trump took out a full-page advertisement in the *New York Times* with a statement that began: "There's nothing wrong with America's foreign defense policy that a little backbone can't cure."[13] He also gave a speech in New Hampshire, did a little polling, and distributed "I (heart) Donald Trump," as in "I (Love) New York," bumper stickers. The newspaper outburst was a bit rich, given that he was essentially slagging off Ronald Reagan, George Shultz, and Caspar Weinberger, who had won the arms race and were about to win the Cold War.

Trump later claimed that he only did all this to promote book sales. The book was a sequence of eleven steps to wealth, a simplistic primer livened up with vicious attacks on enemies like Mayor Koch ("pervasively corrupt and totally incompetent") and wild flights of egotism ("Deals are my art form"). Though it was vituperatively trashed by critics, it sold more than a million hardcover copies.

More important, Trump was in fact thinking seriously about politics. He had tasted the intoxicating honey of a presidential challenge, the beginnings of Potomac fever. The affliction would not go away for long and would possess him entirely eventually.

CHAPTER 2

Donald Trump's Financial Crisis and Recovery

On October 10, 1989, Donald Trump and his organization suffered a heavy blow when three of his senior Atlantic City executives died in a helicopter crash, returning from a press conference at the Plaza Hotel. Stephen Hyde, president of the casino division of the Trump organization, Mark Etess, who managed the Taj Mahal hotel and casino, and Jonathan Benanav, executive vice president of the Trump Plaza Hotel and Casino, were all key executives, shouldering the heavy burden of servicing and grinding down the debt that had been piled on the assets they were managing. The press conference at the Plaza with Trump present was to announce a championship prizefight in Atlantic City between Héctor "Macho Man" Camacho and Vinny Pazienza, the first event staged by the new company Trump Sports and Entertainment. The helicopter had an undetected scrape on the blade which caused the blade to snap at 2,200 feet over the New Jersey woodlands. The helicopter plunged and came apart, killing the three executives and two crew members. Trump telephoned the families ("I have terrible news"), and was clearly deeply shaken and upset by the tragedy. Jack O'Donnell, who was the next in line in the casino company, as president of Trump Plaza Hotel and Casino, said that for the first time in his years with Trump, "I heard fear and uncertainty in his voice."[1]

The Trump Taj Mahal finally had its grand opening on April 2, 1990. The appearance of the vast 120,000-square-foot casino and forty-two-story hotel set a new summit for garishness with its gold, pink, blue, green, and red domes and minarets and giant red-illuminated TRUMP signs, and its opening week was not without mishap. On the Taj Mahal's second day of operation, the Casino Commission shut down its 2,900 slot machines because of a reconciling shortfall of $200,000 on the first night. The missing $200,000 was found in a bag holding open a fire door to admit cooler air to the stifling and over-crowded counting room (which was quickly expanded). Trump returned at the end of the first week with the entertainer Michael Jackson, giving him a tour of the entire gambling floor, and Jackson praised his accommodation at the Taj Mahal, where he was ensconced in the Alexander the Great Suite. Trump went to imaginative lengths to attract increased crowds to Atlantic City, founding an 837-mile bicycle race that ended in front of one of his casinos and was called the Tour de Trump. He eventually sold it to become the Tour DuPont, and it was a modestly successful attraction. More ambiguous in result was the World Powerboat Championship that he paid $160,000 to move from Key West to Atlantic City in October 1989, despite misgivings of several participants that the waters would be challenging and cold and the weather for race watchers could be inclement. High waves delayed events, rain discouraged observers, and the waters were so rough that several boats sank and one contestant flipped his boat and drowned. Trump claimed that the poor weather had been a bonanza for him, as the race watchers were driven into his casinos by the torrential rain and high winds.[2]

An outstanding success was Trump's promotion of prize-fights in Atlantic City. He promoted a long and successful sequence of these main events in his casinos, and for a time Atlantic City supplanted Las Vegas as the prize-fight capital of the world. Donald Trump was instrumental in the career of Mike Tyson, and paid $11 million to hold the title fight between Tyson and Michael Spinks in the Trump Plaza Casino in June 1988. Although the match only lasted for ninety-one seconds before Tyson flattened his opponent, hardly longer than the stirring rendition of the national anthem (in which the last line is drawn out for thirty seconds at such events), Trump grossed $18 million. The casinos in Atlantic City took in $40 million in two days, and the other casino-owners took out a full-page advertisement in the local newspaper that read: "Thank You, Mr. Trump." It was a gracious gesture in a very tough business.

It was in Atlantic City that Trump also got into the beauty pageant business, buying into the American Dream Calendar Girl Model Search in 1992, and in 1996 he took over the Miss Universe, Miss America, and Miss USA contests also. His daughter Ivanka and his wife Marla occasionally worked at the contests, and Donald himself stepped in when Miss Universe, Alicia Machado, ballooned from 118 to 160 pounds during her reign in 1996. He encouraged her to lose weight (something that Hillary Clinton, bizarrely, made a campaign issue in 2016). He also defended Carrie Prejean, Miss California in 2009, for stating her Christian view that marriage was a heterosexual institution involving one man and one woman, though he ultimately parted company with her over some of her photo-shoots. (She remains friendly with him, however, and supported his campaign for president.) He is also credited by Miss Wisconsin of 1985, Melissa Young, with coming to her aid in her "darkest hour" by showing great solicitude for her and her family when she almost died from a blood clot.[3]

From these beauty contests, it was a short step for Trump to branch out into the modeling business, which is where most of the top contestants go after their terms as reigning champions expire. Trump called his operation T Management, and it apparently enjoyed a reasonable success. He was also, publicly, a rather raunchy commentator, and liked to go on Howard Stern's often objectively disgusting radio and television programs and discuss the pulchritude and sex appeal of prominent women.

Trump came on to Stern's program two or three times a year during the 1990s. Stern asked him if he would have liked to have sexual intercourse with the recently deceased Princess Diana, and Donald answered, almost gallantly: "Without hesitation. She had the height, she had the beauty, she had the skin....She was crazy but these are details." Kim Kardashian, on the other hand, suffered from "a fat ass," and Carmen Electra had had "a terrible boob job. They look like two light posts coming out of a body." It made for entertaining, if not elevating, radio and television.

The most interesting appearance, given subsequent history, was when Trump telephoned into the show in 2000 and described his current girl-friend, Melania Knauss, in glowing terms and then handed the future first lady of the United States the telephone, and she purred to Stern and his listeners: "We have a great, great time...sometimes more than once a day." It wasn't Eleanor and Franklin, or even Jack and Jackie (though the sexual derring-do of the Kennedys was probably more energetic and omnivorous), and certainly nothing like Bill and Hillary. Nor was it the height of elegance, but like so much to do with Donald Trump, it was amusing and not what one would expect from a public figure who craves respect. Trump is naturally very humorous, wittily perceptive, refreshingly uninhibited, and a great showman. Melania, as the world now knows, is a woman of great beauty and equipoise.

By the spring of 1990, the extravagance created by Donald Trump's boundless optimism was creating serious problems. He, with Ivana as manager, had spent $50 million renovating the Plaza Hotel to the highest standard, and raising it back to be one of the world's greatest hotels. This brought his outlay on this very prestigious asset, which he referred to as "the Mona Lisa," to nearly $460 million. To handle the overheads in such a well-staffed, high-service hotel and take care of nearly half a billion dollars of debt, revenues would have to reach impossible levels: a full house every night of the year and a huge business in the public rooms.

At the same time, his plans for his Trump Shuttle, bought from the crack-up of Eastern Airlines for $365 million, piled on additional debt. Eastern's twenty-one-tired Boeing 727s were transformed into "diamonds in the sky": leather upholstery, maple paneling, burgundy carpeting, faux marble, and gold plating in the wash-rooms. It was an admirable commitment to quality, which is one of Donald Trump's under-appreciated virtues, at least on those businesses to which he lends his name, all too often overshadowed by his natural aptitude for making tacky or crass comments and by his lesser commercial escapades. But commuters between Washington, New York, and Boston weren't interested in luxury. They just wanted a swift passage, reliable schedules, and a cheap fare. Handing out a Trump casino chip to every passenger favored the wrong audience, as the commuters tended to be purposeful business and professional people, little attracted to Atlantic City. Indeed, only two of these chips were ever redeemed.[4]

The Trump Shuttle lost $34 million in the first half of 1990; the Plaza Hotel, though the exact numbers are not publicly known, must have lost that much or a little more; and though the Taj Mahal Casino had opened fairly strongly, it was taking business from Trump's Palace and Castle also. Trump put his under-used yacht *Trump Princess* and the Trump Shuttle up for sale and drew down in its entirety an unused line of credit for $100 million at the Bankers Trust, while he still had the right.[5] This allowed him to cover interest payments through the spring, but the financial sky had darkened very quickly. After nearly eight years of the Reagan-Bush boom, the economy was slowing. Donald Trump's irrepressible confidence and optimism had met their nemesis in the business cycle, forcing him to meet with his lenders.

There is some disagreement about who called the meeting at Weil Gotshal, the prominent law firm, on the twenty-fifth floor of the General Motors building across Grand Army Plaza from the Plaza Hotel in June 1990, as both Trump and some of the bankers present claim to have done so. But it was obvious to everyone that such a meeting was necessary. The Trump Organization had $3.2 billion of debt, about a third of it in corporate debentures and bonds, and more than $2 billion owed to a group of banking syndicates led by Citibank, Bankers Trust, and Chase Manhattan Bank. Most of the banks—there were seventy-two all told, including European, Japanese, and Canadian firms—had taken the word of the lead banks on the credit-worthiness of the borrower.

When the macro-economic tide turns, and especially when it turns in perfect synchronization to punish the impetuosity of an acquisitive borrower, bankers generally panic, pretend to have been misled, and demand remedial measures. The clever borrower in this unpleasant situation knows that the last thing the banking group wants is to call the loans, bust the borrower, force fire-sales of assets and take large write-offs, or attempt to manage the distressed assets themselves.

Donald Trump was certainly astute enough to know the correlation of forces: he had zero net worth, but he had proven talent—no one could manage his assets better than he could, and no one was better placed to maximize their profits. The banks, by contrast, had not been brilliant lenders; they had no aptitude at all to manage or even evaluate real estate, casinos, hotels, and airlines; and none of these bankers had one cent at stake personally. Donald Trump had everything at stake, as he had personally guaranteed $800 million of borrowings. (The largest piece was $320 million from Citibank, including $135 million for the Trump Shuttle, and $125 million on the Plaza Hotel.) He was staring down the barrel of personal bankruptcy, which would not square well with his plans, ambitions, and, to say the least, ample self-regard. Despite their pious claptrap about the evils of imprudent borrowing (as if anyone but they had advanced the loans), the bankers needed Trump to succeed. It is a form of commercial theater, familiar to everyone who has been associated with a large, troubled corporate borrower or on the credit committee of a serious bank (including the author in both capacities). As one of the Citibank lawyers said later, Trump "was basically worth more alive than dead."

At the meeting, the bankers did not have a spokesman, so after a few disjointed interventions, Trump took over, and with all the charm and respect that he can project when necessary, he acknowledged that he recognized the gravity of the situation. He reaffirmed an absolute commitment to repay everyone a hundred cents on the dollar. He promised to make everyone whole by selling assets on an orderly basis, recouping their intrinsic value, and radically reducing his loans through reliable sources of revenue. As usual, the lenders wanted nothing more than to save face with their superiors and stockholders, to claim that they had bullied the borrower into making promises and concessions, and to confirm that they fiercely defended their institutions. Trump gave them cover to do that.

It must be remembered in appreciating how this crisis was managed and resolved, that Trump entered into these discussions with his private life in turmoil and the subject of incessant and often lurid comment in the press, and that his financial difficulties were aired and amplified and jubilated about by the whole media of the Western World. Most people traversing serious problems with lenders are able to do so free from the glare of publicity. In such circumstances, it is usually possible to downsize companies and pare down assets without the prospective buyers being intoxicated with the conviction that the vendor has no staying power and that it is a bottom-feeders' paradise. Donald J. Trump, forty-four, one of the most famous men in America, admired by many but viscerally despised by many including most of the media, faced a perfect storm of improvidence and on a greater scale than all but a few business-men in American history have experienced. He had to confront the col-lapse of his net worth and of his marriage and of the entire reputation and public persona he had built as a successful businessman, simultane-ously and practically alone, as one of his most trusted collaborators, Jack O'Donnell, abruptly quit as head of Trump's Atlantic City casino opera-tions (as key associates often do in crises, though not, in this case, with-out some grievances against his boss). Trump quickly worked out a draft arrangement with his lenders, but even he was temporarily demoralized by the proportions of his problem and the necessary drastic remedies. But, as always with Donald Trump, he realized the set-back could be represented as the starting point of a brilliant come-back, the perennial moral victory; and this posture, for once, was not mere "truthful hyper-bole."

What was afoot was an astonishing resuscitation of Donald Trump's fortunes. The deal that emerged was that the banking group would take direct liens on almost all his assets and confine his spending to $450,000 per month, dropping within two years to $300,000 a month, and there would be a concerted effort to sell marginal or money-losing assets. (Even very wealthy men would not see this as a huge sacrifice and a hair-shirted existence.)

The banks had the intelligence not to try to make Trump a mendicant and pauper in public, so as not to impair his ability to sell assets. He reluctantly went to the Citibank offices to speak by teleconference in the middle of the night in New York to the Japanese bankers, who had not, at this point, agreed even to these provisions. It took him only thirty minutes to bring them around, and the entire agreement, two thousand pages, was signed at the Weil Gotshal office in the General Motors building on August 21, 1990.

Trump responded to this supreme crisis with astonishing simplicity of method. The banks had demanded that he engage a chief financial officer, not a position he had ever created, and he selected Steve Bollenbach, spotted by Trump on the cover of a finance magazine and identified as someone with experience in the hotel and gaming business in Memphis. Bollenbach accepted Trump's cold turkey call and offer, and joined his company. Trump didn't have the money to promise a believable bonus, so he persuaded Citibank to release its lien on a unit in the old Barbizon Hotel on Central Park South that Trump had bought and the unit became Bollenbach's bonus. Trump convinced the banking group to pay the insurance on the *Trump Princess*—realizing they had little choice, to protect their collateral—but they seized his five helicopters, even though he moved them to undisclosed locations to confound his creditors.[6]

The most ingenious of all of Trump's brilliant improvisations in this very difficult time came over the rail yards on the west side of Manhattan, which he had long hoped could be turned into an immense project, even after Mayor Koch effectively killed the grandiose Television City plan. Trump now proposed "the largest and most technologically advanced" housing complex for elderly people in New York. It would be called Trump City and the promoter of the scheme positioned himself as a champion of senior citizens. It was less offensive to anti-development militants of the West Side than the television project, but they regrouped, as Trump came up with the concept of "underwater zoning," the capturing of submerged land to justify higher building heights, and he was still proposing the world's tallest building. The anti-Trump city planning authorities adopted the technique of drawing Trump ever further into the Byzantine planning and approval process, before opposing the plan, to make it costlier for Trump, whose financial condition had been amply publicized.

A new opposition group sprang up called Westpride, which included a hodge-podge of leftist intellectuals and lawyers, including a former law partner of Mayor Koch, as well as former mayor John Lindsay, historian Robert Caro, and eminent journalists Bill Moyers (former chief of staff of President Johnson) and David Halberstam (who debunked JFK's "Best and Brightest"). They developed their own plan, which still left Trump seven million square feet for his project (down from his initial eleven million), but took down the elevated highway, left it at ground level, and included an attractive waterside park. Trump's buildings would be less imposing, but retain much of their original design.

The new mayor, David Dinkins, advised that the West Side highway had to be repaired at once, as it was becoming unsafe. On advice of experienced counsel, Westpride sent an emissary, who was not to admit whose agent he was, to ask Trump if he would support their project without significant modifications. Trump, who had been trying to flush out something that would transform his position into a viable asset, declined to abandon his own project but told the emissary (Stephen Swid, former co-owner of the 21 Club and chairman of the Municipal Art Society), that if Westpride would bring forth their plan, he would support it. Westpride had immense animus toward Trump; they were embarrassed and unnerved by his response, but met him at seven a.m. at the Cravath Swain law offices.

Donald addressed them for half an hour, starting in his gamecock style, but making amusing references to his financial difficulties and being slightly self-deprecating, and explaining the benign motives for his plan, saying he disliked the existing highway as much as Westpride did. Then, having engaged everyone's attention, he warmly commended the

Westpride plan, said it was better than his own, and sketching on a sheet of paper in front of him, proposed the Westpride Park on one side and a modified version of his plan, largely conforming to what they had proposed, on the other. The effect was the usual astonishment and unease when an ancient foe professes agreement.

Trump personally owed Chase Manhattan Bank $220 million for the acquisition of the railyards, and he got Swid, who was an influential and well-connected man in New York, to tell the bank they had to release him from his personal guaranty for Trump to proceed, but that the bank would retain the property as security and that, when the project went forward, he could undoubtedly sell it at a profit and retire the loan. Just as Trump had used Urban Development Corporation to lever through the Commodore Hotel deal at the launch of his large-scale activities in Manhattan, on this occasion he had levered on top of a civic action coalition, and redirected their hostility to him to achieve their ends and help liberate him from indebtedness.

Opposition to the plan, which proposed an immense 5,700 housing units, spluttered to the end of the process, but complete approval was achieved in December 1992, and in July 1994, Trump sold the property for $338 million, plus a large fee for managing the construction of the project and a share of future profit. He had harnessed the energy of his enemies to be rid of personal indebtedness, then disposed of the entire bank debt with probably $150 million of profit personally and a continuing share of rising profits. It was an astonishing turn of fortune and a salutary tour de force by someone who, no matter how contentious, had demonstrated phenomenal resourcefulness under great pressure. It was the financial version of Napoleon crossing the Beresina.

The deal with the banks did not provide a solution for the $1.3 billion that were attached to the casinos. That would have to be dealt with separately. The Taj Mahal was an operational success, but Trump had been obliged to issue $675 million of the junk bonds he had disparaged and promised never to issue, to get the casino finished and opened. If it had been financed correctly in the first place, it would have been pleasantly profitable, but it was not now covering interest payments. Junk bond syndicates are not as formidable as bankers and did not have cross-guaranties over all of Trump's assets, but they could seize the mortgaged property, not that junk-bond owners would have had any more desire to run a casino than Japanese bankers had to run the Trump Shuttle. The negotiations in the autumn of 1990 took place in the Plaza Hotel and were fierce and ill-tempered, unlike the discussions with the banks, where reasonable decorum is normally observed. But Trump flourishes in this environment too, and with nerves of steel, he allowed the negotiations to break down twice, and he actually went into default.

The bond-holders announced that they would hold a press conference at noon on the day after expiry of the payment deadline, where they were going to announce that they had seized the Taj Mahal. The largest of the bond-holders was Carl Icahn, the legendary raider and asset-stripper, who had bought a lot of the bonds at close to their present trading price. Trump, however, refused to buckle under pressure, and, with Icahn playing a lead role, an agreement was reached an hour before the press conference. Trump knew that if the bond-holders seized the Taj Mahal, they would be required to get the approval of the Casino Commission to change the license holder. While they did so, all of his casino competitors in Atlantic City could raid the Tah Mahal's personnel, the value of the property would collapse, and the bond holders' shares would tank. Trump was right to call the bond-holders' bluff, but it still required great self-possession to do it. The announced deal reduced Trump's interest in the Taj Mahal to 50.5 percent, and made adjustments to the bond offerings to make them commercially sustainable.

There were still problems in the other casinos, and in the week before Christmas 1990, another extraordinarily ingenious move from Trump saved the day and enabled the Trump Castle to keep fairly current on its interest. A lawyer for Fred Trump, Donald's eighty-four-year-old father, arrived with a certified check and bought chips worth $3.5 million. These became the premium creditors of the casino under New Jersey law, and because the money went to a trading account of the Trump Castle, it was not added to the security accessible to lenders. With this money, Donald Trump confounded his enemies again and kept the Castle afloat.

This was only a temporary reprieve, as the Castle and the Palace had yielded market share to the Taj Mahal, and in March 1992 Trump submitted those two casinos to deals with bond-holders that replicated the Taj Mahal deal. They sheared the bond-holders' yield on their debt in exchange for some of Trump's equity, in the normal manner of debt reorganizations.

These deals brought the casinos back to profit and eventually, as Trump worked himself out of the debt abyss, he emerged with half the equity in valuable casinos, after having originally invested almost nothing but borrowed money in them. All three were passed through court on a nod in what are called "pre-packaged bankruptcies" where debtors and creditors jointly request court approval of new arrangements and there is no room for the intervention of other parties and there is continuity in the operations of the distressed business.

In November 1992, Trump arranged another pre-packaged bankruptcy for the Plaza Hotel, and he held a celebration for his financial deliverance at the Trump Taj Mahal. It was an extraordinary self-celebration: eight hundred guests received a Donald Trump mask and were treated to uplifting music based on invincible comebacks, and the host eventually emerged with red boxing gloves, a silk robe, and boxing shorts over his dinner jacket and pants, as the theme from *Rocky* was belted out through the sound system. It was a preposterous performance for someone who had been a party to four bankruptcies, and was even now not out of the woods, but it was magnificent in its tasteless way. He had peeled off his Alexander's (department store) stock, which he had accumulated to get hold of some of the company's prime real estate locations, and the *Trump Princess*, after sailing the world from port to port on orders from the banking group, looking for a buyer, was sold in late 1991 to Saudi prince Al-Waleed bin Talal. He bought the ship for some millions of dollars less than Trump had paid for it when he bought it from the Sultan of Brunei, who had seized it from Adnan Khashoggi. Trump retained a substantial interest in the refinanced Plaza Hotel. (It was a sign of his veneration for it that he never thought of adding his name to that of the hotel.)

Trump was not yet through the financial minefield, though he was well along. He now resorted to a tried and true technique: he set up a public company, issued a Trump "truthful hyperbole" prospectus, and relied on his theory that fame counts ahead of anything else. He aggressively peddled $140 million of stock in an initial public offering by his company Trump Taj Mahal Associates, and he sold another $155 million dollars of casino junk bonds, as the results from the casinos had improved with a reduction in interest costs. The stock was issued in 1992 at $14 a share and it rose over four years to $36. Trump's own stake was then valued at almost $300 million and he returned in 1996 to the *Forbes Magazine* list of the four hundred wealthiest Americans, with about $500 million of net worth. In the course of the four-year rise from its initial price, the Trump casino company bought the Trump castle and the Taj Mahal from Trump and shareholders found themselves responsible for $1.7 billion of Trump debt. The stock sank back to $12 in late 1996, as Trump paid himself $12 million in salary and bonus. The stock descended to 17 cents and, in 2004, it filed for bankruptcy, the fifth such trip to this unfashionable well for Donald Trump. But Trump still profited. He took $44 million of pay and bonuses from the company between 1995 and 2009 (and even sold the company almost two million dollars' worth of Trump Ice bottled water).

Trump publicly referred to this era as an "entrepreneurial" success, by which he meant that he parked a lot of dubious assets on an under-informed investing public who bought into his image-making. It was, taken with all the other maneuvers he executed, a skillful navigation through apparently implacable problems. In 2004, *Forbes* moved him up to a net worth of $2.6 billion. It had been an astounding recovery, and had confirmed Trump in his views that ingenuity and determination would always prevail, and that the power of a brand, the fruit of celebrity, would prove the best of all assets. Few people rise so spectacularly as Donald Trump did; many who do crash. But almost no one has made such a swift and complete comeback, unencumbered by any visible remorse and without even acknowledging that he might have put a foot wrong along the way.

Donald Trump appeared to have a unique combination of desperate cunning, unflagging determination, unshakeable self-confidence, ruthless Darwinian instincts of survival, and a sublime assurance that celebrity will heal all wounds. He now changed his career game-plan to conform with his experiences and observations. He was a vital, and many thought, a sinister, force. But he never merited the derision he received from those repelled only by his vulgarianism, because there was always much more to him than that. He ignored his detractors and was settling on an unimaginably ambitious goal, which he pursued with demiurgic cunning and determination. His obsession with celebrity would drive his enemies to paroxysms of mockery, and then of fear.

CHAPTER 3

Politics Beckons

When the Reagan-Bush handover occurred in 1989, Donald J. Trump, forty-three, was already, as a self-publicizing developer of spectacular sites in the throbbing American heart of Manhattan, a man who loved the spotlights, footlights, and limelight, and an accomplished public relations hustler, but also an agile industrialist and financier, and a patriotic military school graduate who already saw the nation's supreme office as the possible consummation of his accumulation of money and fame. He was now monitoring the currents of public opinion and the political pathways with acute self-interest.

Trump, because of his talents at self-promotion, often of a somewhat grating nature, had been one of the most famous people in the country for some years. His construction of, and name-identification with, radically designed buildings of high quality in choice Manhattan locations, frequent public disputes with local politicians, and general omnipresence in the Manhattan world of celebrity controversy, caused him to be regarded by many with distaste, but also to be regarded by many others—a broad swath of American capitalists, entrepreneurs, and appreciators of showmen—with deep and durable, if vicarious, admiration. Trump had no interest in the usual social and philanthropic eminence of wealthy New Yorkers; he was interested in fame, celebrity, publicity, money, and politics. He began regularly polling American opinion about him, as his name, increasingly prominent and bandied about endlessly in the press, became ever more familiar to the public. He also noted that the political ground and the normal pathways of politics were shifting.

In 1992, after the main party nominations had been locked up by President George Herbert Walker Bush for the Republicans and by five-time Arkansas governor Bill Clinton for the Democrats, billionaire businessman Ross Perot suddenly appeared as a viable, populist third party candidate. Perot's campaign was launched with a tremendous television blitz as soon as the primaries were over. He tried to win over disaffected voters of both parties with an eclectic platform that promised a balance budget, support for abortion, tightened gun control, a stricter war on drugs, trade protectionism, greater care for the environment, and electronic referenda to promote direct democracy. Perot, unlike Clinton, had been opposed to the First Gulf War, successfully fought by President Bush. Perot played to constituencies of both Right and Left, though his appeal as a Naval Academy graduate and Texas patriot, associated with efforts to recover American soldiers missing in action in Vietnam, appealed largely to blue-collar conservatives unhappy with President Bush's support for free trade and raising taxes (after saying he would not).

On the Democratic side, Bill Clinton was a very astute politician, one of a new breed who had never really had any career except politics, nor any real ambition except to be president. Such men as Taft, Wilson, Hoover, Eisenhower, and Reagan had been famous from completely separate careers before they sought public office. Truman, Carter, and Bush had had other careers, and Franklin D. Roosevelt had been sidelined for seven years convalescing with and mitigating the effects of polio. Harding, Coolidge, Lyndon Johnson, and Ford went early into politics (after military service in Ford's case), but none of them were aiming for the White House, and Kennedy and Nixon, who were, at least won some battle stars, got around the world a bit, came from prominent centers (Boston and Los Angeles), and had been a long time in Washington. Bill Clinton ran unsuccessfully for congressman at age twenty-eight, was elected attorney general of Arkansas at thirty, and governor at thirty-two.

Polls had Perot running ahead of both Bush and Clinton prior to the Republican and Democratic conventions, but he abruptly ended his campaign in July, saying he did not want to throw the election to the House of Representatives. However, he burst back into the race two months later, implausibly claiming that he had been forced out by Republicans threatening to disrupt his daughter's wedding.

Perot could not regain his momentum. He looked increasingly out of his depth, unstable, unable to explain in a convincing way how he would balance the budget, and was seen by most as a political charlatan. President Bush seemed out of touch with the Reagan voters who had put him in office in the first place, ran a half-hearted campaign in which he appeared almost to expect to lose, and focused on issues that most voters at the time thought were irrelevant and unseemly even to talk about— namely, Clinton's dodging the draft and his scandals involving women. Clinton, cleverly, positioned himself as a centrist Democrat for whom a disaffected Republican could vote in good conscience, and side-swiped Perot with his pitch to the people of modest means and insecure employment; "I feel your pain" came more credibly from him, a former a trailer park resident, than from the billionaire Perot.

Clinton won the election 44.9 million votes to 39.1 million for Bush, and an incredible 19.7 million for Perot (370 electoral votes to 168 to 0). Donald Trump noted how Bush had lost control of his own party; how a political outsider, making an appeal to discontented blue-collar voters, had amassed a sizeable voting bloc; and how a centrist Democrat had managed to overcome personal scandals to win the presidency (and how he later avoided removal from office after being impeached). None of these lessons were lost on him.

He noted other lessons as well. How Jimmy Carter, and now George H. W. Bush, despite being incumbent presidents, had both been defeated by populist campaigns, and how an independent candidate, even one as successful as Perot, could not win in a two-party system. And he also noted how unpopular an inarticulate, uninspiring, establishment candidate like Bush could be to a discontented electorate. All of these lessons came into play when Trump entered the presidential arena twenty-five years later.

Trump had attended his first national political convention in 1988, when the Republicans chose George H. W. Bush to succeed Ronald Reagan. He told television interviewer Larry King that he came "to see how the system works." He also told King that if he were ever nominated, he might choose African American daytime television hostess Oprah Winfrey as his vice-presidential candidate.[1] (This could be taken as evidence of how much he thought celebrity counted in running for national office.)

His name increasingly popped up in political conversations, and there was serious speculation that he might run as a third-party candidate in 2000, tapping into a conservative electorate unhappy with outgoing President Clinton and unsatisfied with a choice of either Republican George W. Bush (or his primary rival John McCain) or Clinton's Vice President Al Gore.

But Donald Trump also had other things on his mind. On June 25, 1999, Fred Trump died at ninety-three. He had been fading mentally as Alzheimer's had taken hold, and it was painful for his family to see his decline. The funeral was at Norman Vincent Peale's Marble Collegiate Church. Peale was still alive at ninety-five, and still the pastor after sixty-one years, but not well enough to preside. The eulogy was delivered by Mayor Rudolph W. Giuliani, who said that Fred Trump had contributed to making New York "the most important city in the world." Other family members praised their father, as Donald did, but mainly he stressed some of the ambitious projects he had built with his father's encouragement.

Donald Trump has said since that this was the saddest and most decisive day in his life, because of the closeness between his father and himself, and that his father's death may have generated his ambition to be president. Sitting alone near the back of the packed church, and much noticed in the tabloid press the next morning, was the breathtakingly tall and beautiful and magnificently proportioned Melania Knauss, twenty-nine, the Slovenian immigrant and model, who was Donald Trump's current girlfriend. A couple of weeks later, Trump received a thoughtfully worded letter of condolence from John F. Kennedy Jr., as it turned out, on the day that an airplane he piloted himself crashed into the ocean near Martha's Vineyard, killing Kennedy and his wife, Carolyn Bessette, and another passenger.[2]

Donald Trump was now the patriarch of what was a family of varied distinction, including Trump's elder sister Maryanne Trump Barry, a federal district judge, who had just been nominated by President Clinton to the Third Circuit Court of Appeals. Fred Trump's widow, Mary MacLeod Trump, eighty-seven, had never entirely recovered from being mugged and beaten up not far from the family home in Queens in 1991. A delivery truck driver had collared the assailant and handed him over to police, and Donald Trump rewarded the driver (with no publicity) with a check large enough to retire the mortgage on his house, which was on the verge of foreclosure. Mrs. Trump died the next year and her obituary was published in her hometown newspaper, the *Stornoway Gazette*, in Scotland, the land from which she had departed seventy years before to make her way in the new world.

In October 1999, Trump told Larry King on his late-night television program (a favorite place for Trump to air his political bulletins) that, while he was "a pretty conservative guy," he was leaving the Republican Party and joining the Reform Party and setting up an exploratory committee to see if he might run, as a viable candidate, for president. He went on *Meet the Press* with Tim Russert and others, and did not have an easy time explaining slightly flippant things he had said about President Clinton's dalliance with White House intern Monica Lewinsky. He defended his support of a woman's right to a partial-birth abortion, but acknowledged to his assistant, Roger Stone, afterward, that he didn't know exactly what a partial-birth abortion was.[3]

He published a thin volume in 2000 called *The America We Deserve*, in which he said he was thinking of running for president. (He revisited partial-birth abortion and said that after consultation with doctors, he was opposed to it, that he was "uncomfortable" with abortion but still defended a woman's right to choose. In February, he and Melania visited Minnesota Governor Jesse Ventura, a former professional wrestler.) In remarks to a local group, Trump dismissed the leading Democratic and Republican presidential candidates (Vice President Al Gore and Senator Bill Bradley for the Democrats; Texas governor George W. Bush, and Senator John McCain for the Republicans), as "stiffs;" not an entirely inaccurate description.

But on February 19, 2000, he wrote an op-ed piece in the *New York Times* in which he announced that while he had seriously considered running for president, he felt he could not win as a Reform Party candidate because the party was too hopelessly divided. Trump had won two primaries for the Reform Party nomination, in Michigan and California, but then folded the operation. He purported to become a Democrat in 2001, and then supported Fernando Ferrer, borough president of the Bronx, as the Democratic candidate for mayor of New York, saying only a Democrat could now win that office. Ferrer lost the nomination to Mark Green, whom Trump then supported, but billionaire, and nominal Republican, Michael Bloomberg won easily, and remained in office for three terms. This was the beginning of an abrasive political relationship between Trump and Bloomberg. At this point, Trump appeared to be lurching around for a political harbor. His political views, as expressed in *The America We Deserve*, did not change appreciably—a mostly conservative platform, standing on strong national defense, an America-first trade and foreign policy, education reform (including school choice), regulatory and tax reform, health care and social security reform, and tough anti-crime and anti-terrorism policies—but he did not yet have a firm political home in which to express them as a candidate.

Trump continued to believe that in both business and politics, celebrity and fame was more important than money and when British expatriate reality television producer Mark Burnett pitched an idea of a show to him, Trump was interested, though he had reservations. Trump worried about how time-consuming it would be, and he did not like reality television, which he considered to be for "the bottom-feeders of society" (an amusing lapse for Trump into almost dowagerish snobbery). But once satisfied that his part in the show could be shot entirely in the Trump Tower, and that he could work in a great deal of free publicity for his casinos and other properties, he was persuaded. The show would be called *The Apprentice*, and on a handshake with Burnett, they were equal co-owners. Trump's executives, still battle-scarred and shell-shocked from the near death financial crisis they had all just gone through, thought it a waste of time. Trump liked it intuitively and proceeded without consulting anyone; and Burnett and Trump eventually negotiated a deal with NBC, after Burnett failed to agree to a deal with ABC. (Trump refused to work with CBS because it had had declined to televise his Miss USA and Miss Universe pageants.)

The show debuted in 2004, and Trump, hard-working as always, prepared assiduously for his role. NBC had originally thought it might rotate executives in Trump's part; but the network executives were so pleased with his performance that they made Trump the show's star, and his tagline—"You're fired!"—often employed humorously, became part of his national branding. The program was aggressively promoted, and when NBC asked for candidates to be the apprentice seeking to work for the star (Trump), in the first sixteen episodes of the program, two hundred fifteen thousand candidates came forward. *The Apprentice*'s audience rose from an impressive twenty million viewers in its early episodes to a formidable twenty-seven million. The programs were almost continuous advertisements for Trump and his assets, with the rather threadbare theme of Trump trying to help the various contestants learn about his businesses and get on in the world. Trump showed considerable talent as a performer, and he came across as a generous man who regretted having to fire people, though that was an important part of the show.

Trump has always been a highly amusing raconteur, with a gift for tossing off one-liners, and this television experience only added panache to his already greatly accomplished skills as a storyteller, schmoozer, and public speaker. The television experience also softened the public impression of him as a ruthless businessman and narcissistic megalomaniac. He appeared a more human and entertaining man, as well as a capable executive. Trump was proud of the show's high ratings, and was briefly crestfallen when the Fox show *American Idol* did better.[4] Trump explained at this time to one of the contestants that "All publicity is good publicity....When people get tired of you is when you do more publicity, because that's when you become an icon."[5]

NBC's public relations director, James Dowd, was close to Trump at this time, and he observed the metamorphosis of Trump from a well-known but not necessarily likeable businessman to an immensely popular public idol of executive success and performance. Trump implied to Dowd that through *The Apprentice*, he had "won the love and respect of Middle America."[6] Trump also came across in *The Apprentice* as a reasonable person who could say harsh truths with becoming honesty. The political class still regarded Trump as a rich blowhard, useful for donations but little else. Trump, however, saw himself building a persona and popular support that went behind celebrity and business; he was building trust and a political base among middle Americans.

While *The Apprentice* improved and vastly expanded Trump's public image and created new ways for Trump to capitalize on his brand in both business and politics, he assessed his political prospects. After dalliances with the Reform Party and the Democrats, any presidential run he made would be as a Republican. It was by far the best fit for him as a candidate whose major appeal was to blue-collar conservatives; and if his protectionist and anti-illegal immigration positions put him at odds with much of the Republican establishment, which was wedded to free-trade orthodoxy and, in practice, loose immigration policies, his nationalist positions were even more at odds with most Democrats, who saw illegal immigration as a boon to their voter base and free trade as part and parcel of a liberal globalist agenda. Trump was no fan of President George W. Bush, but he couldn't run against a Republican incumbent in 2004, and he knew couldn't defeat either Hillary Clinton or Barack Obama in 2008, as the Republicans had to carry the can for the endless imbroglio in Iraq and the housing bubble and the Great Recession. If he was ever going to have a shot at running for president, and winning, it would have to be the end of the Obama era, when there would be plenty of populist discontent, and Trump's signature issues on trade, immigration, the economy, foreign policy, and the courts, would be to the fore. He was content, then, in the interim to raise his profile and build his bank account.

CHAPTER 4

Rebranding for Profit and Elections

Though he came through his financial near-demise with flying colors, he was chastened by it, and confirmed in his belief that he was better off promoting himself than any particular product or service. He had great admiration for his father, and learned from him the basic business of building, renting, and selling real estate, and dealing with the political system, as one had to do as a big New York builder. But in his desire for celebrity, he had crossed the East River into Manhattan, residentially, vocationally, and in his personality. He was first addicted to the glitz and gossip of rich Manhattan, and then became a leading subject of it, though an outsider to the exalted lions of Fifth and Park Avenues. Then he built upon his public status to project a powerful television personality across America.

Spinning off his television success, he approached premier shirt-maker Phillips-Van Heusen, which had earlier brushed him off, taking the standard, sneering upscale New York view of Trump as a discharged near-bankrupt and blustering mountebank—But his celebrity opened doors, and Trump attended upon them personally in the garment district, and convinced them to design the line of Donald Trump clothing that he wished to market: dark, sober business suits, white shirts, and plain or striped, but not patterned, neckties, that were long enough to reach the waist of even a portly man. This arrangement continued for eleven years. Trump did not put up a cent but received more than a million dollars in royalties every year.

Trump licensed out his name to a startling range of consumer products, beyond clothes to mineral water, fragrances, furniture, décor, sunglasses, wallets, and mattresses. Apart from marketing by the licensees, his products could be had at the Trump Store in Trump Tower (adjacent to Trump's Bar, the Trump Grill, and the Trump Ice Cream Parlor). Donald was never one for half-measures, but, as it happened, he was over-propelled in his branding enthusiasm when he unveiled Trump University at the Trump Grill in March 2005, and declared, apparently with a straight face, that "If I had a chance of making lots of money or imparting lots of knowledge, I think I'd be as happy to impart knowledge as to make money." In fact, what he was proposing was that he make lots of money for imparting a modest amount of knowledge that could be had elsewhere for less. Thus was founded the ill-starred overreach of Trump University.

It was initially an effort to capitalize on the booming real estate business, and there were free seminars in almost every major metropolitan area in the United States. Attendees were led to believe that if they took the real estate success course offered by Trump University, they would prosper beyond their dreams. The authors of this dubious enterprise were careful not to guarantee results, but it was a mass-hustle, that almost replicated the fervor of some of America's most avaricious evangelists and promoters, spanning Aimee Semple McPherson and P. T. Barnum. (Like McPherson, Trump is substantially sincere in most of what he says, even when it is topped out by "truthful hyperbole.") The free recruitment sessions would have a video from Donald, the theme song was the O'Jays' "For the Love of Money," and the chairman of the occasion would end his pep talk with something like "You guys ready to be the next Trump real estate millionaires?"

It was always claimed that Trump himself had hired the "professors," and the whole pitch was get rich quick; "buy it, flip it, forget about it" was one of the mantras.[1] Those who enrolled were assured of "the next best thing to being a Donald Trump's apprentice."[2] When the real estate market softened in mid-decade, Trump University tweaked its pitch to one of taking advantage of a down market. The basic program was $1,495, but the session chairmen were instructed to deduce from the questionnaires the attendees filled out who might be susceptible to upselling, preferably all the way up to the $34,995 "Gold Elite" program. The "alumni" of this highest echelon got a certificate and a photograph with a cardboard cut-out of Donald Trump. This was capitalism of the rawest kind—outrageous, magnificent, unethical, and amusing—and it made Donald Trump a lot of money. (Incredibly, there were six hundred Gold Elite recruits—$21 million for Trump.)

But not everyone was amused. The university was the subject of several class action suits, and the attorney general of New York, Eric Schneiderman, a former longtime Democrat state senator, and whom Trump called (somewhat charitably) a "political hack," sued Trump for misuse of the word "university." Trump put up his customary feisty resistance to legal pressure and only changed the name to Trump Entrepreneur Initiative shortly before he shut the whole thing down in 2010. Trump had promised to give all proceeds to charity, but did not; one of his lawyers claimed that he used it instead for legal fees. In fairness to Trump, the program wasn't entirely a scam, the information provided was a survey crash course in the basics of real estate, and likely no worse than similar courses, and only about a quarter of those who registered asked for their money back. But Trump University was certainly not one of Donald's cleverer moves, and he must surely regret ever having launched such a shabby enterprise.

The real fruit of the branding initiative was harvested in letting out the name Trump for ambitious buildings and building complexes all over the world. Though not without controversy either, this was a mighty bonanza. It was an absolute no-lose game for Donald Trump, and its invention must stand as one of his many remarkable accomplishments. He lent his name to projects, required an up-front payment, and demanded that as an investor he be put first in line among creditors, and had no shortage of suitors. It must perpetually astound the large gallery of his detractors, who have been repulsed for decades that anyone would pay anything to identify with Trump, but many did, and for many it was a wise investment.

In support of his franchisees (to adapt slightly the normal commercial ambit of the word), Donald Trump sometimes implied or even affirmed that his investments in projects bearing his name were much greater than they really were. The most embarrassing example of this was when Trump wrote, of the Trump International Hotel and Tower in Waikiki, Honolulu, in a letter published in the *Wall Street Journal* on November 28, 2007, that "This building is largely owned by me and is being developed by me." In fact, he had no equity interest in the building, nor was he or his company managing it. In a deposition required in a subsequent legal proceeding, he claimed that he had "such a strong licensing agreement that it's a form of ownership." This was bunk of course, but like so much of the unguent liberties he has taken in smoothing his career forward, it is not exactly a lie, though it lends enhanced elasticity to his notion of "truthful hyperbole." There were many other discrepancies between what was strongly implied as the level of Trump's participation in projects and the facts. It is a credit to his record as a quality builder that the use of his name was so prized, by developers, lenders, and unit buyers or tenants. His contracts lending his name to projects generally were extremely advantageous to him, giving him authority over design to assure quality, and leaving him a complete right to walk if the developer faltered or if Trump decided that he was not adhering to Trump standards.

There were many legal problems with disgruntled participants in unsuccessful projects, but Trump had plausible deniability in all cases. Despite the allegations of his enemies and the assorted aggrieved, it was caveat emptor, and he was selling his brand, not guaranteeing performance, and his presence did provide at least a partial assurance that the project would meet fairly high standards. It wouldn't win the gold star of the Better Business Bureau, but it was rarely the subject of successful litigation from complainants. It is only fair to emphasize that the great majority of these projects were successful, and that the Trump name added real value. It is easy, as Trump's enemies have done, to find the turkeys and highlight their often hilarious shortcomings and their impact on pitifully naïve subscribers to the magic of the Trump name. But he never underwrote any of these projects and most of his co-contractants were honest people who succeeded and felt their deals with Trump were valid transactions for received value. Donald Trump the businessman was very aggressive and took all corners on two wheels, but despite some ethical lapses, the licensing of his name to buildings and building projects was much more often than not successful for all parties involved.

In 2007, he created the "Trump Hotel Collection," and roped in a group of genuine luxury hotels happy to put the Trump name atop them. Trump was targeting the most prosperous 5 percent of travelers and between 2005 and 2015 his name sprouted up on grand new hotels in Baku, Dubai, Istanbul, Jakarta, Mexico City, Panama, Toronto, and elsewhere. Some, such as Baku and Panama, had a very troubled history. There were some that didn't get off the ground, but the "Trump Hotel Collection" was a reliable profit center to Trump. Like much of the outright promotional business, it was both clever and cheesy. Trump, a very good golfer, also lent his name to golf courses. Sentimentally attached to his mother's home country, his organization owns not one but two golfing and resort complexes in Scotland, one of which, in Aberdeen, became terribly contentious because of Trump's vehement opposition to a government plan to build offshore wind turbines that he says would destroy the view. As ever, Trump insists that, controversies aside, he is in fact very popular in Scotland, and that while these investments have yet to move into the black, they eventually will, because of the enormous care he has taken in improving the properties, of which he is inordinately proud.

Also controversial were Trump's forays into mortgages and health care, with Trump Mortgage and Trump Network. Trump Mortgage was launched in 2006, just as the mortgage market started to soften, before crashing altogether in the autumn of 2008. This new business was promising swift approvals of applications, but as conditions darkened, Trump took appropriate action to reduce his risk, and as defaults occurred, the volumes were not so numerous that his company had trouble seizing the encumbered properties and holding them until conditions had stabilized. He sold the name Trump Financial to Meridian Mortgage in 2007, and reverted to the sale of his name without risking any of his own money.

Trump Network was a new name Trump sold to Ideal Health, for a share of their revenue, which peddled a vitamin supplement based on analysis of the urine sample provided by buyers. With his customary profit-fueled enthusiasm, Donald Trump announced to a convention of thousands of users in Miami in 2009, that "The Trump Network wants to give millions of people renewed hope...with an exciting plan to opt out of the recession....Let's get out of this recession right now with cutting edge health and wellness formulas and a system where you can develop your own financial independence. The Trump Network offers people the opportunity to achieve the American dream."[3] In fact, it offered $139.95 for a urinalysis, $69.95 monthly for the vitamins, and $99.95 for a follow-up urinalysis every six months. It would be a little harsh to call it a scam, and subscription was voluntary and nothing miraculous was promised, only hoped for, but it was another thoroughly questionable promotion. There were eventually a number of complaints, as was inevitable, and Trump withdrew from the venture when the licensing contract expired in 2011. He was not successfully sued, but it was another dodgy flimflam operation that tarnished the emblazoned name though doubtless at a profit, since, once again, he had not invested a penny.

The next rollout of the equal opportunity, no-fault Trump publicity-generating machine was his foray into international wrestling, which cannot be confused with the continuation of authentic college, Greco-Roman, and oriental wrestling, which are regulated sports. These are the extravaganzas of rigged matches with practically no rules, uproarious antics, and outrageous abuses of officials, but staffed by very talented performers, even if they are not entirely traditional sporting figures. The brilliant but outlandish impresario of wrestling, Vince McMahon, operator of the World Wrestling Federation, happy hunting ground of great celebrities and showmen like Hulk Hogan and André the Giant, became a commercial friend of Trump's when Trump hosted WrestleMania at the Trump Plaza in Atlantic City in the late 1980s.

They agreed to combine their crowd-gathering talents in a mighty roundup of the susceptible called "the Battle of the Billionaires." They had a "show-down" in the Pontiac Silverdome near Detroit, before almost ninety thousand people, on July 19, 2001. In what was portrayed as a contest of their great egos, they sponsored a wrestler to represent each of them in a grudge match to determine which of them was preeminent. They marched down the ramps (fully-clothed fortunately) to the ring and strutted about like giant full-figured roosters before their proxies, the 270-pound Bobby Lashley for Trump, and the 350-pound rippling mountain of tattoos, Umaga the Samoan Bulldozer, for McMahon.

It was an extravaganza of unutterable hucksterism: at a "Fan Appreciation Night" for McMahon a few weeks before in Dallas, pushing the great battle, Trump suddenly appeared on a huge overhead screen and the crowd was littered with dollar bills fluttering down from the ceiling like miniature paratroopers. In another preparatory session, Trump apparently flipped McMahon over a table after a center-ring exchange of vulgarities. After a few more of these warm-ups, the main event finally got going to an immense pay-television audience, and Trump's wrestler won, enabling Trump to shear the hair off McMahon, which he did in a joint triumph of absurd histrionics.

However fatuous the whole business may have been, Trump enjoyed himself, communicated very well with the low-end blue-collar and juvenile following of the sport, and tucked away another fine profit on an initial investment of zero. Apart from the money, Trump was opening up a following with an entire new echelon of the public who would no more have thought that a man of his wealth and education would get involved in wrestling and all its nonsense than that David Rockefeller would appear in a prize-fight in Madison Square Garden. It was a remarkably ambitious and imaginative course for Trump to broaden his base in the multi-layered, intensely cross-threaded society of America, for whatever unspecified ultimate purposes he might choose.

He was also already well embarked on an ambitious schedule as an inspirational speaker, receiving $100,000 per session, telling packed houses how to bootstrap themselves up from obscurity, pick themselves up after a serious setback such as he had endured, and reach for the top. He was giving a couple or more of these speeches most months, and it was another profit center, but also another way for him to meet the public and tap into the opinions and thoughts of middle-class, want-to-get-ahead Americans.

He leveraged his celebrity for cameo roles in other well-known television programs outside *The Apprentice*, including *Sex and the City* and *Saturday Night Live* (the latter of which, nevertheless, has been extremely hostile to him as president). Comedy Central tendered him a full roast, where he showed he could absorb the most barbed ridicule of his many foibles and he responded with self-deprecating egomania, comparing his hair to a wet raccoon, and saying "It must be a great honor for you to honor me tonight." (The only barb Trump could not abide was the charge that he was not really a wealthy man.)

One of Trump's advantages was his versatility, and his willingness, indeed eagerness, to appeal to widely different sections of people. Most celebrities are famous for one thing. They are political or religious leaders, military heroes, movie or television stars, great athletes, or even scientific figures, like Einstein. Trump was different because Trump became famous for a trait, success, an achievement, wealth, and more or less simultaneously as a mark of quality in everything from hotels and casinos to golf courses to wine. He was a developer, a TV star, and even something of a sage, authoring books on success, giving lectures, and unafraid to comment on politics. Trump's garishness and gaucherie often blinds his critics to his talents, which are as manifold as his offenses are to their sensibilities. His critics, even at time of writing, are not perceptive observers; they are straight-men in a monstrous send-up of conventional opinion, tumbled over and rendered absurd in the mighty updraft of the main event of Trump's career.

To a man of Donald Trump's self-confidence, the idea of his becoming president of the United States was not at all outrageous. He had brushed shoulders with politicians and met presidents, and he was not at all intimidated by them and did not believe that they had any special powers or talents or mystique that he lacked. In fact, he had qualities that some of them didn't. He was a rich celebrity whose tastes were not to hobnob with the swells and socially eminent benefactors, but, crucially for a presidential candidate, to harvest the affection of the lower middle and working classes of America who were not appalled, but rather, to some degree, inspired, by his bravura, buffoonery, and raw egotism, for behind it they saw an outrageously successful version of themselves, and one who, they intuited, understood them and their desires, fears, and hopes.

It was in this period that this author first got to know Donald Trump beyond mere social pleasantries. My associates and I owned the *Chicago Sun-Times* and its low-rise building on the Chicago River just south of the Wrigley Tower. The building was an obvious candidate for redevelopment, which to us was a potential source of a windfall profit. We commenced a normal bid process, and as Trump appeared to be the competitive winner, our American directors all warned me to "keep (my) hand on the company's wallet," that Trump was a scoundrel who could not be relied upon for anything. We were accordingly cautious and vigilant when he was the winning bidder, and followed advice to assure that he could not lay off on us any superfluous expenses such as jet fuel bills for his airplane. But he came in on budget all the way through and there were no significant issues. He started out promising to build the world's tallest building, but after the September 11, 2001, attacks on the World Trade Center, he scaled the project back to about 1,270 feet, still an imposing sight on the skyline.

He delivered exactly what he had promised under our contract, and it is a generally admired building, ninety-eight stories designed by the distinguished firm Skidmore, Owings & Merrill, and undoubtedly built to an extremely high standard. Donald and Melania came voluntarily to our annual shareholders' meeting in 2003, and he intervened to speak very flatteringly of the manner in which my associates and I had conducted our side of the complex negotiations over the Chicago property, and I will say that I found Trump a good deal more ethical and honest than many other businessmen and corporate directors I have known.[4] Melania was charming and her arrival in Donald's life seemed to settle him. Trump's marriage with Marla Maples had semi-publicly broken down in syncopated lurches, as it had begun, but without public acrimony.

Donald had happened upon Melania Knauss at the famous Kit Kat Klub in 1998, and was so astounded by her startling beauty and sultry, confident poise, that he effectively ditched his date, the formidably attractive and capable Norwegian businesswoman, and bearer of a famous name in that country, despite its awkwardness in English, Celina Midelfart. Melania modeled her way out of late-socialist Slovenia to Milan, then Paris, and in the mid-1990s, New York. She seems to have led a fairly restrained private life, and has had no difficulty silencing media that have insinuated otherwise (collecting 2.5 million pounds from the London *Daily Mail* in 2014 for writing that she had something to do with an escort service). Once she was Trump's companion, she had a relaxed view of the relationship, as in her cameo appearance on Howard Stern's radio program confirming the couple's robust sex life. She appeared on the cover of the British edition of *GQ* in January 2000, lying sideways on a bed in Trump's airplane, naked except for diamond jewelry, with the headline "Sex at 30,000 feet. Melania Knauss earns her air miles."

Donald and Melania were married at Palm Beach's Bethesda-by-the Sea Episcopalian Church on January 22, 2005. This and the Roman Catholic St. Edward's Church just beyond the Breakers Hotel and Everglades Club to the north, are two of America's better known society churches. The events board in front of Bethesda a few weeks before the Trump wedding had announced a visiting homilist who would speak on the theme "The Lord is my Shepherd, even in Palm Beach." The denomination was apparently a compromise between Donald's Presbyterianism, which doesn't have a suitable church in Palm Beach, and Melania's Roman Catholicism, where marriage to a twice-divorced man would have required a few prior formalities before it could be conducted in a church. It was a packed congregation, studded with celebrities from the entertainment, media, casino, and political worlds (including the Clintons), but with little representation from the couple's neighbors in the great salons of Fifth and Park Avenues and South Ocean Boulevard. (The author's wife had a very convivial conversation with flamboyant promoter and impresario Don "Only in America" King who was sitting just behind us in the church, before the bridegroom appeared, looking very serious, with a slight pout and his soon to be famous contumelious lip.) A very grand reception went very late at Mar-a-Lago.

The relationship has apparently lasted smoothly for nearly twenty years and has produced Donald Trump's fifth offspring and third son, Barron (the name he gave himself on the telephone when pretending to be his own public relations advisor during previous marital problems). Melania is a devoted mother, ignores the snide imbecilities of her husband's media lampooners, is well-liked and respected by the public, and always makes an excellent and tastefully glamorous impression when she goes abroad. She is neither an employee of her husband nor a rival nor a scene-stealer; she is neither cloying nor bossy. She is confident and relaxed, cool and poised, looks whimsically on some of her husband's eccentricities, but is always very supportive. Her English is markedly accented but perfectly fluent and comprehensible. (She speaks several other languages also.) She exudes an exotic and mysterious composure that is often more becoming than the opinionated and busy nature of some of her recent predecessors as first lady. She never appears to the public to be either short-tempered or over-eager to please or impress. Her only historic rival as a glamorous chatelaine in the White House is Jackie Kennedy.

The decks were already fairly clear for Donald Trump to try his theories of celebrity in a race for president, but he would have to be patient. He was seeking the office, not the other way around.

CHAPTER 5

Preparing to Seek the Grand Prize

Trump had supported George W. Bush for president in 2000, though he wasn't especially active in the campaign. Like most Americans, he enthusiastically backed the president's energetic policy against terrorism after the September 11, 2001, attacks on the World Trade Center and the Pentagon. He claims to have disapproved of the Iraq War of 2003, though earlier he had said to Howard Stern that he "guessed" he would approve such a war, which was unleashed six months later. That is a reconcilable position and he was prescient in describing the war as botched just a few days after it began.[1]

In any case, when defense secretary Donald Rumsfeld and the appointed Iraq administrator Paul Bremer dissolved the armed forces and police of Iraq and told the four hundred thousand people involved that they were unemployed and without benefit but could keep their weapons and munitions, it is hard not to wonder what they were thinking. Trump was already a war critic by the time this ordinance took hold, and he remained so; a strong advocate of fighting terrorists, defending the international interests of the United States, but not of plunging unthinkingly into foreign wars, and not of taking on the task of building democratic states where there was no precedent or fertile ground for one. Having opposed the Iraq War more or less in the first place, Trump was appalled, as were most Americans, at the fiscal, strategic, and humanitarian disasters that Bush and Obama had managed to fashion from it.

By 2008, Trump's own extensive polling confirmed and amplified other polls, which showed that the country—suffering from war fatigue, big government Republicanism, and a looming economic crisis—was disgusted with the performance of all branches of their government, except the military. The whole political battle in 2008 was for the Democratic Party nomination between Hillary Clinton and Barack Obama, as the banking crisis and the ensuing Great Recession, as well as the interminable open sore of the Iraq War, assured the defeat of the Republican nominee, Senator John McCain, who though a distinguished man, was an inept blunderbuss as a presidential candidate. Obama's masterly victory over Hillary Clinton offered Americans the opportunity to put the racism of their national past behind them by electing him their president, which they happily did, twice, given the Republican alternatives on offer—first McCain and then the equally inept Mitt Romney.

Some space must be allowed for the maturation of Trump's political judgment during this period. He has been taxed, for instance, for having sent Democrat Eliot Spitzer a hand-written letter of congratulations when he was elected attorney general of New York in 1998 and for having supported Spitzer when he successfully ran for governor of New York in 2006. Spitzer was a very belligerent and draconian prosecutor, who didn't hesitate to intimidate boards of directors of a target with threats of spurious indictments, and as governor was forced to resign in 2008 after a prostitution scandal, taking with him the sympathy of no one. Trump described Spitzer in 2013 as a "horrible governor and attorney general." This has been cited as evidence of Trump's inconstancy,[2] but that is not a reasonable conclusion. It came fifteen years after Trump's congratulations to Spitzer on being elected state attorney general, and is not an unjustified opinion of Spitzer's performance in office.

Moreover, while Trump's political views remained largely constant, his party affiliation did not, as he tried to find and support a party that reflected his own beliefs. Trump changed political parties no less than seven times between 1999 and 2012. Trump initially saluted Barack Obama's qualities as a gifted politician, when he was elected a United States senator from Illinois. But Trump became a sharp critic of Obama as president, and was one of the leaders in the early 2012 polls to take the Republican Party nomination and challenge Obama, then running for reelection. Not content with attacks on Obamacare and other elements of Obama's rather thin record of accomplishment, Trump embarked on the hare-brained allegation that Obama was not eligible to hold the office of president because he was not born an American. Obama finally produced his long form birth certificate and the whole issue collapsed.

Obama drew extensive laughter when he asked, in Trump's presence at the annual Washington Correspondents' Dinner in 2012, if Trump would now move on to the question of: "Did we fake the moon landing?" The comments rankled, but Trump declined to run for president in 2012, and instead campaigned for Mitt Romney, and went to what he hoped would be Romney's victory party in Boston on election night. He was apparently quite upset by the result, and fired off a torrent of comments in his newly favored medium, Twitter, calling the election, in words that he would make familiar in another few years, "a total sham and a travesty." He called upon Republicans to "fight like hell and stop this great and disgusting injustice....We can't let this happen. The world is laughing at us."[3]

This is somewhat Trump's technique: if he didn't win, it was fixed—and then he will claim to have won anyway. In this case, he could claim victory by pointing to Republicans maintaining their majority in the House of Representatives, but he also had a more personal plan. Less than two weeks after the election, Trump filed a patent and trademark application on Reagan's slogan of twenty years before: "Make America

Great Again." In 2012, Trump turned sixty-six. If he was going to make a serious attempt to crown his career with the uniquely great office of president of the United States, it was 2016 or never.

Issues on which he had experience and expertise—real estate (via the housing bubble), banking, the economy—had risen to prominence. During the 1990s, Trump had watched in rising dismay as President Bill Clinton had inflated the housing bubble, by executive order and legislation, enjoying the political benefit of increased home ownership at no apparent cost to the taxpayers, as well as the tangible gratitude of the building trades unions and real estate developers. As Trump was one of the country's greatest authorities on most aspects of real estate development, he was increasingly concerned with the problem, especially after his own recent debt crisis.

And after the economy almost collapsed in 2008, he consoled himself with the spectacle of the bankers who had put him on the rack (crying like starving children for government assistance to avoid the complete failure of the banking system). It would have been a challenge to make Donald Trump a greater cynic than he already was about the claims of probity and impeccable motive of the captains of industry and capital, but the shambles of international finance in 2008 and following years managed it. The politicians from right to left who had enabled and fostered the crisis, led by Presidents Bill Clinton and George W. Bush and Senator John McCain, locked arms and blamed the crisis on private sector greed, and then acquiesced in the legislative demand for greater powers to assist the federal government in preventing what had occurred, despite the fact that Congress, the president, and the federal bureaucracy already possessed all the powers they needed to avoid it, and, in fact, were the chief architects of the problem.

In 2009, President Obama had entered office with a strong mandate and the good will of everyone, including Donald Trump, as the absurd and unjust color barrier to the nation's highest office was shattered. Indicative of the wave of hope that accompanied him into office and for a time after was the award, on October 9, 2009, not nine months into his presidency, of the Nobel Prize for Peace. The reason given was his

"Extraordinary efforts to strengthen international diplomacy and relations between peoples." This was nonsense, and the secretary of the Norwegian Nobel Association, Geir Lundestad, stated six years later that the award was an attempt to "strengthen" Obama's position and not a reward for anything he had done, and that it was a mistake. George W. Bush's trigger-happy war-making and nation-building, capped out by the economic debacle of the housing debt crisis and Great Recession, so demoralized America and the world that the articulate, suave Obama, representing multiethnic tolerance and racial justice, was accepted at face value by almost everyone. This made the disappointment of his ineffectual performance in office more bitter.

He enjoyed a respectable personal approval rating, probably because the country did not want to digest the thought that the first non-white president was not a good president. But in fact, he was not. Polls revealed that the American people thought their country was on the wrong track, and on a wide range of policy issues opposed President Obama. Objectively, the twenty years from 1996 to 2016 gave the country the worst economic crisis since the Great Depression, and with the exception of the Great Depression, the worst since the 1870s; as well the worst peacetime public sector debt accumulation in American history with only 1 percent per capita GDP growth to show for it.

More than a trillion dollars had been squandered in Iraq, to hand three-fifths of it over to Iranian influence and reduce the rest to violent civil and sectarian war. An oceanic flood of desperate refugees was loosed upon the Middle East, North Africa, and Europe, as the United States itself continued to admit unassimilated masses of illiterate Latin American peasants as undocumented migrants. Gross Domestic Product per capita growth declined from 4.5 percent in the last six Reagan years to 3.9 percent in the Clinton years, to 2 percent under George W. Bush and 1 percent under Obama. In Obama's eight years, food stamp use and the percentage in defined conditions of poverty sharply increased. The work force shrank by more than ten million people, though the population grew; and twenty-three million single Americans between the ages of thirty-five and fifty-four, the prime of a person's working life, were completely idle. A great many of them were sustained on immobi-lizing anti-depressants supplied by expanded Medicaid access.

All three recent presidents had blundered in foreign policy. In the case of North Korea, that mismanagement had led to the point where the incoming administration in 2017 would be facing an imminent nuclear threat from Pyongyang. With regard to Iran, a distinct minor-ity of Americans approved of Obama's attempt to placate the Iranian theocracy, the principal terrorism-sponsoring state in the world, with a slightly and conditionally delayed green light to deploy its own nuclear weapons.

Donald Trump got around the country a great deal and had an enormous number of contacts in almost every section of the population. He could see opinion building like a pressure cooker, especially among blue-collar conservatives alienated not just from the direction President Obama was taking the country, but from the establishment Republican Party that was supposed to offer a political alternative. Trump himself did not take naturally to mastering policy issues, but he had a good idea of what a very large number of people were against, and he knew from his preliminary run in 1987 and again in 2000 that a third party could not win. There would be no incumbent president running in 2016, and the country was angry at both parties. Both George W. Bush and Barack Obama, by normal measurements, had been unsuccessful presidents, and the first unsuccessful presidents to be reelected. Presidents who had been unsuccessful in the past, either did not seek reelection (Pierce, Buchanan), or sought reelection unsuccessfully (Van Buren, Benjamin Harrison, Hoover, Carter). Some presidents were adequately successful but were politically out-maneuvered (John Adams and John Quincy Adams, Cleveland, Taft, George H. W. Bush); and Polk and Hayes were successful presidents but declined to seek reelection. Trump, then, approached 2016 in an almost unique position, where there would not only be no incumbent, but where the American people, reelecting for a lack of other choices, two unsuccessful presidents, were now looking for a dramatic change. That, he realized, offered an opening for a non-establishment candidate.

Trump, however, did not spend the Obama years entirely torque-
ing up for a possible presidential run. The coils of the casino industry
were not so easily snipped. An inordinately lengthy time was required
for Trump to get free from the imbroglio of Atlantic City. He was
dogged by press skepticism about the proportions of his net worth,
though there was no longer any question about his solvency. The
casino boom in Atlantic City from which he had profited had followed
the traditional path to a bust. Too many casinos were built, neighbor-
ing states sought the same revenues and licensed their own gambling,
and Atlantic City was a decrepit and somewhat out-of-the-way place.
The contraction of the Atlantic City boom was painful and difficult,
and Trump's casino company had gone into bankruptcy again in 2004,
and the same fate appeared to be stalking it in 2009. Trump was getting too old, and generally prosperous, for this now, and rather than
take it through the wringer of bankruptcy again, he simply retired
from the company, saying that his economic interest in it was no longer material. It was an agile effort to side-step the issue, but Carl Icahn,
Trump's old and astute ally in many battles, opposed him this time.
Trump was supporting a proposal, sponsored by a hedge fund, that
the company go through bankruptcy yet again, but give Trump 10
percent of the emergent company in exchange for use of his name.
Icahn led a competing offer that would remove Trump completely,
adding publicly the acerbic reflection, that if Trump's name was so
valuable, "how come they (the casinos), went bankrupt three times."
Trump didn't answer, but Icahn's bid was unsuccessful.

Relations with Icahn were patched up (and the strength of the Trump
name has been demonstrated), but the casinos again went into the tank
in 2011. The Trump Castle Casino was finally sold for about 8 percent
of what Trump paid for it, though he had taken a lot of profit from it
over the years, and he parked most of the capital loss on bond-holders.
As always when in retreat, he congratulated himself—in this case, for
departing the Atlantic City Casino business at the right time. The Trump
Plaza and Taj Mahal casinos went back to the bankruptcy trough in
2014, as four of Atlantic City's twelve casinos closed, in a Darwinian

effort to restore commercial viability to a down-sized industry. Icahn returned to the fray and gained control of these assets in 2016. By this time, he was a public supporter of Trump as a political candidate, but was guarded in his commendation of him as a businessman. It was messy, but Trump had at least got clear of it all well before there was any need to start organizing politically for 2016.

The subject of Trump's wealth, not that it much matters to anyone except himself, as he is obviously a very wealthy man by the standards of all but a handful of people in the world, is difficult to assess precisely. He owns the commercial space and three-story penthouse in the Trump Tower, the Trump Building at 40 Wall Street, a number of valuable properties on East 41st, East 57th, and East 61st Streets, all prime locations. He has a sizeable interest in and the management of 1290 Avenue of the Americas, a forty-three-floor, top-end office building, and a substantial number of very high-quality golf courses and many lucrative real estate branding and licensing agreements. He owns Mar-a-Lago, a money-spinning private club in a unique location, built from one of the greatest and most famous mansions in America. He owns parts of many other projects, none of which seem now to be controversial. It could probably be assumed that Trump has substantial other assets that are not visible, and that his income streams benefit from the most agile tax planning that can be had. The Federal Election Commission in July 2015 released filings from Trump indicating a cost value of his assets of $1.4 billion, against liabilities of $265 million, but his campaign, presumably thinking it a vote-winner, said that the real asset values were about $10 billion (likely the customary truthful hyperbole but probably not more than two or three times the real figure). He made, and did not inherit, billions of dollars, and became a television star and remained one for many years, and in his first try at politics, was elected president of the United States; whatever happens after this, he has already had a career of astonishing achievement, though he is still unlikely ever to lead a cotillion.

Another subject that his always noisy critics focused on was his charitable endeavors. Trump frequently cites his charitable donations, and his enemies just as frequently try to debunk them. In May 2016, a long-standing critic in the *New York Post*, David Fahrenthold, exposed that Trump had promised to donate a million dollars of his own to veterans' causes, but had not done so. There had been many stories trying to pick holes in Trump's filed claim of having donated $102 million to bona fide charities between 2011 and 2015. This was shown to include the donation of free rounds of golf at his many fine golf courses, and other such prizes auctioned at charity benefits. There was particular emphasis on the donation of a free, chauffeured ride given to tennis star Serena Williams to attend a tennis tournament, and the donation of a framed, autographed portrait of himself. The value of the autographed portrait was $1,136.56. Trump was understandably irritated that such an item (submitted by his accounting staff), should be hyped in the obsessively negative press, and angry that it overshadowed his donation of more than one hundred million dollars to certified benevolent causes.

In response to Fahrenthold's sniping, Trump called a press conference at the Trump Tower, and announced that he had successfully canvassed donations of $4.6 million dollars for veterans' causes, and that he had, as he had promised, made a personal cash donation of one million dollars to the Marine Corps-Law Enforcement Foundation, bringing the total contribution to $5.6 million dollars—short of his target of $6 million, but still a tidy sum. He handed over this total, and noted that interest on the gift would quickly bring it to the campaign goal. For a man claiming such wealth, coming up with nearly $6 million did not require a backbreaking charitable campaign, but he had done what he had promised and should not have been subjected to the carping insolence of penurious journalists, who are poorly qualified to judge the generosity of others. At his press conference, Trump attacked the media treatment of his charitable activities as "dishonest" (frequently it was), and he singled out one television reporter as "a sleaze" (on normal probabilities, quite likely an accurate description). Trump was serving notice not only that he would not hesitate to attack the press as events unrolled, but that he knew how profoundly the public distrusted the media, and, in his opinion, with good reason.

As on several previous quadrennial occasions, speculation of a possible Trump campaign for the presidency was bruited about in the media, though it was understood that this time, it would be a contest for the Republican nomination, which was thought to be wide open, with no clear leading candidate for the first time since Barry Goldwater and Nelson Rockefeller contended for the honor of being buried by President Lyndon Johnson in 1964. Trump had spruced up and been more selective in his pursuit of public approval in the preceding decade. Not only were there no more ludicrously entertaining wrestling appearances, but he phased out unpromising applications of his brand, and did fewer profitable but lightweight inspirational addresses; further, he consigned to the complicated and incomprehensible attrition of litigation any and all disgruntlement over Trump University. But the polyglot army of his critics and skeptics were confidently lying in wait for him, and the more febrile opponents publicly beseeched him to test his real popularity in the field where they were both self-styled experts and presumptive king-makers and -breakers. He must make the race, comedian Stephen Colbert and others shrieked, so he could make a complete and irredeemable ass of himself, and satisfy America and the world that the country had not been battered by improvident events into seriously considering such a buffoon for its highest office. As an unfriendly duo of biographers put it: "Late-night comics only hoped he would stay around long enough for them to milk his candidacy for a few laughs."[4]

Almost nobody took such an initiative seriously. Trump had considered running for governor of New York in 2014, and he did not, at first, renew his contract with NBC for his ever-popular program, *The Apprentice*. Many skeptics snarkily assumed that Trump dropped hints of political ambitions merely to keep his name in the news, increase his brand visibility, and boost his ratings. The polite and civilized media, whose politeness rarely extended to Trump, accepted that Trump might be popular with up to 20 percent of the public, but it was not imaginable to any audible commentators except former House speaker Newt Gingrich (who had himself given Mitt Romney a respectable run for the Republican nomination in 2012) that Trump could possibly win a series of primaries in the glare of publicity and with all the baggage he carried from past bankruptcies, indiscretions, and assorted affronts to the conventional wisdom, not to mention generally accepted versions of good taste. If the nation's greatest blowhard and most vulgar capitalist, leader of the flat-earth level "birther" movement complaining that Obama was ineligible to be president, a known appreciative reader of the *National Enquirer*, was even considering such a move, it could only be for an ultimate publicity blow-out, the satiation of his own lust for publicity no matter how negative, and a stratospheric escalation of his tawdry and unlimited brand-building mania.

But Trump was in all respects a unique candidate, and had a unique political positioning—the appeal of which his critics didn't understand. Only one person, Donald Trump, came forward to challenge the whole political establishment—to call the Bushes incompetent, the Clintons dishonest, Obama a failure, the press toadies, the pollsters flacks and lackeys, much of the financial community greedy hypocrites, and Congress a bipartisan group of self-serving and inept insiders who were just gaming the system for their own incumbencies and the devil take the country and its voters. Came the day and the man, on June 16, 2015, the all-time red-letter day in the history of the Trump Tower. Trump's campaign manager, Corey Lewandowski—a Republican campaign organizer in New Hampshire, whom Trump had hired on the basis of a thirty-minute interview—had written a campaign announcement of under ten minutes. Trump descended the escalator of the grand foyer of the Trump Tower, with Melania and his children, and spoke for forty minutes. The atrium was packed, though some may have been attracted by offers of free Trump tee-shirts and hats. He was fluent, emphatic, and entertaining, and gave a foretaste of what was to come.

He emphasized the issues of illegal immigration; the loss of manufacturing jobs, sacrificed to disadvantageous trade deals and an unquestioned belief in the virtues of freer trade; the sky-rocketing national debt; and Islamic terrorism. He accused the Obama administration, including former secretary of state Hillary Clinton, of not recognizing Islamic terrorism for what it was, and of failing to defend the country adequately against it. Trump promised to finance his own campaign and severely criticized what he regarded as the corruption of the entire political system, from the buying of candidates through dishonest campaign financing, to the buying of votes in Congress by lobbyists. On illegal immigration—in a country with an estimated eleven to twelve million illegal residents—Trump applied the dentist's drill directly to the politically correct nerves of the Left by saying that illegal immigrants from Mexico were not Mexico's "best people" and included inordinate numbers of drug dealers, drug addicts, rapists, and other criminal elements, though he conceded that mixed among them were, "I assume, some good people." He promised "a great, great wall" to end the absurd porousness of seven hundred miles of open country, without even a fence between the United States and Mexico, like the much longer, but uncontroversial border with Canada. The United States, he said, had become "the dumping ground for the world's problems."

He promised to promote economic growth, to repatriate jobs with an incentive tax structure that would stop mollycoddling Wall Street deal-makers, to reopen and renegotiate unsuccessful trade agreements, to end the freeloading of America's so-called allies and the insolence of its enemies, and to redefine the national interest in a coherent line between George W. Bush's hair-trigger adventurism and Barack Obama's pacifistic, Panglossian quest to have America's allies and enemies change roles and places.

The initial reactions, entirely predictable, were mainly expressions of horror, leavened by jubilation from much of the media that the dingbat billionaire had jumped with both feet on a land-mine in his first appearance. It was almost too rich a payout on their hopes for a spectacular fiasco than they had dared to imagine possible. The "blowback," as Trump called it, was tempestuous: NBC ostentatiously canceled its arrangements with Trump (meaningless given that he had pulled out of *The Apprentice*, but indicative of the network, and most other networks' invertebrate response to controversy); NBC also declined to carry Trump's beauty pageants (but he was selling out of them anyway at a handsome profit); and Macy's cancelled its sale of Trump's clothing line, as his campaign announcement was "inconsistent with Macy's values" (a moral canon whose existence had not previously been suspected). Spanish-language networks Univision and Ora (partly owned by Mexican billionaire Carlos Slim, a large investor in the financially challenged *New York Times*), and NASCAR, severed their (tenuous) connections with Trump, as did even the Serta Mattress Company (not a heavy blow to the Trump Organization), all to the cacophonous jubilation of most of the media. Hillary Clinton piled on, saying, in the wake of the Charleston shooting, which happened the next day, when a twenty-one-year-old white man shot and killed nine people in an African American church, that Trump had "said some very inflammatory things about Mexicans. Everybody should stand up and say that that is not acceptable."

This was the beginning of the mighty Democratic smear steamroller that claimed Trump supported and incited racist violence. It was an unjust but not entirely surprising charge; his comments on Mexicans were provocative but not inflammatory. Hillary Clinton's statement, however, was the first in a long line of assertions that tended to confirm a suspicion that there was no argument to reelect the Democrats on their merits, nor any amber waves of enthusiasm for Hillary to harvest, only the potentialities of discrediting the Republicans. At this stage it was enough to attack a dark horse candidate for that party's nomination.

A bifurcation had already begun, between the conventional liberal wisdom, encompassing all the Democrats and at least half of the Republicans, 80 percent of the national media and 95 percent of the entertainment industry, and probably three quarters of the limousine liberal community in and in close touch with Wall Street on one side; and a section of popular opinion that was not well represented in the leadership groups of the country but was, from the first days of the Trump campaign, evidently a good deal larger and more capable of flexing its muscles at the polls than complacently received and robotically repeated civic-worthy opinion had remotely thought possible. The day before, former Florida governor Jeb Bush, son and brother of presidents, had announced his candidacy, and revealed that he had a war-chest of $100 million in a PAC (Political Action Committee), called Right to Rise USA.

Jeb Bush was assumed to be the favorite from the start, and Trump's assurance that he would have no PAC and would accept no contributions, was assumed to be irrelevant as his campaign was not expected to last for more than a few weeks; an amusing sorbet, a circus of the bumptious, before the country got down to choosing between the latest offerings of the Bush and Clinton families that the American political class, with singular lack of originality, would be offering for its delectation, this political season. Almost undetected, the political earth was starting to tremble and a seismic shock had begun to ripple across the country.

CHAPTER 6

Storming Babylon

The Republican Party chairman, Reince Priebus of Wisconsin, who had done a good job of clearing up the Republicans' financial problems and getting a smooth trans-party consensus on the center-right, telephoned Trump and asked him to moderate his message, or the stresses on the party could become dangerous. Trump was hounded by the media with accusatory questions bellowed from salivating mouths, through bared teeth, and with nostrils flared, but he fairly calmly held his line, citing reasonable journalistic evidence that was not entirely easy to dismiss, and stressed that he was in favor of immigration, including Mexican immigration, but was opposed to immigration that was not applied for and accepted according to fair criteria. He opposed immigration chosen by foreigners, imposed on the United States without its approval, and especially as a means of moving criminal elements out of Mexico and other Latin American countries into the United States. Some Republican candidates agreed that it was a legitimate issue, but most

rushed to join the feel-good bandwagon that the tenor of Trump's comments was unnecessarily provocative. Trump's rational response to
criticism, and his confident repetition of his argument, often with escalating flamboyance, quickly pushed his opponents along a path they
wished in any case to follow, of demonizing him as an extremist, a racist,
and a person of questionable mental stability as well as nauseating vul-
garity.

The Bushes and Clintons were not dynasties in the American political tradition of the Adamses, Roosevelts, and Harrisons, where the
presidents were at least a generation apart, and all were elevated on
meritocratic grounds (and in the case of the Roosevelts were sixth cous-
ins, though Franklin Roosevelt's wife was Theodore Roosevelt's niece).
The Bushes and Clintons emerged as quasi-dynasties because George H.
W. Bush was the first president to have politically ambitious sons, since
Taft and Theodore Roosevelt, and theirs didn't get a presidential nomination, and Bill Clinton was the first president to have an electorally
ambitious wife. The result was that for thirty-two years, eight straight
terms (1981–2013), one or other member of the two families was president, vice president, or secretary of state, and four years after that stretch
the standard-bearers of both families were the favored opening candidates for their parties' presidential nominations. The presumption that
the ascent of one or other of these heirs was foreordained left them both
more vulnerable to an alternative scenario than all but a very few people
saw.

Donald Trump opened his active campaign right after his announcement at the Trump Tower, and pulled a large crowd that packed out the
auditorium in Des Moines, Iowa, and brought the crowd to its feet in
complete spontaneity many times. In early July, Trump went to Phoenix,
Arizona, and advanced sales required the event be moved to a bigger
hall, where more than four thousand people were squeezed in like the
proverbial sardines, and thousands more were outside. The response was
so enthusiastic, it was a happening—and the crowd and the speaker
revved each other up. Someone shouted "Build a wall!" which Trump
had already promised to do, and he said "We will take our country

back!" He was well aware of how he was warming the atmosphere, in a state that had hundreds of thousands of undocumented Hispanics in it. An introductory speaker was the eighty-four-year-old former Maricopa sheriff Joe Arpaio, who gave part of his speaking time to the parent of a girl killed by a Mexican gang member in Los Angeles in 2008. The deceased girl's brother later disapproved of the politicization of the case, but it resonated well with the audience. Arpaio invoked Richard Nixon in saying "The Silent Majority is back."

Long-serving Arizona senator John McCain said (of Trump), "He fired up the crazies." This was rather insulting in a state where McCain was in a neck-and-neck race for reelection. Trump referred to McCain as a "dummy," which was also uncalled for, though it was, like a great many of Trump's comments and much of his conversation, good for a laugh. A week later, answering questions from Republican pollster Frank Luntz before an auditorium of evangelical Christians in a small town in Iowa, Trump, when pressed on what he had said about McCain, attacked McCain's statement that he had been speaking to "crazies….He called them all 'crazies.'" He defended his Phoenix audience but added that McCain was a "loser," one of his favorite pejorative descriptions. Luntz shouted over audience applause that McCain was a "war hero." Here Trump imprudently responded, "He's a war hero because he was captured. I like people that weren't captured, okay?" This was a serious discourtesy to a man who had been repeatedly tortured in eight years as a prisoner of the North Vietnamese, and who refused early release unless all his comrades were released too. (McCain's father was a distinguished admiral.) Trump simply could not resist his knee-jerk impulse to counterattack anyone who criticizes him.

On Lewandowski's advice, he held a press conference, where the questions, on the assumption that the media could kill the candidacy, were extremely hostile. One of those present was long-shot rival candidate Mike Huckabee, former governor of Arkansas, who told his campaign aide, Chip Saltzman, that not only would Trump escape the McCain episode unscathed, his numbers would go up. Incredibly, they did. Polls in mid-July, after the Hillary blast and the McCain incident had reverberated heavily, showed Donald Trump leading a field of seventeen candidates, all of them at least somewhat plausible. Head-scratching among the professionals of both parties began in earnest; at time of writing, it has not stopped.

The first Republican candidate debate came in August 2015, and as the polls were showing Trump as the leading candidate, he was placed at the center of the group and received the first question. Bret Baier of Fox News asked if any candidate who could not pledge in advance to support the party's eventual nominee would raise a hand, and only Trump did so, with the qualifier "I can totally make that pledge, if I'm the nominee." He saw the danger of doing so in a Republican audience, but as it was known that he had changed parties seven times in fourteen years, and he was running as much against the Republican establishment as against the Obama-Clinton Democrats, he felt it was both the honest and tactically preferable response. The most loaded question of the night was from the glamorous and articulate Megyn Kelly, who asked why Trump had called women "fat pigs, dogs, slobs, and disgusting animals." Trump expressionlessly responded, "Only Rosie O'Donnell," and when Ms. Kelly pushed the point, Trump railed against political correctness. It was a fairly unscarred escape from the question, but Trump said after that Kelly was hostile: "There was blood coming out of her eyes; there was blood coming out of her whatever." This was construed by the "Never-Trumpers," as anti-Trump Republicans were already starting to be called, as a vulgar reference to menstruation but Trump responded that that was a "sick" interpretation, and that all he had meant was that she was very hostile. Trump had cleared the first hurdle, and while not taken seriously by the media, was obviously not going to vanish in a trice.

The game began of how to quantify how significant a voting bloc the discontented "Archie Bunker" voters were (named after the politically incorrect working class lead in the 1970s sitcom *All in the Family*). Opening estimates were generally that Trump could pull 20 percent or so of the Republican vote, but that when the field narrowed, and other candidates passed him, Trump would fade away, having soaked the campaign for all the publicity he could. At this task, he was already an over-achiever;

the media hostility and skepticism had garnered him huge attention, and even though most of the exposure was intended to be negative, Trump was proving his point that all publicity was valuable. He was pulling very large crowds wherever he went, and though there were hecklers and picketers, Trump supporters were very numerous and demonstrative. The level of outrage of much of the public for the wars, recession, debt, violent crime, foreign policy blunders, illegal immigration, and economic stagnation had still not registered with the complacent media. Trump's support level, as the only candidate in either party not steeped to the eyeballs in the failures of the last twenty years, had not yet been noticed by the somnambulant, flaccid media and political establishment. The Trump aberration rumbled on, gathering strength like a tornado.

The Fox debate had attracted twenty-four million viewers, the highest total ever for such a thing and the networks, desperate for content, started running Trump rallies live. He generally made hilarious jokes and punchy declarations and generated a great deal of mirth. They had no idea of the consequences of giving him hundreds of millions of dollars of free attention. It was designed to sink his campaign by exposure, but to the media's dismay, many Americans liked what they saw, and rallied to Trump's banner. Trump did not need or buy advertising and paid for the events themselves by selling "Make America Great Again" hats and tee-shirts and other campaign paraphernalia. He was not only paying for his own campaign; at times, he was making money from it. Inconceivably large numbers of people, including many missed by the pollsters (because they had not voted or responded to polls for decades), liked his message and attended his rallies. And he was, as always, a great showman, and an entertaining, if often somewhat outrageous, public speaker. The conventional wisdom, though discommoded, was tenacious: the crowds were there, but it was entertainment and the rigorous campaign to come would banish the interloper.

Trump regularly attacked the media, often singling out individual reporters or pundits as "low-lifes" and "liars" and so forth. He departed the usual labored courtesy of the election campaign and was quite dismissive of several of his opponents and debunked the entire political system as a corrupt gravy train for the insiders, while the condition of the country deteriorated. "We don't win any more," he said, referring to the United States and its recent experiences in war and trade. Each week it became clearer that Trump had called it right and had a much better judgment of the state of public opinion, from all his television, product-branding, beauty contests, boxing and wrestling matches, and catering to the millions of people who gambled away a lot of their income. While he lavishly disparaged the media, he was very accessible for interviews, where he generally held his own in this early stage before policy questions became quite precise. And because he was such a phenomenon, most questions put to other candidates were about him. He took over the news, and his opponents assumed they were putting out the fire, but it kept spreading.

The Trump campaign only had five employees and this diminutive group determined its tactics as it went along, watching the news on Trump's airplane as they flew between campaign meetings. The media predictably took up the charge of Trump's rivals that he had "no ground game" and that his campaign would implode (they eagerly anticipated Trump becoming a casualty of his allegedly self-destructive exploding ego), but Trump pointed to his small entourage and cited it as an example of business efficiency. My good friend, Mark Steyn, a very experienced political journalist, attended a Trump meeting near his home in New Hampshire, and was in the press circle before the event. He was impressed at the absence of scurrying and officious aides; Trump was in the midst of conversation with several people when he heard himself being announced, as is traditional on such occasions: "The next president of the United States...," and said, "Let's get back to this when we finish—see you later," and strolled nonchalantly to center stage. He did resume the conversation later, and his manner was in all respects disarming.

Instead of leaking research and gossip about rivals, Trump just trotted rumors out directly, no matter how frivolous. Thus, as time went by, to establish that Senator Lindsey Graham had given his private cell phone number to Trump, he gave it to a crowd of thousands, and he repeated spurious stories about Senator Ted Cruz's father having had an association with Lee Harvey Oswald. (Cruz's father had been a Cuban Communist once but a connection to Oswald was neither believable nor relevant.) He even accused Cruz of philandering and adultery, though Trump was hardly an appropriate source for such priggish comment.

Trump also revived the practice, from a century before, of hurling personal abuse at other candidates. Standards of courtesy had descended a very long way from Ronald Reagan's Eleventh Commandment: "Never speak ill of another Republican." It had even descended from when Theodore Roosevelt called William Jennings Bryan an imbecile. Donald Trump was more direct: "Little Marco" (Rubio, senator from Florida); Lyin' Ted (Cruz), "Low-Energy Jeb" (Bush), and ultimately, "Crooked Hillary." It was undignified, of course, but there hadn't been much dignity left in presidential elections for a long time, and it was good entertainment.

Much of the public considered Trump's unorthodox behavior a welcome antidote to the pomposity, platitudes, and absurd self-importance of the other candidates. The people had heard all they had to say before and were tired of it. And the other candidates had no idea how to respond. Former Texas governor Rick Perry, who fumbled out of the Republican nomination contest four years earlier when he couldn't remember the name of the third government department he would abolish and said, "Woops," decided he had nothing to lose with a frontal attack, and denounced Trump as a "mean-spirited...demagogue (and) a cancer on conservatism." Neither Trump nor even the anti-Trump media paid much attention and Perry soon dropped out of the race. (Trump eventually made him secretary of energy, one of the departments Perry was going to abolish.) Jeb Bush, scion of a family of gentlemen as he is, was flummoxed by Trump's tactics, and finally simply said, "Donald Trump is a jerk—it felt good to get that off my chest." Such delicate reproaches were not going to turn what was a heavily running tide by late summer.

Trump personally liked some of the candidates and did not mock them: Dr. Ben Carson, New Jersey's Governor Chris Christie, and Arkansas's Mike Huckabee. Scott Walker, the very respected governor of Wisconsin, who had faced down militant public service unions and the persecution of his political supporters by an egregiously partisan Milwaukee U.S. attorney, dropped out a few weeks after Perry. He had led in Iowa, where his quiet personality and strong performance in office were popular—he called himself "radically normal"—but Trump's personality and the strength of the Trump story, no matter how hostile the person who told it, over-powered the less assertive candidates. Walker urged others to withdraw to allow more conventional and moderate Republicans to rally around an alternative to Trump. It was only September 2015, the first primary was not until February 2016, and Trump was already attracting calls for a unitary stop-Trump candidate to prevent the Grand Old Party from falling into the hands of the great vulgar philistine, roughneck, and ogre, whose candidacy was greeted with howls of glee, mockery, and execration announcing a summer festival of fun and farce just three months before.

On November 13, 2015, there were a series of terrorist incidents in Paris; a suicide bomb was detonated in the national football stadium (where the president of France was attending a match) and three groups of ISIS (Islamic State) gunmen attacked restaurants and cafes and opened fire in a crowded theater, killing a total of 130 people. Trump had been amenable to the admission of some refugees, if they could be screened properly, but now changed course to attacking Obama's policy of admitting 110,000 refugees, which, when truthful hyperbole was applied to electioneering, he represented to a raucously cheering corn-fed Texas crowd in Beaumont as 250,000 refugees. He promised to "beat the shit" out of ISIS, and repeated his familiar histrionics about building a wall.

On December 2, 2015, a married Muslim couple, the husband born in the United States and his wife a recent legal immigrant from Pakistan, killed fourteen and injured more than thirty in a shooting attack at an office holiday party in San Bernardino, California. They made no serious effort to survive the incident and, in a shoot-out with police, fired eighty-one rounds, injuring several policemen, and were killed by a fusillade of 440 rounds from many angles and a variety of weapons. It was an alleged case of Islamist self-radicalization. President Obama and Secretary Clinton declined to use the expression "Islamist extremism," and Obama called it "workplace violence." Trump issued a terse statement, but reserved his main reflection on the terrorist incident in California for the anniversary of the attack on Pearl Harbor, December 7, 2015, when he spoke at Mount Pleasant, South Carolina, aboard the retired aircraft carrier *Yorktown*, permanently secured as a museum and war memorial. He called for a "total and complete shutdown of Muslims entering the United States until our country's representatives can figure out what the hell is going on" which he later refined to a ban on people from certain largely Islamic countries, which had become failed states or were actively hostile toward the United States. The initial reaction by the media, the Democrats, and the Republican establishment to Trump's remarks was extremely hostile; Jeb Bush, for instance, tweeted that Trump was "unhinged." Trump's own small council of advisors had warned him of a potential backlash against his apparently reactionary stance. But he was cheered almost deliriously on the *Yorktown* and polls shortly revealed that most Americans thought he was the only candidate who had any idea how to deal with the terrorist problem as it crept into the United States.

By this time, Trump was leading most polls among Republicans, and running closely with Hillary Clinton for the presidency. It was still generally assumed that when the debates became more policy-specific, and the race thinned out a bit, and irritated voters felt they had got their anger out of their systems, Trump would fall behind Bush, Rubio, and Cruz, or at least one of them. But at the end of 2015, the race was almost over, though that was still not widely seen. Rather than crumpling like a burst balloon as had been anticipated, the Trump campaign's popularity was expanding and actually sucking the air out of the room for the other Republicans.

The Iowa caucuses were the first test of real voters, in January, and that race is generally won by whoever pulls the evangelical Christians. Trump was advised to ignore Iowa, because of his marital past and raffish big city manner and financial controversies and association with gambling and contests of pulchritude between semi-naked women. But when polls showed him falling behind Ben Carson, he started barn-storming the state, questioning the intelligence of voters who would prefer Ben Carson to himself. Carson fell away, but Ted Cruz, a quasi-evangelical Christian who in his final play for the nomination four months later would claim in Indiana that "God told me to run for pres-ident" (not even Donald was going to try that one), pulled ahead, as the national media suddenly recirculated the story that Trump had no "ground game." (This would be far from the most imaginative of the reasons they would devise to convince their viewers and themselves as the election year unfolded that Trump could not win.)

At the end, they were very close, but on the night of February 1, Cruz won Iowa after putting it about that Carson was quitting the race and that Carson's supporters should vote for him. It was a bold stroke, but when Cruz started playing hardball with Trump, he would be facing a fastball, brushback expert, who threw at the cheek-bones of his oppo-nents with greater zeal and force than anyone in American national politics since the Civil War. Trump made a brief concession speech on caucus night, but claimed that Cruz had not won Iowa: "He stole it," an allegation Ben Carson supported. Trump was annoyed and slightly embarrassed, but his showing in Iowa had been, all things considered, remarkably strong. Even with a movement of Protestant pastors behind him, Cruz had won only 27.6 percent of Iowa's caucus vote to 24.3 per-cent for Trump and 23.1 percent for Rubio. Ben Carson was fourth at 9.3 percent, and if any of the other candidates, including the massively financed Jeb Bush, was going to make a race of it, they would have to be heard from in New Hampshire.

The media tried to represent it as a stinging rebuff for Trump, but it wasn't and in New Hampshire he was ready and had been campaigning intermittently since 1987. Three nights before the New Hampshire vote, Christie blasted Rubio in an all-candidates' debate and said he was just a talking box who couldn't run anything; Rubio froze and repeated a canned statement about how Obama knew that he was ruining the country and was doing so deliberately. Rubio's statement had been irrel-evant the first time round, but repeating it made Rubio seem like an idiot.

Christie had ignored the knock of opportunity at his door four years before, and this was his desperation play to get into contention. He killed Rubio without resuscitating himself.

Lewandowski, who was from the Granite State, and Trump's young and beautiful communications director, Hope Hicks, set out their stall carefully and Trump called at police stations and campaigned to small groups with his customary inexhaustible energy. This was a decisive moment, as New Hampshire primaries have often been, including for John F. Kennedy, Richard Nixon, and Ronald Reagan. Trump said his team had "learned a lot about the ground game in a week," and on primary day, February 9, his campaign slapped the mouths of the skeptics by taking the state 35.2 percent to 15.7 percent for Ohio governor John Kasich who had put his full effort there, 11.6 percent for Cruz, 11 percent for Jeb Bush, 10.5 percent for the mortally wounded Rubio, and 7.4 percent for Christie. The New Hampshire primary is usually won in both parties by the candidate who proves to be the nominee, so this was a major victory. The comfortable assertion that Trump could not break through the ceiling of 20 percent GOP support had been raised to 25 percent after Iowa and was now at 35 percent. Confidence that the unimaginable Trump candidacy could be resisted within the Republican Party now depended on far-fetched notions that self-destructive indiscretions would rally primary voters to a stop-Trump candidate.

The thought that Trump might actually have struck a deep lode of electoral anger and ambition to punish the orthodox political class was still unable to penetrate the imaginations of the commentariat. On a worst case, the conventional wisdom was sheltering in the certainty that if Trump limped through to the nomination, he would be bombed by Clinton as Goldwater had been by Johnson, with 61 percent of the vote to 38.5 percent in 1964, and as McGovern was by Nixon by a similar margin in 1972, which in the present electorate would be a plurality of thirty million votes. Since a Trump victory was unthinkable to the knowledgeable, no one thought about it aloud, except Newt Gingrich, Ann Coulter, and Trump's influential supporters on the talk radio circuit, who had tens of millions of followers, such as Rush Limbaugh, Laura

Ingraham, and Sean Hannity. Senate majority leader Mitch McConnell of Kentucky said, as reported by the *New York Times* and not denied, that if Trump were nominated, "We'll drop him like a hot rock," and run the Senate campaigns separately from the presidential election.

The campaign moved to the South, starting with South Carolina on February 20. Again, in the debate before the primary, it was widely thought that Trump had gone too far. When Jeb Bush had defended his brother, the ex-president, and said that he was securing the country while Trump was putting on a down-market reality television show, Trump reminded the audience that the World Trade Center towers had been brought down by suicide skyjackers while George W. was the president. (Trump had claimed that Bush lied over Saddam's possession of weapons of mass destruction, but under heavy questioning from the media, retreated to the assertion that he should not have been so confident that Saddam did have such weapons.)

The live audience booed, but Trump, as always, was unrepentant and compounded this controversy by getting into an imbroglio with the pope (who does not have a large number of co-religionists in South Carolina). Flying back from Mexico to Rome, the pope had said, in evident reference to Trump's promise to build a wall on the border with Mexico, that this was "not Christian." Trump replied that the Vatican had "massive walls," and that "If the Vatican is attacked by ISIS, which everyone knows is its ultimate trophy, I can promise you that the pope would have only wished and prayed that Donald Trump would have been president." Trump won the exchange and the pope's remarks were gratuitous, but Trump didn't need more controversy. The next day, he told a story that is generally believed not to be true, though it has been about for many years, that General John J. Pershing, while suppressing a Muslim revolt in the Philippines in the early twentieth century, ordered the execution of fifty Muslim rebels, had the firing squads' bullets dipped in pig's blood, affronting Muslim sensibilities, spared one of the men sentenced to death, and told him to tell his people what had happened. This was a story that circulated in military schools such as the one Trump attended in New York.

Trump won the South Carolina primary easily, with 32.5 percent of the vote. Rubio, buoyed by the endorsement of the popular governor of South Carolina, Nikki Haley, eased in ahead of Cruz, 22.5 percent to 22.3 percent, with Kasich, Carson, and Bush all between 7 and 8 percent. Bush suspended his campaign that night. The Bush era in the Republican Party, a coincidence arising from Reagan having made George H. W. Bush vice president, was over. With Jeb, in many ways a more appealing candidate than family members that preceded him, the family's luck ran out. He hit a buzz saw with Trump, and the country considered the Bushes tainted by the unprecedented and infuriating decline of America, which seemed to have fallen overnight from being the world's sole superpower to being a country mired in recession, endless war, and cultural self-doubt.

It was clear that, unlike the other candidates who could raise themselves up to some extent in states where they could concentrate time and resources, Trump was going to pull a large number of voters everywhere in the country. It was the last chance to put up a stop-Trump candidate, and it was only February. Cruz, a Texan, had been counting on South Carolina, and a big clean-up in the following southern primaries. This was obviously not going to happen, and nor was there an obvious principal alternative to Trump. Rubio, if he had not been so shamefully demolished by the departing Christie, who soon dropped out and endorsed Trump, might have been able to do it. But the Trump steamroller seemed unstoppable.

The primaries now came down swiftly, and the vote percentages of Trump, Cruz, Rubio, and Kasich are repeated in that order after each state: Alabama (43, 21, 19, 9), Arkansas (33, 30.5, 25, 4), Georgia (39, 23.6, 24.4, 6), Massachusetts (49, 10, 18, 18), Tennessee (39, 25, 21, 5), Vermont (35, 32, 17, 9), Virginia (33, 10, 19, 30). The Massachusetts result was especially astounding. The Republicans had no chance of winning the state in a presidential election (Reagan in 1984 was the only Republican to do so since Eisenhower in 1956), and even the Republicans are very liberal, but Trump romped over his rivals. It was clear from these primaries that Trump had the strongest and least regional base of Republican support, which meant that even if every other candidate dropped out, leaving only one anti-Trump stalwart, Trump still had a very good chance of winning.

All the ridicule of the media, the howls of outrage and mockery of the sophisticates and of the sensitive, the bunk about ground games— none of it counted for anything. The Republican field wasn't weak: Bush, Kasich, Christie, Huckabee, and Walker all were or had been popular and successful governors; Cruz and Rubio and Rand Paul were articulate and well-publicized senators, but they were instantly passé—they were all identified with the decrepit failure of war, recession, stagnation, debt, and international embarrassment and humiliation of the past twenty years. Trump was the only contender who wasn't, and who understood the populist groundswell that his competitors missed, and he was now unstoppable among the Republicans. It still never seemed to dawn on anyone that he might not be any pushover for Hillary Clinton either (and she had her hands full dealing with a revolt from the Left led by the independent Democratic senator from Vermont, who had been elected to the Senate as a socialist, Bernie Sanders).

Just before the Illinois primary on March 15, there were clashes with anti-Trump protesters, and at a Trump rally in Ohio the next day, an unarmed but angry and belligerent man tried to storm Trump's platform at the airport. Trump's instinct was not to duck or run, but to clench his fists and turn to face the commotion. Security removed the man without serious incident, and when Trump resumed his speech he joked with his audience, "I was ready for him, but it's much easier if the cops do it." Trump dealt with a lot of hecklers and neither he nor his followers had much toleration of them, though, it must be said, the interlopers never showed any disposition to witty repartee. This was not a British election meeting and these were not effete audiences. Donald Trump was speaking to his followers, a great many of whom believed that he was the first candidate for the nation's highest office since Reagan, with the possible exception of Bill Clinton at his best, who cared a rap for them or spoke their language.

Trump had lots of private as well as official security and would urge them to remove disorderly or disruptive people: "Get him out of here!"

or "In the good old days this didn't happen because of the rough treatment they got," or "I'd like to punch him in the face," or even "Knock the crap out of him." The best response was: "Try not to hurt him. If you do, I'll defend you in court." It was a bit crude but Trump genuinely identified with the general feeling of being angry at what had happened to the country, impatient for a change of approach, and irritated by attempts to prevent him from speaking to large crowds of supporters. He was accused of inciting violence, but that was an unjust rap; he refused, on behalf of his evidently very large following, to be intimidated by physical threats or vocal interruptions. When asked if he had encouraged violence at his rallies, Trump replied, "I truly hope not...we have some protesters who are bad dudes." That was a fair summary (and was later confirmed with revelations that Democratic operatives had paid for "bad dudes" to disrupt Trump events) but did not spare him from the charge by his now fearful, rather than merely contemptuous, enemies, that he, and not those who came to prevent him from speaking or being heard, was inciting violence.

Kasich won his home state of Ohio in the primary of March 15, 47 percent to 36 percent for Trump and 13 percent for Cruz. This was an achievement, but Kasich was a successful governor who had been reelected by more than a million votes, and he only beat Trump by 220,000 votes, and gave an eccentric victory speech in which he urged people to "take a widow to dinner...and embrace a stranger in the mall," (advice, which if followed, would have led to a startling increase in sexual assault charges across the state). On the same day, in Florida, in a winner-take-all primary, Trump bombed Rubio out of the race in his home state 47 percent to 27 percent, with 17 percent for Cruz, and 7 percent for Kasich. Cruz was finally the last viable man standing against Trump when they got to Wisconsin on April 5, though Kasich remained in the race hoping to present himself as the ultimate anti-Trump Republican in a longshot bid to consolidate the anti-Trump vote both in the remaining primaries and possibly at the Republican convention. Cruz won Wisconsin by 48 percent to Trump's 35 percent, to 14 percent for Kasich. Cruz had some success rounding up spare delegates where states had not elected pledged delegates, and outsmarted the local Trump organizations in North Dakota and Colorado. But Trump caught on quickly, and on April 19 in New York, after playing up Cruz's earlier derision of "New York values" hammered the Texan 60 percent to 17 percent and 23 percent for Kasich, and took eighty-nine of ninety-six delegates. It seemed that there might still be a very slender chance to deny Trump a majority on the first ballot, keep him out until the pledged delegates were free to vote as they wished, and get the party grandees, such as they were, to broker something, as in olden times, either for Kasich or for some other establishment-favored candidate.

It was a madly improbable idea, but it the was the only hope the Never-Trumpers had before the showdown in the general election, where the conventional wisdom, shaking but still afloat, held Clinton to be unbeatable, despite the desperate bruising she was taking from the preposterous Sanders. The Vermont senator had worked and lived in a Stalinist kibbutz even after the Twentieth Communist Party Congress had denounced Stalin; he had even taken his honeymoon in Khrushchev's Moscow. If Trump was a change, Sanders was an off-the-wall democratic Marxist representing the sylvan little state of Vermont with his heavy Brooklyn accent. The presidential race was becoming steadily more surreal with Hillary Clinton and Donald Trump standing in the wide center, in policy terms, between the far leftist Sanders and the gun-toting, Bible-thumping, Texan prosecutor Cruz who was pitching his campaign to the corn-cobbers and the wool-hats.

The Cruz dream died in Indiana on May 3: Trump carried the state 53 percent to 37 percent for Cruz and 7 percent for Kasich. Cruz said he had "left everything (he) had on the field in Indiana," having, in a desperate gambit to swing more voters his way, announced Carly Fiorina, former CEO of Hewlett-Packard and former U.S. Senate candidate from California (but, fatally, much more loved by the conservative establishment than by conservative voters), as his running mate. He and Kasich suspended their campaigns. (They didn't officially withdraw, in order to receive public funding for campaign expenses.) Hillary Clinton eventually retained control of the Democrats, relying on ex officio delegates, the same group that had taken the nomination from her eight years before, when she ran even with Barack Obama in the primaries. (She did defeat Sanders in the primaries by 16.9 million to 13.2 million votes, but more than half her delegate lead was provided by unelected super-delegates.)

As the nominating process in both parties lumbered to its weary end, there were plenty of disturbing statistics for those who confidently assumed that the Clintons would be moving back into the White House. A strong Republican candidate—an Eisenhower, a Nixon in 1972, or a Reagan—can take Pennsylvania in a presidential election, but the primary results in that state generally indicate a substantially larger number of Democrats than Republicans. In the primaries on April 26, 2016, the Republicans got almost 49 percent of the total vote, although there was a ding-dong battle between Clinton and Sanders on the Democratic side. Trump won the Republican primary, 57 percent to 22 percent for Cruz and 19 percent for Kasich, and there appeared to be indications that he was pulling significant numbers of blue-collar Democrats (who had been dismissed in that state eight years before by Obama as preoccupied with guns and religion). Noteworthy was that significant numbers of Trump supporters in Pennsylvania (and elsewhere) were voting for the first time in some years. In Indiana on May 3, while it is generally a 55 percent or so Republican state, Trump took 53 percent of the Republican vote, which amounted to 92 percent of the entire number of Democratic votes in a hotly contested battle between Clinton and Sanders (which Clinton won narrowly in the state). Trump was getting stronger rather than weaker as the campaign progressed. Instead of being worn down by the febrile animosity of the sophisticated media, he was pulling a steadily greater wave of people who were more pleased than offended by his round-house attacks on the bipartisan misgovernment of the recent past, always delivered with panache and large dollops of hyperbole, truthful and otherwise. Hillary was still the favorite, but it was no time for the complacency still unctuously exuded by the Republican Never-Trumpers and their Democratic analogues. Comfortable America took its summer holiday feigning serene confidence, but nagged by a concern that matters were getting out of hand. They were.

Almost no respectable opinion could yet imagine that Donald Trump, of all people, might actually be on his way to the White House (as chief occupant). It was too unthinkable, but to take a phrase from segregationist Dixiecrat candidate George C. Wallace in 1968, Trump had shaken the governing elites of the country by their eye-teeth, and it was far from over. In a year that was supposed to produce a Bush-Clinton rematch, the American political class was in shambles.

CHAPTER 7

The Republican Nominee

A s the dust settled and Trump prepared for the convention, the ambiance within Republican ranks was far from conciliatory. Many within the Republican establishment—including former presidents George H. W. Bush and George W. Bush, former governor Jeb Bush, former presidential nominee Mitt Romney, and Ohio Governor John Kasich—let it be known that they would not be supporting Trump, and House Speaker Paul Ryan said he was "not ready" to support the apparent nominee. Trump replied that he might remove Ryan as chairman of the Republican convention. On June 2, however, Ryan said he would vote for Trump and he was confirmed as convention chairman. There was squabbling within the campaign itself, and Trump fired Lewandowski and replaced him with Paul Manafort, a more seasoned political professional, whose chief job was to make sure Trump had a sufficient number of committed delegates to stave off attempts by anti-Trump agitators to release delegates from their pledges and block Trump from getting the nomination. Senate leader Mitch McConnell, Senator Jeff Sessions of Alabama, and former presidential and vice presidential candidate Robert Dole, and several governors and former governors, including Rick Perry of Texas, who had denounced Trump as a "toxic demagogue" before quitting the race, endorsed Trump. McConnell said that the wishes of the voters in the primaries had to be respected.

On June 12, a Muslim gunman born in the United States killed forty-nine people and himself in a gay night club in Orlando, Florida. Trump repeated his demands for restriction of Muslim immigration (which was not relevant to the facts of the tragedy) and did so, in part, to argue that he (and America) were tolerant of homosexuals in a way that Muslim radicals were not. He also implied that Obama was too friendly with America's enemies. The media, and the Left, took this badly, accusing Trump of picking on one minority group, while trying to appease another, and not understanding the alleged nuanced diplomacy of Obama.

The rising contumely in the media got worse when Trump accused the judge in a class action suit against Trump University of being biased because of his Latin American heritage. The judge had Hispanic parents, was born in Indiana, and was a member of various Hispanic legal organizations including the San Diego La Raza Lawyers Association, and Trump undoubtedly believed he was merely telling the blunt truth, but it was at least a provocative thing to say. Senator Lindsey Graham of South Carolina went too far when he said Trump's remarks were "the most un-American thing from a politician since Joe McCarthy. If anybody was looking for an off-ramp, this was probably it." Ryan denounced Trump's words as "absolutely unacceptable....the textbook definition of a racist comment." This was over-stating it too, and Ryan did not retract his support of the candidate, but Trump was being perverse in aggravating the sore regions of his party. Trump stated that he refused to be politically correct and that his whole interest was to make America great again, which could not be achieved with more political correctness. He said that his wife, sitting beside him in the back of a massively armored car with windows an inch thick, and a huge security unit holding back thousands of people outside the Trump Tower, asked him "Are you sure that this is what you want for the rest of your life?" Of course it was.[1]

On July 5, the FBI director, James B. Comey, held a press conference to announce that after a criminal investigation of a year into Hillary Clinton's use of a private email server while she was secretary of state—an investigation that included looking into the destruction of evidence: the erasure of 33,000 emails, many of which were government property and had been subpoenaed by Congress—that he would not recommend a prosecution. The attorney general, Loretta Lynch, had inadvisedly met on an official aircraft on the tarmac at Phoenix airport with former president Bill Clinton on June 29, and there were loud calls for her recusal from the Clinton email investigation. She said she would abide by the advice of the FBI director. It later came to light that she had asked and Comey had agreed that the investigation should be called "the Clinton matter" rather than an investigation. It also later emerged that Comey had written a draft exculpation of Mrs. Clinton six weeks before he interviewed her or other key witnesses, including close aides Cheryl Mills, Heather Samuelson, or Huma Abedin. Moreover, there was some evidence that Lynch knew beforehand that Comey would not recommend charges against Hillary, so her agreeing to abide by Comey's advice was not much of a concession to the impartial administration of justice. At his press conference on July 5, Comey explained in detail that Clinton's conduct and that of some of her entourage had been "extremely careless," but concluded that "no reasonable prosecutor would bring such a case." He did not elaborate.

It eventually emerged that a rabid Clinton supporter in the counter-intelligence service of the FBI, Peter Strzok, had changed "grossly negligent" (a crime) to "extremely careless." The same FBI official would later be exposed as a prominent figure in an anti-Trump movement within the federal bureaucracy in late 2017.

Two days after his press conference, Comey was questioned closely by the Republican-led House Judiciary Committee and acknowledged that a number of Mrs. Clinton's utterances on the subject of her emails, some of them to FBI investigators, had been inaccurate. He did not speculate on whether her statements had been honestly mistaken or deliberately untruthful. This was the first time that the FBI had revealed the results of an investigation rather than handing its recommendation discreetly to the Justice Department, and it was never explained why Lynch had invited Comey to do so rather than, after her recusal, giving it to the deputy attorney general, Sally Yates. This is where this matter lay until October 26, though there were audible rumblings of discontent that his decision was improper and suspect. Hillary Clinton claimed it was a complete vindication, though she acknowledged that she had "short-circuited" the truth.

The Republican convention in Cleveland opened on July 16, and came right after a terrible terrorist incident on the Promenade des Anglais in Nice, France, on Bastille Day, July 14, that killed eighty-six people, and the murder of eight policemen and wounding of nine in Dallas and Baton Rouge by black militants on July 7 and 17. The convention was supposed to be an informal Trump celebration, but was sobered by the theme of American decline under the Obama administration, marred by the boycotts and rebellions of anti-Trump Republicans (including that of Governor Kasich who refused to attend a convention held in his own state), and by the amateurism and stupidity of a speechwriter giving the poised, beautiful, and popular Melania Trump a speech that plagiarized directly from a speech by Michelle Obama, making Mrs. Trump a blameless victim of the inadequacies of her husband's campaign staff.

Trump revealed the identity of his vice presidential choice, Governor Mike Pence of Indiana, who was well received, though CNN (generally known as the Clinton News Network throughout the campaign because of its relentless partiality) falsely claimed that Trump had changed his mind and wanted to dump Pence. The other alleged contenders had been New Jersey Governor Chris Christie and former House Speaker Newt Gingrich, but Christie had too much political baggage, as would become apparent, and Gingrich was better suited to commenting on Trump than serving under him (though his wife Callista became Trump's United States ambassador to the Holy See).

The convention was generally rather rancorous, with the predictable fierce attacks on the Clintons, especially on their financial integrity and her past appeasement of Islam, including her refusal to utter the words "Islamist extremism" and her alleged negligence in the killing of the U.S. ambassador and three other Americans during a terrorist attack in Benghazi, Libya, in 2012. The convention also gave lots of air time to people whose family members had been murdered by illegal immigrants, an issue that particularly agitated Trump but also that was certain to produce negative comment from the liberal media. Trump, however, refused to be cowed by media criticism and had already written the media off as an overt enemy of his campaign. Former New York mayor Rudolph Giuliani gave an address that would have led a foreign visitor to believe that no one in the country could set foot outside their homes at night, or in many places even during the day, without fear of physical assault. It was one thing to make America great, but something different to try to incite hysteria about the state of public security. An official of the National Rifle Association explained how Hillary Clinton would take away everyone's firearms; Governor Christie conducted an in absentia mock trial of Hillary Clinton and worked the crowd up, chanting, "Lock her up!' and "Guilty!" There was a prime-time film called *Hillary the Horrible*. It was already clear that the Democrats were going to scorch Trump as a racist, sexist, crook, and idiot, even if this were the only subject where the Clintons, Obama, and Sanders could agree. Trump, in the Irish football expression, was "getting his retaliation in first." It was going to be an epic mud-slinging match, and, in Pentagonese, both candidates were "target-rich environments."

Trump emulated the law-and-order theme Richard Nixon emphasized at the 1968 GOP convention, where he drew huge applause for such lines as "No one will use the American flag for a doormat, in this country or any other, while I am the president." In their Trump biography, *Washington Post*'s Michael Kranish and Marc Fisher wrote the Republican convention "presented TV viewers with a vision of a country in deep trouble, unsafe, weak, governed by rigged systems and by people who had dishonest, even evil intentions. Speakers described a country that had lost respect abroad and hope at home, a country nearly at the mercy of...terrorists. It was a gloomy picture of a nation in decline, a society that had lost its identity."[2] Naturally, this was not a theme to bring the patriotic Republicans at the convention to their feet cheering, but interspersed with vehement expressions of hostility toward Hillary, it armed the faithful with a grim sense of what they were fighting against. (One delegate proposed that Hillary be hanged on a gallows without further discussion, and another suggested a firing squad instead.)

Hillary Clinton put out a widely played television advertisement in the middle of the Republican convention, accusing Trump of having "No self-discipline, no self-control, no sense of history, no understanding of the limits of the kind of power that any president should impose upon himself." It was the scolding of a schoolmarm. The country was uncomfortable with both candidates; but Trump had a huge and ardent following; Hillary was Bill's (wronged) wife, the only woman in the race, and not Trump, but few could regard her with enthusiasm, it was more a sense of resignation that she was next in line for the Democrats no matter how unlikeable or ethically tainted she might be. The Cleveland Republican convention had a number of memorably odd moments; one was when runner-up Ted Cruz spoke and did not mention the nominee, urging Republicans to "Vote your conscience," a pretty corny and unsportsmanlike exhortation, which drew tremendous booing and catcalls. Then Donald Trump himself walked on stage to waves of applause. It wasn't party unity, but it wasn't a staged and forced exercise in Clintonian non-spontaneity either.

Trump wound it up with a seventy-six-minute harangue to a television audience of thirty-five million, rather more than Mitt Romney had reached four years before. He spoke from a teleprompter to be more systematic and structured than he generally was in his frequently hilarious but often rather syncopated and discursive addresses he gave to big crowds on the hustings. He fear-mongered and lamented for fifteen minutes, before easing into attacks on his opponent. This set the crowd on fire with chants of "Lock her up," and less polite calls. The candidate didn't sign on with the chants, and instead raised his hand and said,

"Let's defeat her in November." This comparatively statesmanlike stance was varied somewhat with the assertion that Hillary Clinton's legacy would be "Death, destruction, terrorism, and weakness." He promised to win against the woman responsible for "terrible, terrible crimes."[3] But he also invited Silicon Valley billionaire Peter Thiel to be the first openly gay man to address a GOP convention and went out of his way to promise that, as president, he would protect the LGBTQ community, and when this drew applause, he paused to thank the convention for approving sentiments favorable to gays. Despite the smears of "homophobia," Donald Trump was the most pro-gay GOP presidential nominee in American history, and one who managed that feat while also being a sincere defender of religious liberty, with overwhelming support among white evangelical voters.

He relied implicitly on his claimed status as an efficient and bold businessman to get the quick resolutions he promised for difficult problems like crime and drug abuse, hit all his usual hot buttons again, and ended: "I'm your voice. Believe me." He didn't get a huge bounce from his convention and the country that wasn't already won over by him would take some persuading, but it wasn't as disorderly a convention as it could have been given the Republican establishment's disdain for its own nominee. There would be no traditional gentlemanly wait for the other side's convention, and Trump launched his formal assault on the White House at once.

It was generally still assumed Hillary Clinton would win safely enough, but there was not now a consensus that it would be a romp. Trump personally was confident. After the distance he had covered against all odds, he had some reason to be.

Trump brought Kellyanne Conway, an experienced pollster and political strategist, on board on July 1, and in August she replaced Manafort as campaign manager, as he had proved contentious, and there were media attacks on his former position as an advisor to pro-Russian president Viktor Yanukovych of Ukraine. On the same day as Ms. Conway's elevation, Trump brought in the head of Breitbart, a lively but somewhat conspiratorialist news service, Steve Bannon, as chief executive of the campaign. Bannon is an interesting intellectual Catholic, with a good background in the Navy, finance, and film-making, but also cantankerous and cranky, and as journalist James Delingpole noted, "the most terrifying boss you could ever have….He's short-tempered and when he roasts you, he's very foul-mouthed. But he is a genius as well, a political visionary."

Trump was impressed by Kellyanne Conway and she brought a renewed sense of direction, discipline, and focus to the campaign, though, inevitably, there were conflicts with so many powerful personalities working together. Conway was the first female campaign manager of a winning presidential bid, continuing Trump's history of promoting talented women in largely male-dominated fields, but neither she nor he got credit for that, such was the media hostility against them.

In late summer, Clinton was leading in all the polls, but only by between 1 and 7 percent. Trump's achievement, whatever happened next, was amazing. In the entire history of the country, the only other major party nominee for the presidency who had never held a public office, even an unelected one, or a senior military position, was Wendell L. Willkie, lawyer, utilities executive, and public intellectual, who ran a strong but unsuccessful campaign against Franklin D. Roosevelt in 1940. Trump was also the wealthiest presidential nominee ever, and the oldest person ever nominated for president by a major party for a first term.

Almost all the media had guffawed in uproarious disbelief at every stage of Trump's candidacy and assumed right to the end that it had been a brand-building move to enable him to sell more neck-ties, mineral water, or deodorant, and that he had just struck it lucky to do as well as he did. It also propagated the myth that all Trump's followers were blue-collar reactionaries, when it was clear from the huge vote he pulled in many Republican primaries, including Massachusetts, Pennsylvania, New York, and Florida, that he was taking a big chunk of the middle class, and a surprising number of non-whites of all ethnicities. That he offended the comfortable Left as a reactionary did not mean that he really was a reactionary, only that he was politically incorrect and prepared to say how catastrophically misgoverned the United States had been for the last twenty years. He stuck to his lines that he was in favor of immigration but not illegal immigration, and in favor of health care for everyone, but not on a coercive and dishonest basis such as Obama had put across (as in famously false promises that patients could keep their doctors and that their premiums wouldn't go up).

Trump was in favor of charter schools because, like most parents in the country, though his own children had gone to private schools, he held teachers' unions responsible for the net decline of the IQ of the American public in the last generation (a shockingly underreported story). He was in favor of foreign trade, but not of immense trade and current account imbalances that resulted in American unemployment. Trump was concerned with the environment, but opposed to throwing millions of people out of work and paying billions of dollars to foreign governments because of unproved theories of global warming and how to combat it. Much of the country, as it turned out, considered these policies he opposed to be, in Napoleon's phrase, "lies agreed upon." And although he often put it a bit simplistically, he favored a sensible definition of the national interest, and the retention or development of the level of military strength necessary and sufficient to protect that interest, while pursuing neither the military adventurism of George W. Bush nor the pacifistic defeatism of Barack Obama. He was not an isolationist and favored alliances, but not alliances where "allies" gave the instructions, and Americans did the work and paid the bills. To his visceral opponents, this was knuckle-dragging demagogy. To tens of millions of others, annoyed and in many cases unnerved by financial insecurity and national embarrassment, it was plain-spoken truth.

So sudden and profound had been the disintegration of the liberal Democratic and look-alike Republican consensus, the commentariat embarked almost unanimously aboard the good ship *Clinton*, not realizing it was already sinking. Distinguished conservative opinion leaders like George Will, Bret Stephens, David Frum, and David Brooks; almost every writer at *National Review*, the *Weekly Standard*, and *Commentary*; and Bush-inclined neoconservatives sitting in right-leaning think tanks denounced Trump as a brainless, vulgar, dangerous charlatan and barbarian. It was an uncontrollable reflex, whose causes could be understood and explained up to a point, but which became the source of a barrage of mindless and irrational fulminations. With a few exceptions, this obloquy from the highbrow Right continued even after Trump's policy successes cemented his as the most successful first year for a conservative president since Reagan, if not Eisenhower. In a moment of truth, *Weekly Standard* editor Bill Kristol acknowledged his loathing for Trump "is bringing out my inner liberal."

Trump greeted it all with amusement; he knew that these people controlled no votes, influenced few, and were talking to themselves, and that it would be a valuable gift to run against the Washington and New York and Los Angeles media and entertainment communities that had not got anything right for decades. Self-important, polysyllabic pundits were precisely the sort of people who would be ignored and despised by the "great unwashed body of America" of Jack Kerouac: "Whither goest thou, America, in thy shiny car in the night?" (Kerouac asked in his *On the Road*.) The answer in 2016 was not necessarily to Hillary Clinton. The conservative columnists' antics reinforced Clintonian over-confidence, as did the cloying deference of Hollywood stars. The country might be able to take all the opinionated airheads of the movies on the big or little screen, but they had no more interest in what Beyoncé or George Clooney or Meryl Streep thought about politics than they wished baseball stars to remove their appendix or super models to extract their wisdom teeth. Donald Trump was the champion of transforming celebrity into political influence, and he dismissed Clinton's Hollywood entourage as idiots and poseurs. (Many were.)

On July 23, just before the opening of the Democratic convention, WikiLeaks released a large number of Democratic National Committee emails that showed that the party executive was strongly in favor of Clinton over Sanders and had violated obligations of neutrality. Emails of the party chairman, Debbie Wasserman Schultz, revealed the DNC had tried to rig the convention, and Wasserman Schultz, amid great controversy, was obliged to resign, and was booed from the podium as she did so. At a lively press conference from his Doral golf course on July

27, Donald Trump joked, "Russia, if you're listening, I hope you're able to find the 30,000 emails that are missing." The humorless and befuddled media, unable to take a joke, concluded that Trump had incited treason.

The Democratic convention was in Philadelphia from July 25 to 28, and was a full return broadside of ad hominem fire at the Republican nominee, as well as a celebration of the Bill Clinton and Obama years as if they had not been interrupted by the George W. Bush interregnum and had been an uninterrupted four-term coruscation of good government and unchallengeable progress. Trump was portrayed as a racist, a sexist, an inciter of violence, a crooked businessman, totally unstatesmanlike, an ignoramus, and a disruptive interloper in the inexorable progress of liberal Democratic America, by a litany of speakers from a host of former and aspiring incumbents that included both Clintons, both Obamas, Vice President Joe Biden, and Senator Tim Kaine of Virginia (who between them, had spent or were about to be nominated to spend the formidable total of fifty-two years in the official residences of the president and vice president).

At one point during the convention, then–first lady Michelle Obama gave a stirring speech about the merits of taking the high road in politics, including the much-touted phrase "when they go low, we go high." Unless Hillary Clinton had thought Mrs. Obama was referring to budgetary expenditures on attack ads, she was not inspired by the speech. The Clinton election strategy was unprecedented in two relevant respects: it shattered all records for most money spent by a political campaign on attack ads ($400 million), which consisted of the highest proportion of personal attack ads (more than 60 percent), described in a study on campaign spending published by the Wesleyan Media Project, as "devoid of policy discussion." All told, Clinton and her allies spent a staggering $250 million on personal attacks, ten times more than Trump, who not only spent less, but focused far more on policy (70 percent of his ads). Given this obscene quarter-billion-dollar smear job, it is miraculous that Trump's approval rating is as high as it is. It is also amazing (and alarming) that the media so uniformly accepted that Mrs. Clinton's campaign was taking the high road, and that Trump was taking the low road when he responded to her attacks.

Personal attacks might make for a perfectly good partisan argument up to a point, but in the case of the Clinton campaign it was not accompanied by any policy program that was emphasized enough for the voters to notice it. Obama's audacious and hopeful promise to bring about "change we can believe in," though well received after the failures of the George W. Bush administration, had gone unfulfilled to the point of fueling the Trump fires of discontent. Obama might be impeccably cultured, conversationally fluent, and polished and presentable but after his eight years in office, the country felt more divided than before, and in a state of decline.

While there was no great warmth of affection between the Clintons and the Obamas, they locked arms, mounted their soap-boxes and rang the alarm bells in opposition to a mighty ogre who represented a categorical rejection of their joint incumbency and of the politically correct group-think of the liberal elite. The heyday of fear and smear was at hand, and the enemy was not a gentleman or an amateur. The Clintons and Obama faced far more than they bargained for.

For the Democrats to turn the tables on Trump's rhetoric about Muslims, given the high level of public concern about the admission of Islamic terrorists or people who were apt to become radicalized once inside the country, the Democrats sent to the podium Khizr Khan, a lawyer who had emigrated from Pakistan in 1980, and his wife, Ghazala. Their son, Humayun, had died in Iraq in 2004 in a suicide bombing while serving in the U.S. Army and had been posthumously awarded a Bronze Star and a Purple Heart. Mr. Khan spoke of his son and objected to the earlier Trump proposals to ban Muslim immigration, saying, "if it was up to Donald Trump, [his son] would have never been in America." Mr. Khan spoke calmly and graciously and asked if Trump had ever read the Constitution, and produced a copy from his pocket and offered, somewhat gratuitously, to lend it to Trump. Mr. Khan concluded that "Trump had sacrificed nothing and no one." It was a reasonable effort to snag Trump on his earlier reckless call for a temporary ban on the admission of Muslims to America, but it was also a rather shabby exploitation of natural sympathy for any family that has lost someone in war, serving with distinction in the country's uniform. The next week, on a political television interview program. ABC's George Stephanopoulos raised the subject, and Trump replied that Mr. Khan "looked like a nice guy to me." Trump wondered if Mrs. Khan did not speak because she was not allowed to speak. Stephanopoulos asked what Trump had sacrificed for his country, and he replied that he had worked very hard, created many thousands of jobs, built some very fine buildings and projects, and added his work for and contributions to veterans' causes, including a Vietnam Memorial in Manhattan. Trump was heavily criticized, including by a significant number of Republicans, for "belittling" Mr. Khan, and his polls slipped generally, by several points.

Speaker Paul Ryan was always among the first Republicans to wring his hands over Trump's less guarded reflections, and on this occasion, he said they were "beyond the pale." Trump declined to endorse Ryan's reelection, after Ryan said Trump's nomination was "not a blank check." Trump, never a believer in unilateral verbal disarmament, dismissed the Khan controversy. He said that Khan was being ferried about the entire country as a Democratic campaign speaker, and had attacked him (Trump) and pointed out that the story was not about Mr. Khan, but about "radical Islamist terrorism in the U.S." Khan was effective initially for the Democrats, but Trump issued a further statement that Mr. Khan's son was "a hero to our country and we should honor all who have made the ultimate sacrifice to make our country safe. While I feel deeply for the loss of his son, Mr. Khan, who has never met me, has no right to stand in front of millions of people and say I have never read the Constitution (which is false) and say many other inaccurate things." In the second of the presidential debates, when the subject came up again, Trump said that Captain Khan "would still be alive today if I had been president in 2004." The issue subsided without lasting effect. (I debated with Mr. Khan in Britain shortly after the inauguration of the new administration. He was very courteous and amiable, and sincere in thinking Trump was hostile to Muslims, but completely inflexible and repetitive in his inaccurate opinions. We parted cordially.)

Hillary and the others weren't as good at throwing invective around as Trump was, and they didn't have as vulnerable a target as he had when he attacked their performance in office. She couldn't separate herself from the flat-lined economy and massive debt increases of Obama without splitting her party, which was fragile enough after the tremendous charge of Bernie Sanders, whose voters Trump was pitching to with his claim that Sanders had been "shlonged" (New York Yiddish for "screwed," which was a lingua franca Sanders and Trump both knew from their upbringing in the outer boroughs of New York City).

If the Republicans had had their popular New York mayor speak to their convention, Rudolph W. Giuliani, the Democrats had theirs with Michael R. Bloomberg. Bloomberg had initially thrown in his lot with Jeb Bush, angling for the position of secretary of state, and when that campaign imploded, largely under the Trumpian onslaught against "Low-Energy Jeb," Bloomberg had cast his lot with Clinton. He had run for mayor of New York originally as a Republican, only the fifth Republican mayor of New York in a hundred years, but Bloomberg had become an Independent, and, as of his appearance at the Democratic convention, a Democrat. Bloomberg called Trump a fraud who had inherited his money (untrue and, in any case, not a bad thing) and had much less money than he claimed to have, and was a "con." Bloomberg is a much wealthier man than Trump (apparently his company is worth around $35 billion) and has had a relatively uncontroversial and brilliantly successful career. Bloomberg, seventy-three, risked his entire political future, such as it was, on Clinton winning. He gambled, and, for once, he lost. (Mayors of important cities have rarely done well in American history. Only Grover Cleveland, who had been mayor of Buffalo, was elected president, and the only other nominees who have been mayors were DeWitt Clinton of New York City in 1812 and Hubert Humphrey of Minneapolis in 1968.)

The campaign was off and running and promised to be one of the nastiest in American history. On August 2, President Obama, speaking at a press conference with the prime minister of Singapore, said: "The Republican nominee is unfit to serve as president. He keeps showing it." He repeatedly claimed that Trump favored the Ku Klux Klan, a monstrous outrage. On the same day, the Koch Brothers, who reportedly raised and contributed more than $800 million for the 2016 elections, announced that they were not supporting Donald Trump. Also on the same day, Trump expressed the fear that the election could be rigged with the votes of illegal aliens. Obama dismissed this, saying "there is no serious person out there who would suggest somehow that you could even rig America's elections." (A few months later, he and almost everyone in his party were suggesting that the election had been rigged by the Russians.)

August 2 was an especially eventful news day; typical of national media denigration of the Trump campaign, when the candidate joked after a baby cried in its mother's arms at one of his rallies on that day, and he suggested having the infant ejected, CNN and other networks claimed that he had actually threatened to have the baby forcibly removed from the rally. Trump regaled his tens of millions of Twitter followers with this report as indicative of the media's dishonesty, and drew huge applause over it from his very large campaign crowds.

The Democratic candidate, massively financed and organized, and supported by most of the media, poured out every lurid detail of Trump University; the illegally admitted and underpaid Polish workers at the Trump Tower building site; the supposed racial discrimination of Trump and his father as landlords; tax returns Trump refused to make public, contrary to modern tradition (though he claimed he would do so when the challenges to them by the IRS had been resolved); the many bankruptcies, with their screw-jobs on debt-holders and rough treatment of some employees; and the less specific allegations of whipping up hostility to immigrants and Latin Americans and Muslims. Hillary Clinton and the Democratic campaign orators, including former presidents Bill Clinton and Barack Obama, roasted him every day for fifteen weeks as a mendacious hypocrite.

On August 3, Trump lost an important judgment on the Trump University case, rendered by Judge Gonzalo Curiel, whom he had already suggested was biased because of his Latin American heritage. The next day Melania Trump debunked claims that she had once worked illegally as a model in the United States, and the following day, as Karl Rove, President George W. Bush's political manager, compared Trump's electoral position to that of Walter Mondale, who lost forty-nine states to Ronald Reagan in 1984, the BBC, always anti-American and especially hostile to Republicans, proclaimed, "Trump Campaign on the Brink," and asked: "Should Donald Trump throw in the towel before the inevitable November knock-out?" On August 7, Ohio governor John Kasich declined to say if he would support Trump, whose campaign he described as "disturbing and alarming," and predicted he would not win Ohio.

On August 9, Evan McMullin, a former national security advisor to the Republican leadership in the House of Representatives, ran as an independent in Utah, with the declared object of splitting that state's Republican vote and delivering it to Clinton.

Trump made no effort as the campaign progressed, to moderate the predictable impact some of his foibles would have on the country. He continued to refuse to release his tax returns. And he gave passing attention to some rather wingy conspiracy theories, such as that President Obama was secretly a Muslim and that conservative Supreme Court Justice Antonin Scalia had not died from natural causes. Trump was easily portrayed as a credulous reader of shabby tabloid media (he was also an omnivorous reader of newspapers) addicted to controversy, showmanship, and hucksterism, and there was some truth in that. But his endless barrage of tweets, aside from showing how little he slept and driving his critics to paroxysms of outrage, both stirred up his supporters and acted as a counterbalance to the hostility of the media.

Unctuous and self-important groups of establishment Republican thinkers and former officials solemnly produced petitions and open letters denouncing Trump, which were often jubilantly highlighted in the *New York Times*. These pundits, almost none of whom actually knew Donald Trump, proclaimed he was unsuited to govern. One group, whose "warning" surfaced on August 8, declared that Trump "would be the most reckless president in American history...would weaken the United States' moral authority," and disputed that Trump knew about or believed in the Constitution, and stated that Trump had "demonstrated repeatedly that he has little understanding (of the nation's) vital national interests, its complex diplomatic challenges, its indispensable alliances and democratic values," and added, with immense condescension, that "Mr. Trump has shown no interest in educating himself." The conclusion, like a child stamping his foot, was that "None of us will vote for Donald Trump," although they volunteered that "many of us...have doubts about Hillary Clinton."[4]

It was such an ineffably pompous document, Trump almost certainly gained support when he promptly replied that the signatories were "the ones the American people should look to for answers on why the world is a mess, and we thank them for coming forward so everyone in the country knows who deserves the blame for making the world such a dangerous place." He dismissed them as "the failed Washington elite" trying to hang onto power, and correctly identified them as largely implicated in the debacle of the Iraq War, and of having been associated with the campaigns of people that he defeated in the primaries. They piously repeated the usual Clinton mantra that Trump was temperamentally unsuited to the office he was seeking, that "He does not encourage conflicting views, lacks self-control and acts impetuously. He cannot tolerate personal criticism,"[5] and declared that he could not be trusted with nuclear weapons. They also tried to make the case that Trump's use of the slogan "America First" implied fascist sympathies. It was an impenetrably fatuous outburst of snobbery from a very tired and generally second-rate congeries of former junior officials few members of the public could identify or remember. A number of them had very, or at least somewhat distinguished careers, such as Ken Adelman, Ellen Bork, Tom Donnelly, Niall Ferguson, Robert Kagan, Michael Mukasey, John Negroponte, Daniel Pipes, and Robert Zoellick; but most were irrational zealots like Max Boot, insufferable snobs like Eliot Cohen, or just tired hacks of the kind that are always numerous and vocal in Washington. A few Republican legislators followed in the same line, including Senator Lindsey Graham of South Carolina. It was all pretty stuffy and pretentious. Trump irritated many and often did himself no favors with his flippancy and his indiscriminate references to quack ideas, but there was no reason to dispute his sanity, disparage his intelligence, or imply that these petitioners were anything more than a washed-out group of mediocrities, partisans, and frightened establishment Republicans. This and some similar exercises in self-importance had no discernible impact on the race.

As it heated up, the campaign was unedifying and rarely substantive, but rarely dull; less statesmanship than entertainment, which was Trump's forte.

CHAPTER 8

Race to the Wire

At Wilmington, North Carolina, on August 9, Trump accused Hillary Clinton of seeking to repeal Americans' constitutional right to bear arms through her gun control proposals. This was a serious exaggeration, but not an uncommon one in political campaigns. He said "if she gets to pick her judges, nothing you can do, folks. Although [with] the Second Amendment people, maybe there is."[1] Without asking for clarification on what he meant, the jackals in the pro-Clinton media reported he had called for Mrs. Clinton's assassination. He clarified that he was only referring to the well-known and frequently demonstrated political influence of Second Amendment enthusiasts, and their chief lobbying arm, the National Rifle Association, to get their way.

The Democrats and their media allies would not let it go in their desire to exploit what they thought a vulnerability of Trump's about incitement to violence. Tom Friedman, the absurdly partisan Democratic sympathizer who comments on national and international affairs (very predictably) in the *New York Times*, wrote "And that, ladies and gentlemen, is how Yitzhak Rabin got assassinated." It was a false and scurrilous statement, but it is doubtful that this controversy had any lasting impact because it was so manifestly untrue; in fact, it would eventually be proven to be the reverse of the truth as liberals themselves delighted in publicly imagining Trump's assassination. Still, Trump did not help himself by adding in September that Mrs. Clinton's secret service detail should disarm themselves and "let's see what happens." Trump was not promoting violence at all—in this case, he was trying to underline the effectiveness of guns for personal protection—but his belligerent spirit of "We won't take it anymore," which appealed to tens of millions of people, was easily construed by those who viscerally disliked his strident egotism and bluntness as betraying a tendency to violence. Most of these controversies, based on different interpretations of ambiguous statements, reinforced people where they were and did not move large blocs of opinion durably in one direction or another.

Trump too was on the offensive every day of the campaign. On August 11, he referred to Obama and Hillary Clinton as "co-founders of ISIS." The anti-Trump media went through their ponderous fact-checking process to establish that the accusation was not literally true, as if Trump had claimed that Obama and Clinton had personally set up an organization calling for a new Muslim caliphate. There were widespread media reports on August 11 that Reince Priebus had threatened to withhold Republican National Committee funds from Trump and consign them to Republican candidates for other offices. There was no actual evidence to support this allegation; it was vehemently denied on all sides, and was one of the early egregious examples of what Trump called "fake news." On August 16, 123 people who claimed to be Republicans, including two congressmen (Reid Ribble and Scott Rigell), eight former congressmen, and twenty-seven former members of the Republican National Committee, signed a petition making the request that the media had already attributed to Priebus. The petition declared that "Donald Trump's chances of being elected are evaporating by the day," and excoriated his campaign "of anger and exclusion," which has "mocked and offended millions of voters, including the disabled, women, Muslims, immigrants, and minorities...(and) shown dangerous authoritarian tendencies" and favored "illegal and unconstitutional measures." It was pretty hysterical and RNC chairman Priebus rightly ignored the petition when it arrived. By this time, the country was well aware of the negatives of both candidates and of the Republican establishment's hostility to Trump.

In the Trump-led counter-offensive, the Clintons were represented as sleazy operators of a pay-to-play casino that had transformed the Clinton Foundation into a straight influence-peddling operation where Canadian businessman Frank Giustra had pledged $131 million and Russian interested parties paid Bill Clinton $500,000 for a canned speech in Moscow, as rewards for President Clinton's assistance in negotiating, and Secretary Clinton's offering her approval under national security requirements, of a lucrative sale of substantial American uranium resources to Russian and Kazakhstan interests.

Trump charged official corruption and emphasized the problems with Mrs. Clinton's emails. Clinton alleged unethical business practices by Trump. There was some truth to both sides and Trump seemed narrowly to get the better of it, if for no other reason than that the questionable Clinton Foundation antics involved much larger sums than did the controversy over Trump University, and her public service misconduct involved far more serious breaches of ethics, and possibly the law, than anything Trump had been plausibly accused of in the conduct of his myriad businesses. It was a bare knuckles battle from start to end.

Clinton carried the banner for women out to break the ultimate glass ceiling, and also accused Trump of misogyny, which given his track record in employing women—including his campaign manager—was hard to sustain. He came back with explicit attacks on the peccadilloes and wild indiscretions of President Clinton, accusing Hillary of being an enabler who had dismissed accusations of sexual harassment and worse against her husband as coming from "bimbos." In the opening stages of the campaign, Trump generally got the better of that exchange too. But Clinton scored more heavily with allegations of hostility to non-whites, which was an easy if cheap shot to make given Trump's support for enforcing and tightening the nation's immigration laws, and mocking his complete political inexperience. He righteously denied the charge of racism and came back quite strongly, accusing her of complicity in failing to defend America's border with Mexico and of pandering to millions of illegal immigrants (whom she hoped to turn into Democratic voters). He endlessly chided her inability to utter the words "Islamist extremism" and condemned her as a foreign policy failure as secretary of state. This was a close match. Clinton had the edge in experience and precise knowledge of policy issues, and took full advantage of Trump's tendency to over-claim, over-accuse, and over-simplify.

The Clintons and the Democrats played the game of identity politics to those groups they liked to consider their own—ethnic minorities, women, public employees unions—but there was also a large body of moderate opinion that was comfortable with the Clintons, who were a known political quantity and undoubtedly experienced and competent and in no sense extreme. Hillary Clinton had not had any great impact as a senator or secretary of state, but at least she knew the ropes of government. Because of his tendencies to shoot from the hip and throw haymakers with every sentence, Trump delighted those disposed to agree with him, but appalled skeptics, and worried the judicious. Essentially, both candidates had huge negatives; neither was trusted personally, and both had natural followings, but Trump had many more true believers because of his engaging style and the depths of resentment against the political establishment; he reaped the benefit of being a complete outsider. But he also was the less knowledgeable candidate. He replied to the charge of inexperience that Hillary Clinton's experience was that of someone steeped to the eyeballs in bad and failed policy.

It became a titanic struggle between Mrs. Clinton and the Democrats' ability to represent Trump as a crooked and half-mad egotist and impostor, and his ability to rouse resentment against the Clintons as personifications of the decline of America while they immersed themselves in financial greed and the moral hypocrisy of Bill Clinton's philandering like a rutting panther while she strutted the country as a priggish scold and virtue-sodden feminist.

In the early days of the campaign, and at stages through it, I was on American television news comment shows, essentially as a token source of the view that Trump was not a completely implausible candidate. Early on I encountered a barrage of well-known Democrats so confident that they demanded to know why the respectable elements of the Republican Party had not deserted their nominee as they had Goldwater in 1964. I stated the obvious, that the positions of the two Republican candidates and the stature of the two Democrats, were hardly comparable, Goldwater was effectively opposed to federal civil rights legislation and appeared to be contemplating a greater level of escalation in the Vietnam War than the country was comfortable with, and President Johnson was well respected.

There were massive allegations that Trump was lying whenever his lips moved, and opposition media regularly released what they purported to regard as authenticated lists of Trump's falsehoods. PolitiFact, a partisan political fact-checker, had already declared him the author of the Lie of the Year of 2015, through an uncountable multiplicity of lies, and asserted that 76 percent of Trump's assertions were "mostly false, false outright, or pants on fire lies." (Trump would win this distinction again in 2017.)

Norman Ornstein of the conservative American Enterprise Institute gave a more sober appraisal—that Trump was a graduate of a milieu, the New York real estate development industry, as well as the world of television virtual reality, where the truth was routinely departed from, and that Trump, the grand impresario, had entered "an environment that was ripe for bombastic, inflammatory, outrageous statements without having to suffer the consequences,"[2] where extreme partisanship, public cynicism, general disregard for traditional expertise, and accumulated public anger did not discourage his natural tendencies to hyperbole and did not really punish lapses into fabrication. Other less partisan observers counseled caution and warned that Trump often insinuates things without stating them, and engaged in deliberate vagueness, leaving him, in the words of past American political controversies, "plausible deniability."

Trump also had the improvident knack of enabling his opponents to impute to him an unseemly respect for undemocratic leaders. That, in turn, assisted them in implying that he had anti-democratic tendencies himself. Trump frequently expressed respect for Russian leader Vladimir Putin, saying that he could be a valued ally in fighting ISIS, and that he was a much stronger and more astute leader than Obama (almost certainly true, but untimely and not strictly relevant). He was skeptical of Obama administration and Democratic Party claims that Putin was behind the release of stolen U.S. government intelligence, or the hacked DNC emails published by WikiLeaks, or conducting a cyberwar against Hillary Clinton. This played into the natural Democratic claim that Trump and his campaign collaborators had had compromising business dealings with Russia. No one seemed to foresee how quickly this sort of charge would grow into a dangerous monster lurching about the American political landscape.

Trump also said that, while disapproving of the severity of the Chinese government in suppressing the Tiananmen Square occupiers, he recognized their strength and purposefulness in doing so, and considered the occupiers of the country's principal public space to be "demonstrators." He was practically correct; the regime of Deng Xiaoping did not fold as the Shah of Iran did; and no government could tolerate the country's main square being occupied indefinitely by dissidents. But, as is so often the case with Donald Trump, his selection of the words to express his views was far from optimal. Not without eventual irony, he said of the "maniac" Kim Jong-Un that he deserved "credit" for liquidating rivals to his authority. He even gave Saddam Hussein credit for taking out domestic terrorists, without suggesting that Saddam was a terrorist himself. The spontaneity Donald Trump had always had of putting out his views unsubtly and without regard to the range of possible interpretations of them, especially by opponents, created unnecessary problems for him. He commended Turkey's Recep Tayyip Erdogan for putting down an attempted coup d'état, and made the perhaps correct point that

Iraq and Libya would be better off if Saddam and Qaddafi had been left in power in those countries.

On August 17, the media widely credited the opinion of far-left film-maker and general misfit Michael Moore that Trump "is purposely sabotaging his campaign because he never wanted to be president." It is illustrative of the poor quality of media coverage that such nonsense from such a silly source was circulated seriously as a news story. This sort of ill-founded speculation—and a new example occurred every few days—assisted Trump in reviling the national media as untrustworthy and partisan (which was certainly true).

It was as this story was spread across the country that Kellyanne Conway was formally confirmed as campaign manager. Trump had had three managers in six months, but his campaign was a fairly smooth professional operation by now, although he was spending much less than Clinton, and had a relatively small entourage. Trump always maintained that these campaigns, like governments themselves, were vastly overstaffed. On August 25, the British leader of the successful campaign to leave the European Union, Nigel Farage, spoke at a Trump rally in Jackson, Mississippi, and said "I wouldn't vote for Clinton if you paid me." On August 31, Trump met with the president of Mexico, Enrique Pena Nieto, and they had a very civilized discussion about Trump's concerns over illegal immigration and the trade gap between the two countries. Pena Nieto stressed that he had also invited Secretary Clinton to visit, but that she had declined. He pledged to stay entirely out of the American election process. Trump went from Mexico to Phoenix and there delivered a thoughtful and thorough speech about his immigration policy, which, in a familiar pattern, was panned by most of the media as racist. On September 3 he spoke to a pan-evangelical meeting in Detroit and gave a very moderate address outlining policy areas where he thought the federal government could be much more useful to the African American community. The *Los Angeles Times*–University of Southern California and Rasmussen polls, considered as outliers by the political establishment, steadily showed the candidates neck and neck.

Trump did not campaign in California, New York, or Illinois, where it was assumed Clinton would rack up heavy majorities, and he did not spend too much time in states where he was expected to win easily, even large states such as Texas. He concentrated heavily on a number of quite large states where he had to win, or there seemed to be a possibility that he could win despite them being traditionally Democratic states. It was assumed that Florida, North Carolina, and Ohio would be relatively close, and Trump had to win them all, with sixty-four electoral votes, to have a chance of election. He also focused on Pennsylvania, Michigan, and Wisconsin, which were long shots, but there were undoubtedly many discontented working-class voters, who thought their Democratic Party had been taken over by the liberal elite, millennial progressives, and left-leaning minority activist groups, and that they had been forsaken. Trump directed his message to them and demonstrated his immense stamina with a punishing campaign schedule through those states. Presidents had been elected five times before with fewer votes than their chief opponents, and Trump was clearly trying to game the electoral system to do it again.

There were persistent questions about Mrs. Clinton's health, especially when on September 11 she fainted within camera view while returning to her car after a ceremony marking the anniversary of the 2001 terrorist attacks. After an initial attempt to cover it up, and once the footage leaked, her campaign acknowledged that she had been suffering from a bout of "walking pneumonia." In the medical circumstances, her perseverance was admirable, but what was seen was her physical infirmity in comparison with her apparently inexhaustible opponent, who seemed never to tire.

Hillary Clinton made a serious tactical error on September 9 when she told an LGBT fundraiser with Barbra Streisand at New York's Cipriani Restaurant that "You can put half of Trump supporters into what I call a basket of deplorables. Right? Racist, sexist, homophobic, xenophobic, Islamophobic, you name it. Unfortunately, there are people like that and he has lifted them up. He has given voice to their websites that used to have only 11,000 people, and now have eleven million. He tweets and retweets offensive, mean-spirited, hateful rhetoric." She added that some of these people were "irredeemable" and "not America." In part she was pitching to her non-straight audience (which had no valid grievance with Trump) and in part she was expressing frustration that her solid media support was not opening a cavernous lead for her because of Trump's dominance of social media and the talk shows. Trump had made no homophobic comments and his only complaints about immigration were illegal entrants and incipient terrorists. Clinton back-tracked two days later, saying she had "grossly over-generalized," but Trump and his team hammered her across the country as an elitist infected with the bigotry of a failed establishment class, now frightened and desperately trying to retain its incumbency through smears and demagogy.

Trump revealed a thoughtful child-care policy, partly drafted by his daughter Ivanka (who was just about as startlingly beautiful and stylish as her stepmother), but the media paid little attention because it did not fit their narrative. The next day, there came something that did. Trump called a press conference to bury the nonsense about where Obama was born, once and for all, but did so by claiming that the allegation was originally made by Hillary Clinton, and that he, Donald Trump, had resolved it by compelling the president to produce his birth certificate. Then, without skipping a beat, he introduced a group of highly decorated veterans of the armed forces who supported him (but had nothing to do with the birther controversy, inane as it was).

Four days later, Trump met with the president of Egypt, General Abdel Fattah el-Sisi, who had not been impressed by the Bush-Obama demand for free elections in Egypt. After the Muslim Brotherhood won the election, el-Sisi was also unimpressed by the championship of the Brotherhood by Obama and Republican senators John McCain and Lindsey Graham, virtually conducting their own foreign policy, and all asking for great deference to the Brotherhood. This was an astonishing bipartisan display of bottomless political naiveté. Trump and el-Sisi had a very cordial discussion, and, as with his meeting with the Mexican president, the meeting with el-Sisi reinforced the seriousness of Trump's candidacy and his ability to speak knowledgeably with foreign leaders.

Trump had rarely spoken from a text and while his spontaneous addresses were often rollicking occasions, they were discursive, and the media were generally unconvinced that he had any ability to give a prepared and sequentially coherent direct speech. However, his first such address, a foreign policy speech on April 27, and his address to the Republican convention, a blood-curdling partisan effort, were both coherent and apparently effective. But it was generally assumed that in a debate Trump, with his impressionistic and undisciplined style, and lack of detailed familiarity with most policy issues, would be at a heavy disadvantage to Mrs. Clinton, who had been a policy wonk and high-office holder for many years. The first of the three debates between the presidential candidates was at Hofstra University in New York on September 26. Trump started well, but Clinton clearly won the last half of the debate, though not catastrophically so for Trump. There was an all-time record of eighty-four million American viewers.

Trump did expose the moderator, Lester Holt, of his old network, NBC, as another partisan pseudo-neutral when he switched roles with Clinton and debated Trump about the police habit of random stop-and-frisk, a practice that Trump endorsed as necessary to reduce the level of violent crime. Holt claimed that it was declared unconstitutional by New York courts as largely singling out African Americans and Hispanics. Trump responded, with exact knowledge, that this was a New York verdict by an anti-police judge that the new, leftist mayor of New York, Bill de Blasio, had refused to appeal, but that in many other American communities, stop-and-frisk was entirely legal and frequently imposed. Trump won the exchange and emerged well above the low bar the Democrats and their media allies had set for him as an inarticulate and ignorant wind-bag. It was still generally thought to be a Clinton win but without any clangorous misstatement or revelation of extremist or uninformed views by Trump that came remotely close to forfeiting the election. But no one would know that from watching the debate coverage on CNN or MSNBC, where Trump's total collapse was reported on a daily basis throughout the campaign.

Clinton had championed former winner of Trump's Miss Universe contest Alicia Machado, whom Trump had taken issue with when she put on a good deal of weight during her "reign" as Miss Universe. Ms. Machado accused Trump of being like (Venezuelan dictator) Hugo Chávez and the inevitable Adolf Hitler[3] and was recruited as a Clinton campaign spokesperson.

There were unctuous complaints about Trump's ungentlemanly remarks, but there were no votes on this one for Clinton. Most polls showed the Clinton lead opened up slightly for a few days, but then narrowed again, to 2 to 4 percent. That could be a six to seven million plurality, and if the margin in California, New York, and Illinois came close, as was indicated, to accounting for such a lead, it still possessed the potential to be a cliff-hanger election. Even at this late stage, with barely a month to go, there was no sign of Clinton pulling away.

On October 7, WikiLeaks released a series of transcripts outlining Clinton's deep connections with Wall Street, many of them from very well-paid speeches, including one to Latin American bankers, where she put all her cards on the table for free trade and unrestricted immigration. Taking these comments with remarks released from an address to New York bankers, the picture emerged of Hillary Clinton as a rather conventional globalist leftist happy to use trade agreements as a way of equalizing income with poorer countries, and an ardent green crusader, but in both cases, finessing it in public, given the realities of public opinion. To the Latin Americans, she said: "My dream is a hemispheric common market, with open trade and open borders, sometime in the future with energy that is as green and sustainable as we can get it, powering growth and opportunity for every person in the Hemisphere." To the Wall Streeters, she said: "Politics is like sausage being made. It is unsavory, and it always has been that way, but we usually end up where we need to be. But if everybody's watching, you know, all of the back room discussions and the deals, you know, people get a little nervous, to say the least. So, you need both a public and a private position."[4]

Her opening of the policy kimono to the Latin Americans was incautious and a debatable take on the national interest. The fact that she had been highly paid to say such things to these audiences exposed her as a rank hypocrite, both cynical and naïve. This would have been a bigger source of damage to her candidacy than it was if the Democrats had not decided on this day to explode their largest grenade—the now-infamous Billy Bush tape.

With a month left, Trump was right on the back of Clinton in the polls. On October 7, when it must have been thought to be too late for Trump to recover from it, the *Washington Post*, having been fed it by NBC, released an audio-video of a conversation between Trump and another member of the ubiquitous Bush family, Billy Bush (of NBC) from 2005, in which Trump offered the lewd reflection that a celebrity, by virtue of his status, can get away with almost anything with women, including grabbing them "by the pussy." The media and the Democrats (generally more or less co-extensive groups), erupted in righteous outrage, as did many of the Republicans who had been looking for an excuse to desert their party's candidate anyway. The party chairman, Reince Priebus, ran for cover and all but disowned Trump. So did Mitt Romney, who had already blasted Trump as totally unqualified and altogether a bad man (to which Trump responded by reminiscing about Romney beseeching him for financial assistance in the presidential campaign four years before, when Romney had been the electorally incompetent nominee). Speaker Paul Ryan, whose support of Trump had been extremely tenuous, and frequently withdrawn as if by a person tempting an animal with a treat, announced that he was "sickened" by the remarks and disinvited Trump from a joint public appearance they were going to make in Wisconsin in a few days. After brief further reflection, Ryan said he would no longer "defend or support" Trump's campaign (not that he had done much of either) and authorized all Republican congressmen to take as much distance as they wished from the nominee.

Aghast and supercilious murmurings in the New York City and Washington, D.C., salons parroted the indignant fulminations from highbrow commentators, who insisted in unison that Trump's lewd remarks were so boorish they disqualified him from being president. It was all ahistorical revisionist bunk. Lyndon B. Johnson, John F. Kennedy, and William J. Clinton, among other occupants of the White House, engaged in conduct so lascivious, exhibitionistic, and indecent it would have made Billy Bush blush.

Melania Trump referred to her husband's remarks (they were just married when Trump made the comments but had been together intimately for seven years before that), as "offensive and inappropriate," but not currently relevant to her or to election issues. Trump himself issued a video statement after a few hours stating that "Anyone who knows me knows these words do not reflect who I am. I said it, I was wrong, and I apologize." He continued: "There is a big difference between the words and actions....Bill Clinton has actually abused women and Hillary has bullied, attacked, shamed, and intimidated his victims."

This was a bold gambit from the great counter-puncher. The Clintons retained a moral silence, happy enough to have the latest WikiLeaks revelations overshadowed. But the noisiest spokespeople among the Anti-Trumpers shrieked like jungle parrots that Trump must not be seriously considered for the country's highest office, and perhaps two dozen Republican candidates at different levels renounced support for the Trump candidacy. Among them were senators Ayotte (New Hampshire), Crapo (Idaho), Fischer (Nebraska), Flake (Arizona), Gardiner (Colorado), Kirk (Illinois), Lee (Utah), McCain (Arizona), Murkowski (Alaska), Portman (Ohio), Thune (South Dakota), Toomey (Pennsylvania), a sprinkling of congressmen and governors, including Kasich, and a few quasi-luminaries of the past such as former secretary of state Condoleezza Rice.

They could be called, in a famous Hollywood phrase (from *Casablanca*), "the usual suspects," and for few of them was it anything but a happy and even vindictive leave-taking. Trump's comments were certainly very damaging, coming so indiscreetly to a media person from a fifty-nine-year-old billionaire who was an educated man, well brought up in a civilized and traditional Presbyterian family and at a military academy where young men are taught to be officers and gentlemen. No one wants or expects a male presidential candidate to be a eunuch or a prude, but this was a serious lapse of judgment, even for a man who was at the time a celebrity and not a candidate. What he had said had nothing to do with being president, but he apologized for it and he deserved to have his apology, which must have been sincere (in the electoral circumstances), accepted. There was also the other matter Trump was about to elaborate, of the difference between idle talk about sex and unseemly, or even criminal, sexual activity.

The next debate was two days later, and Trump started out on the afternoon of the debate with a press conference with three women who had given affidavit evidence that Bill Clinton had attempted to force himself upon them sexually, with varying degrees of success, and a fourth woman, Kathy Shelton, a victim of violent rape whose assailant had been acquitted because of his counsel Hillary Clinton's manipulative use of criminal procedure, a matter Hillary Clinton had been recorded boasting about, amid laughter. Trump developed his theme, with his usual theatrics, about idle, unserious observations by himself eleven years before and the flagrant delicts of his opponent's husband whom she had facilitated and who was now proposing to return to his old hunting ground in "the people's house," the White House. Trump had ignored the demands that he withdraw in favor of Pence, and took the position that what he had said to Billy Bush was an aberration, "locker room talk" from many years before, that he had apologized for it, and that none of it had anything to do with this election. It seemed that both campaigns had been prepared. The Democrats' friends in the media had unleashed their secret weapon and Trump had his counter-charge: that the Clintons were the most hypocritical, unvirtuous couple in American presidential history.

This had been, from the start, such a shabby campaign, that the blow was not a mortal one for Trump, though it was a heavy hit. None of the participants in presidential debates going back to 1960 had been under as much pressure as Trump was now, in this second debate, with many of his most influential partisans calling for him to withdraw from the race. Most commentators thought that the best Trump could do now was to salvage his presidential candidacy, staving off calls that he step aside for Pence, and then go down to an inevitable, decisive, but not unprecedentedly one-sided defeat in the election.

The candidates entered the debating arena at Washington University in St. Louis, Missouri, without shaking hands and in a clearly grim atmosphere of total war. Trump's entire campaign was on a knife-edge. His was a boffo performance. Trump was calm, clear, spoke fluently and on subject, side-stepped the Billy Bush fiasco with remarkable agility, dismissing it as the dirty tricks of his opponents to introduce a red herring like this at the end of the campaign. He had apologized and that was the end of it.

He regained the offensive in references to the Clinton Foundation's pay-to-play activities, and Hillary's alleged dishonesty about her tens of thousands of deleted emails. He promised a "special prosecutor" to look into the murky area of the Clintons' activities, and when she said "it is awfully good that someone with the temperament of Donald Trump is not in charge of the law in our country," he interjected: "Because you'd be in jail," which was hilarious but of course outraged the humorless media who alleged, hysterically, that Trump was acting like a Latin American dictator threatening to jail his opponents, when in fact he was, facetiously but effectively, standing up for the rule of law to which Hillary was apparently immune. It was a superb performance throughout the debate; there is disagreement among polls about who won (and most polls were, as events proved, skewed to be pro-Clinton anyway) but even Clintonians acknowledged that Trump had done well. Under intense pressure, Donald Trump had clearly saved his candidacy from collapse, and was still in the race. He had shown the same icy and confident determination under terrible pressure that he did at the worst of his simultaneous financial and marital crises in 1990. In her Goebbels-like whitewash of an election memoir, Hillary Clinton claims to have been the author of a magnificent clutch performance because of Trump's attempt to "get inside (my) mind." In fact, all she had to do was show up, and she still only managed to debate her way to, at best, a draw.

Trump was certainly still trailing, but Republican Party chairman Preibus rallied to him, based entirely on Trump's debate performance;

vice presidential nominee Mike Pence, who had been ominously quiet for two days, tweeted his congratulations and continued support: "Proud to be with you in this campaign." It had been rumored that Kellyanne Conway had quit as campaign manager but she tweeted a photo on Melania's iPhone that showed the three—she, Melania, and Donald Trump—riding together in good spirits to the debate. Other Republican spokespeople were quite buoyant after the debate in their television interviews. The Democrats came back with specific allegations of their own against Trump of harassment of women. Among a movement of opportune complainants coming out of the woodwork after many years, Jill Harth had filed a suit against him in 1997 alleging groping of her "private parts and relentless harassment." Trump denied all of it with his customary strenuousness. Mud-slinging darkened the skies and filled the media.

The battle was a straight reciprocal character assassination. Every issue was now magnified to present Trump as a quasi-fascist revolutionary directing street thugs, to bring the wheels of democracy to a grinding halt if he did not win. He regularly suggested that the political system, not to mention the election, was "rigged" with, among other things, the media acting as Democratic propagandists (which was demonstrably true). Trump continued to counter this with his dominance of social media and talk radio. Lively and exotic blogger and television commentator Ann Coulter, a strong Trump supporter throughout the campaign, occasionally presented the election as a crusade not to inflict upon America the "spectacle of Hillary wallowing around the White House in her neon pantsuits for eight years."

Trump denounced Hillary Clinton as "Crooked Hillary," as he had effectively attacked his primary opponents as "Little Marco" (Rubio), "Lyin' Ted" (Cruz), and "Low-Energy Jeb" (Bush). By all traditional standards, Donald Trump should not have got past the early primaries, and was not expected to, and should not be a serious contender now, but he was. Trump slathered the national media relentlessly as liars and lackeys of all those in both parties who had failed the nation and now wrote petitions about Trump's mental health and ethics. On October 11, a WikiLeaks dump of purloined or hacked emails revealed that media commentator, former presidential primary debate chair, and Democratic National Committee official Donna Brazile had leaked questions to Mrs. Clinton in advance of a candidates' debate. The media shuffled and fumbled through their embarrassment at this naked bias (for Clinton over Sanders). Again, Trump hammered it very hard and humorously to his large audiences, taking full advantage of the high exposure the media had to give him in search of viewers in this highly competitive unfolding story. Whatever anybody thought of either candidate, almost everyone was fixated on this extraordinary campaign.

One of the vulnerabilities of Trump, and of American conservatism generally, was that conservative candidates relied heavily on the endorsement of Rupert Murdoch, a brilliant media owner and innovator, who has a near monopoly on mainstream right-wing news. At eighty-five on election day, and with a long background of deserting every politician he had ever supported and who had helped him, in every country, except Ronald Reagan, who was presumably assisted by the two-term limit in this respect, Murdoch was an invaluable but potentially fickle supporter, and his national American newspaper, the *Wall Street Journal*, had been fair though sometimes skeptical of Trump, while his national television news network, Fox News, had been mostly supportive.

On October 19, at the third debate in Las Vegas, Trump acknowledged of Hillary, "She has experience—but it's bad experience; the experience of having got our country into this mess, domestically and in the world." In the end, that appeared to be the final battle line—Trump standing for change against an establishment that had brought America to economic and strategic decline, foreign policy retreat, and a crisis of moral and historical self-doubt, and Hillary having as her only real argument that Trump was too scarily racist, sexist, and ignorant to be president. That argument certainly had its appeal to certain audiences, but it also had its limitations. Trump wasn't an extremist if you peeled the onion a little, and examined him in more depth; he was moderate and sensible in most policy respects, but blunt and provocative. As he had demonstrated many times, he could capitalize on the resentment of the disaffected without frightening most of them back into the camp which had generated their discontent in the first place. In sum, he portrayed Clinton as the queen of the May in a cavalcade of national decline.

Of prominent newspapers, only the *Las Vegas Review-Journal*, the *Washington Times*, and the generally scurrilous *National Enquirer* (in loyalty to Trump as a regular reader), endorsed Trump. *USA Today*, which normally did not endorse anyone, declared Trump to be "erratic" and accused him of having had "a checkered business career and to be a serial liar," and said he was "unfit for the presidency." This was a widely held view. Trump had assaulted the entire American political class, and they did not take it in good spirits, or, generally, respect their assailant, or, right to the end, have any idea what a serious threat he was to them.

According to the Federal Election Commission, Clinton had outspent Trump in their presidential campaigns $564 million to $333 million. Counting the Political Action Committees (PACs) and Super PACS, Clinton outspent Trump, $1,191,000,000 to $648,000,000 dollars. Trump contributed about $60 million dollars of his own money to his campaign, flew on his own aircraft, and when possible, staged events in his own hotels, and resorts. By the standards of other democratic countries, these are unimaginable amounts of money spent on an election, and the role of money in American public life is unlike anything in the history of the West.

In the last debate, as on many occasions in the last stages of the campaign, Trump again declared that the political system was to a substantial degree a "rigged" system, and promised that if he were robbed of victory, he would contest the outcome. He was widely accused, with the usual exaggeration, of "threatening to upend a fundamental pillar of American democracy, and...raising the prospect that millions of his supporters may not accept the results on November 8 if Trump loses."[5] Trump clearly enjoyed exploiting the reflex of his opponents to impute to him the most extreme intentions, and then settling things down with condescendingly placatory assurances. There was nothing alarming in his statement that he would not have the election stolen from him, and he calmly assured media questioners that he would not dispute the result if, as he expected, he won. The third debate was generally reckoned to be a draw, but on balance, Trump had considerably exceeded expectations in the debates, as it was widely anticipated that he would be eviscerated as a mere blowhard by his supposedly encyclopedically knowledgeable opponent. (The irony was that November 8 would mark the beginning of a concerted effort on the part of Clinton and a large contingent of her millions of supporters to invalidate the election—an effort that continues with allegations, utterly unsupported, but pursued with dogged if ludicrous determination, that the Russians somehow stole the election for Trump.)

An endless procession of Hollywood personalities attacked Trump and appeared with Clinton to try to gin up the attendance at her rallies. A catalogue of their inanities would be a lengthy and painful recitation, but the most commendably original was the vocalist, and all-round showman, Madonna's promise to fellate any wavering male voter who went for Clinton. Trump's standing in the polls the following day rose a point, but it is not clear that the two occurrences were related.

One mighty and surprising twist of the plot remained—the last drop of a tawdry, yet in a way gripping, drama was about to be wrung by an unexpected player, suddenly appearing in one of American history's most portentous cameo roles. Win or lose, Donald Trump had exposed the political elites of America in the ghastly infirmity of their jaded complacency, and had offered an alternative that almost half the electorate considered to be preferable.

CHAPTER 9

President-Elect

The slugfest continued unabated into the last days of October, when the FBI director, James Comey, abruptly reappeared at center stage. On July 5, he had purported to close the file on Hillary Clinton's misuse of a private email server while secretary of state, and of the emails on her server that were government property, and of the truthfulness of her responses to investigators of the "matter," as the attorney general had told Comey to describe it instead of an "investigation." On October 28, eleven days before the election, he announced in letters to members of the Congress that the FBI had come upon a new batch of emails and was reopening the investigation of Mrs. Clinton. As Comey was advised by senior colleagues, it was not FBI practice to make any announcements about investigations, but Comey thought that chasing down these emails would take until after the election, that the practice was "guidance" rather than a firm rule, and that in the circumstances, he had to make this development known. It aroused immense controversy.

The emails in question were discovered on the server of former congressman Anthony Weiner, and were between Mrs. Clinton and Weiner's estranged wife, Huma Abedin, who was Clinton's assistant. Weiner was being investigated on unrelated matters. The FBI assigned additional personnel to deal with the new discovery quickly and Comey wrote the members of the Congress again on November 6, just two days before the election and reaffirmed his judgment that no prosecution was warranted. This suspenseful sequence of events assured that Comey's conduct was almost universally criticized by both sides in what everyone now conceded was a close election, though a Clinton victory was still generally anticipated. The *New York Times* estimated the chances of a Clinton victory at 92 percent; the Huffington Post at 98 percent. Comey, having alienated everyone as he sought the limelight, had one more mighty turn as a starring political celebrity, and America would not have long to wait for it.

The Democrats believed that there was no reason to justify an additional public statement as the new emails were deemed inconsequential. The Republicans thought Comey had done the minimum to maintain any credibility of a thorough investigation, but had reopened and again closed the case in order to make his whitewash of Clinton, despite his heavy criticism of her conduct, as convincing as possible, as if he had conducted two thorough and separate investigations producing the same exculpatory result, even though he acknowledged Clinton's conduct was blameworthy. Despite Comey's refusal to recommend prosecution, Mrs. Clinton's view, in her election memoir, was that she had been "shivved three times by Jim Comey"—counting his initial press conference and his reopening and closing of the investigation as three separate affronts.[1]

The campaign went to the last day with the storm of counter-charges reaching a cacophonous peak. Election Day was November 8, 2016. The campaign was a mere appetizer compared to the results.

I had the good fortune to be one of a few color commentators who lasted the whole evening from seven p.m. to the end at 3:30 a.m. (Eastern Time) on Wednesday, on the principal Canadian television network, CTV. Adrienne Batra, the peppy, young editor of the *Toronto Sun,* and

I were among the very few in Canada or the United States who called it a 50-50 race with a slight advantage to Trump. The Sunday before, I had been the token non-anti-Trumper on my friend Fareed Zakaria's CNN program *GPS* (for Global Public Square). It was like a Clinton cheerleaders' rehearsal with a dissonant voice allowed solely in deference to the minimal requirements of pluralism. I was part of a panel made up entirely of Democrats, led in articulate fervor by the Obamaphilic editor of the *New Yorker*, David Remnick. Immediately prior to our discussion, we listened to a surrealistic debate between two pollsters about whether Mrs. Clinton's victory two days later would be by 5 percent or 7 percent of the total vote. This, it struck me, was an irrelevant conversation, because American presidential elections are not won by total vote counts. While Clinton would obviously rack up tremendous majorities in liberal states where Trump did not campaign—namely, California, New York, and Illinois—Trump would, it seemed to me, likely win an adequate number of other states, many by narrow majorities, to carry the Electoral College. (The winner in almost every state takes all that state's electoral votes no matter how narrow the margin.)

I had the impression from the primaries that the chief polling organizations were sampling a model of voters that did not account for the large numbers of Archie Bunker, irate, blue-collar "deplorables," as Mrs. Clinton had called them. Clinton was the candidate of continuity, of a broad liberal Bush-Clinton-Bush-Obama consensus that had governed Washington since the departure of Ronald Reagan. Trump, jarring and erratic though he often was, represented the rejection of that liberal consensus. He was the champion of those who felt they were losing their country to elites who did not share their values and their patriotism, and of those who had been disappointed and left out from the benefits of a globalism that favored transnational elites and foreign (or illegal immigrant) workers, in their view, over American blue-collar workers. The opposition of the political establishments of both parties, and of the media, and of the functionaries, including the academic ones, of the sloppy, shabby, bumbling, and discredited cadres of the old order, these voters regarded as a badge of honor for the formidable, if often outlandish, Republican contender. Many would feel, as I did, a foreigner, what Franklin D. Roosevelt said of his ostensible mentor but later rival, Alfred E. Smith, FDR's predecessor as governor of New York and a Democratic presidential nominee: "I loved him for his enemies." (I know the Clintons also, especially President Clinton, and have always found them very intelligent and unfailingly courteous, but they had had their turn and Mrs. Clinton's campaign was unimpressive.)

These were my views as the evening began. Kentucky and Indiana reported first and gave heavy majorities to Trump, the anticipated result, but if any credence had been attached to the Trump-smear-scare, his lead would have been narrower even in those normally Republican states. His majority in the two states was almost a million votes. There was not a ripple in the ranks of my fellow panelists, who, apart from the *Sun* editor, were uniformly dismissive of Trump's candidacy, including my old friend Lloyd Robertson, Canada's senior news anchor, gracious and mellifluous as he had been on the country's airwaves for more than fifty years. We all had a break for fifteen minutes or so each hour to stretch, eat pizza, drink coffee, and watch all the other networks on screens in the green room.

Trump led all night. The early confident assertions of the imminent emergence of the great Clinton invincibility slowly faded into a tense acknowledgement that it was a very close election. In monitoring the American networks, I saw my former employee (at the *Jerusalem Post*), Wolf Blitzer, as he scrambled like an asphyxiated roach between electoral maps in the CNN newsroom, desperately trying to unearth a thread of plausible data that would conduct Hillary Clinton to the White House. The expectation of an inevitable Clinton victory slowly, excruciatingly shut down; the people had spoken, but had not followed the script that had been handed to them.

My fellow panelists, some of whom were rabidly partisan (but in every case, very civil and pleasant, and for the most part, only so partisan because they had bought the media and Democratic line that Donald was a madman, a degenerate, and a crook of the first water), became rather dejected around midnight, as Trump still led, and the big "battleground" states had all gone Republican. These were the supposedly knife-edge contests in Florida, North Carolina, and Ohio, which Trump won by, respectively, 113,000 votes, 173,000 votes, and 447,000 votes, despite the lack of Ohio Governor Kasich's endorsement of his party's nominee. I felt moved to tell my fellow commentators, on camera, and in complete sincerity, that they should not be such defeatists; that the result was uncertain and that their faith in a one-sided victory had been misplaced but that the result was still a toss-up. Trump was leading but it all depended now on Michigan, New Hampshire, Pennsylvania, and Wisconsin. All but New Hampshire (only four electoral votes) had been assumed to be safe for Clinton, including by Mrs. Clinton herself, and as we progressed wearily past one a.m., these states were deemed too close to call, though Trump was leading in Michigan and Wisconsin.

As the world awaited the results from the key states, the analysis on all the networks turned from a sniggering mood of participating in a Clinton coronation to a much more serious, not to mention panicked, discussion of what might actually happen. The discomfiture of poor Blitzer (the greediest employee I ever had, and among thousands of journalists, that was a signal distinction) and his fellow liberal hysterics across the networks and cable news channels was palpable and almost oppressive, though gratifying. At two a.m., when asked by my co-chairperson, as the senior champion of Trump's possibilities from many hours before, to give my prediction, I said that I had never thought Trump could win Michigan, and still did not, and that I was astounded by Wisconsin, which had not voted for a Republican in a presidential election since Ronald Reagan. But with Trump leading by 85,000 votes with 93 percent of the ballots counted, unless the uncounted ballots were all from the African American districts of Milwaukee, he seemed likely to win that state. In Pennsylvania, I had always thought Trump an underdog, and I still thought the election as a whole, and the election in Pennsylvania in particular, was in doubt, though as the ballots kept getting counted in Pennsylvania, Clinton's early lead was steadily diminishing.

As I was winding up this studious effort at absolute impartiality, one of the technicians, when the camera was on the panel, came forward and pointed at the electoral vote totals, that now had flipped Wisconsin to the Republican candidate and showed Trump at 275 electoral votes, five more than needed for a majority, and that he was now the president-elect. After three minutes, as no one had picked up on this, though the technician was waving his arms about as if he was directing the landing of torpedo bombers on the flight-deck of a storm-tossed aircraft carrier, I gently suggested that the election result appeared to have been determined. Wonder and incredulity contested for mastery in the reactions of everyone on all the networks, even, up to a point, myself. Between 2:30 and 2:45 a.m., all the main networks and news agencies declared Donald Trump the next president of the United States.

Mrs. Clinton's campaign manager, the hyper-combative John Podesta, came out to speak in the candidate's place and said she would speak (later) in the morning and for everyone to go home. He did not comment on the outcome of the election or acknowledge that it was clear Trump had won. Donald Trump and his family and chief political collaborators, already swaddled in the vast apparatus of the U.S. presidency, proceeded in an immense motorcade the several blocks from the Trump Tower to the New York Republican election headquarters at the New York Hilton. (As the winning candidate was about to address the country, I whispered to Lloyd Robertson, quoting Monty Python, "Now for something completely different.") Donald Trump spoke with exquisite tact and magnanimity at 3:15 a.m., gave no hint that he was surprised by the result, and said he had had a gracious call from Mrs. Clinton. He promised to try to encompass the wishes and ambitions of all Americans. He acknowledged that it had been a "complicated" campaign and urged a spirit of civility: "To all Republicans and all Democrats and Independents…I say it is time for us to come together as one united people."

When the full vote was in, it was clear how close the election was, and how astutely Trump had exploited the vagaries of the Electoral College system. The final vote would be 65,853,516 for Clinton to 62,984,825 for Trump, to 4,489,000 for the Libertarian Gary Johnson, 1,457,000 for the Green candidate, Jill Stein, and 732,000 for the Utah independent, Evan McMullin. If it had been a quest for the highest number of votes, as in a French presidential election, Trump would have campaigned in California, New York, and Illinois, and narrowed the gap. If there had been a run-off between the top two candidates to obtain a majority, as there is in France, Trump would have taken most of the Libertarians and independents and Clinton most of the Greens, but Trump would probably have won anyway. Illustrative of the Clintons' decline, all polls confirmed that Trump won the white women's vote.

There were unusually wide disparities in the individual states: fourteen states and the District of Columbia cast more than 60 percent of their votes for one or other of the candidates. Trump crossed this threshold in Alabama, Arkansas, Kentucky, North Dakota, Oklahoma, South Dakota, Tennessee (where his lead was 653,000 votes), West Virginia, and Wyoming. Clinton took more than 60 percent of the votes in California (a lead of 4.25 million voters, an astounding state-wide victory, the margin of which alone amounted for more than her lead in the popular vote nationally), Hawaii, Maryland (735,000 lead), Massachusetts (905,000 lead), and the District of Columbia.

Trump, in his railings against big government, the lobbyists, and the national media, had run against the interests of almost every adult resident of Washington, D.C. Even allowing for that, Clinton won the District's three electoral votes by the unheard of margin of 282,830, 90.5 percent, to 12,732, 4.1 percent. In other words, counting third-party candidates, the nation's capital voted 96 percent against its incoming president. In Illinois and Indiana, neighbors by geography but not by politics, Clinton carried the larger Illinois by 945,000 votes (56 percent), and Trump took Indiana by 525,000 votes (57 percent). In the home state of both candidates, New York, Hillary Clinton led by 1.73 million votes (59 percent). Trump's biggest plurality in terms of sheer number of votes was in Texas, where the margin was 808,000 votes: 52 percent for Trump, 43 percent for Clinton), and the narrowest race was in New Hampshire, where Clinton finally won by 3,200 votes (a margin of less than half of 1 percent).

In the states where the election was won, Trump took Michigan by 11,000 votes (barely a fifth of 1 percent of the total), Pennsylvania by

46,000 votes, seven-tenths of 1 percent, and Wisconsin by 23,000 votes, 77/100ths of 1 percent. These states have, respectively sixteen, twenty, and ten electoral votes, and Trump, with all other results unchanged, needed one of the three to win. A shift of just 40,000 votes between the three would have won for Clinton, in an election where nearly 137 million people voted. On the other hand, even if those 40,000 votes had changed in Clinton's favor, if 16,000 people had voted for Trump instead of Clinton in Nevada and New Hampshire, Trump would have won those states and would still have won the election, 270 electoral votes to 268.

Trump won thirty states and the second elector in Maine, and Clinton won twenty states and the District of Columbia. The turnout was about 55.5 percent of those eligible, but many Obama voters sat it out, and many previous non-voters came out for Trump, but it is impossible to be very precise about the size of these shifts. Substantial numbers of Latin American voters favored Trump, despite his comments on immigration, presumably because they had come to the country legally, or their parents had, and they thought others should. The African American vote, understandably, fell well short, as a percentage and in absolute numbers, for Clinton compared to what it had been for Obama.

After a slight shuffling of individual electors, Trump was elected by 304 members of the Electoral College to 227 for Clinton, with seven other votes cast for people who had not contested the election. Trump was tactically astute in where and how he campaigned, but he was also lucky. It is hard not to sympathize to some degree with Hillary Clinton. Unlike her husband, Mrs. Clinton was an infelicitous candidate: she had exactly tied the primaries against Barack Obama in 2008, but was denied the nomination by the ex officio "super delegates"; and though in 2016 she turned these tables on Bernie Sanders to some extent, she was again denied victory after winning the popular vote in the election, and was only the sixth candidate in United States history to have achieved that dubious distinction, though she won the popular vote by a larger margin than any of the five such previous defeated nominees, which made it all the more disappointing (or infuriating).

Trump, however, could claim the distinction not only of winning the election but of winning more votes than any previous Republican candidate for president. It was also impossible to withhold from Trump the credit for such a stunning and unprecedented upset. With nothing but his own ingenuity, intuition, and stamina, and not even much of an investment of his large personal fortune (he spent less than 7 percent of what the Koch Brothers did supporting their approved candidates), he became the oldest (in a first election) and wealthiest victorious presidential candidate, and the only one never to have sought a position of public service, civil or military. The Republicans, also contrary to predictions, retained control of both houses of the Congress, but only by fifty-two to forty-eight in the Senate, and Trump was not popular with the majority of Republican legislators, whom he had severely criticized for being wobbly and ineffectual (reasonable criticisms as the coming months would confirm).

Among other developments, populism had triumphed. If any Bush, Clinton, or Obama is heard from as a coming candidate for the presidency again, it will be on a straight meritocratic basis and after the appropriate interval when spurs are won and the country is exposed to other families—the old-fashioned way, as it was for the Adamses, Harrisons, and Roosevelts.

What occurred was the supreme triumph of populism in American history and in the modern democratic world. Even Andrew Jackson had been a prominent general, albeit in Gilbert and Sullivan wars and in crushing the natives almost as brutally as Mussolini did the Ethiopians, and he had briefly been a senator and congressman, and ran once (and was the leading vote-getter in a four-way race) before he was elected president. Politically, Trump came from nowhere.

Among the great Western nations, only the traditional republics of the United States and France have the constitutional and psychological ability to conduct a full national exercise in populism with previously untested candidates. Some of the criticism of this election as demagogy was justified on both sides, though not the charge of mob-rule leveled against Trump by the Democrats. In 2016, populism was the only avenue to national renovation for America, as it probably was in 2017 for France, when that country elected a political newcomer as president and a new party to predominate in the National Assembly.

The election of Donald Trump electrified the world and stunned the American political community, which had never imagined such a turn of events to be possible; and when the outcome was announced, economists, with all the weather-forecasting skills for which they are so notorious, immediately went on many of the networks predicting a stock market crash. In reality, in Tokyo, Singapore, Sydney, and Hong Kong, where the stock exchanges were already open, there were sharp upward moves. The London Stock Exchange, the second most important in the world, rose all day. The continental European exchanges advanced in lockstep, and when New York opened, it delivered a powerful vote of approval to the voters' choice, though Trump had never been a favorite in Wall Street, nor had he much use for its services or, with a few exceptions, regard for its leading figures. Nevertheless, the American stock rally that began on news of his election would take the stock market to ever-more record-breaking highs through his first year in office. (Among those stunned by this reality have been the writers and editors of the *Economist* who had been hysterically hostile to Trump since he first surfaced as a contender, and have remained so, serving as yet another exemplary illustration of how intelligent people, on the subject of Trump, have simply lost their minds.)

The stupefaction of reeling American liberals soon transmogrified into denial, clinical depression, demonic demonstrative activism, blood-curdling threats of civil disobedience and obstruction, and even the guerrilla resistance of violent self-styled "anti-fascists" (or Antifa). The Left had not imagined it necessary to compose any contingency plans in case of defeat, and now, shattered and fragmented, it turned to the streets, to round-the-clock denunciations of Trump on cable news channels like CNN and MSNBC, and to daily editorial barrages on nearly every page of the *Washington Post* and the *New York Times*, both of which took the absurd position that the defeat of their favored candidate meant that American democracy was now endangered. Protest demonstrations arose almost spontaneously in New York City, Chicago, San Francisco, Oakland, Philadelphia, and Seattle, and the next day in Portland, Oregon, where violent window-smashing and petty vandalism by semi-professional urban guerrillas in ninja-outfits continued for several days. Women purporting to wear elaborate head-gear intended to simulate vaginas, demonstrated in Washington. Madonna, who had so recently offered her physical favors almost indiscriminately, announced to cheers that she had thought of "blowing up the White House" (presumably after the Obamas had departed it). To the liberal media, which had just received a stunning rebuff in the election, and to the generally somewhat resentful anti-American world, the whole future of humanity was put in doubt by the election of this raving and garish buffoon who was unqualified to be, and should not be, president. On November 10, Will Rahn of CBS Digital put up a piece called "The Unbearable Smugness of the Media," in which he chastised his colleagues in the press for failing to notice the strength of the Trump movement, and for subscribing to the Clinton view that Trump supporters were just a bunch of louts and failures. He correctly predicted that the media's reaction to Trump's victory would not be self-reflection that they had failed in their professional duty to cover the story fairly. Instead, they would conclude that there were more louts in the country than they had realized.

Trump called on President Obama at the White House on November 10 and they had a cordial chat. Four days later, Obama urged the country to "Give Trump a chance." The day before Obama's common sense appeal, the *New York Times*, in a letter to subscribers, signed by the publisher and the editor, and instantly reprinted all over the media, acknowledged that "Donald Trump's sheer unconventionality (led) us and other news outlets to underestimate his support among American voters." The *Times* had been irrationally hostile from the start and has continued to be so, without interruption by a single noteworthy pro-Trump story. (Trump referred to the paper as "the failing *New York Times*" throughout the campaign, because of its poor financial results and stock price, and the fact that it had issued junk bonds to Mexican mega-billionaire Carlos Slim to make up operating and capital losses.)

Trump tried to improve the media and political atmosphere by granting an interview to the *Wall Street Journal*, which, after overcoming its initial skepticism, had become more supportive as the campaign wore on. As an olive branch to Democrats, he hinted that he would be prepared to keep parts of Obamacare.

In an interview on November 13 with the CBS show *60 Minutes*, Trump again tried to conciliate Democrats, saying that, when it came to illegal immigration, his focus would be on deporting illegal migrants who had been convicted of crimes, which he estimated at two to three million people, and that, as long as the border was secured, he envisioned a normalization procedure for the other eight to nine million people who had entered the country illegally. The media, in what must be considered an outright act of collective dishonesty, purported to regard this as a proposal to expel two to three million innocent people, while allowing the rest to be normalized. There were, within a few days, completely unfounded but widespread media reports of chaos in the effort to recruit White House staff for the incoming president. In fact, in short order, Reince Priebus was appointed White House chief of staff and the controversial populist intellectual Steve Bannon was designated chief strategist, on November 14.

On November 17, Trump proposed that lobbying be prohibited for five years after leaving office, rudely interrupting the notorious Washington practice of people going directly from government into intensive lobbying of their former workmates dishing out government patronage. The next day, clearing away a significant irritant, he settled all the Trump University lawsuits for $25 million. He now had much more important work than dabbling in such indignities. The vice president–elect, Mike Pence (who had conducted a very effective campaign and undoubtedly won his debate with his Democratic opponent, Senator Tim Kaine of Virginia), was booed and harassed by the audience and even the cast at a performance of the musical *Hamilton*, in New York. This was a startling indication of the poisoned political atmosphere in the country. There would be no "honeymoon period" for the new administration; indeed the Left took the position that there should be no tolerance or respect for the incoming president and his administration at all.

On November 22, Trump told a meeting with reporters and editors of the ("failing") *New York Times* that he did not want to "energize" the so-called "Alt-Right" (which had become a portmanteau for the extreme Right, though that had not been its original meaning) and that "I disavow this group."

Between November 18 and December 16, in a very well-organized flow of plausible and respected candidates for key positions, Trump and his transition team announced his selections for key administrative positions. His nominees included: Jeff Sessions, senator from Alabama and Trump's principal early supporter in the Congress, for attorney general; Betsy DeVos, a well-known supporter of charter schools, for education secretary; South Carolina governor Nikki Haley for ambassador to the United Nations; Congressman Tom Price, a doctor, for secretary of health and human services; Elaine Chao, wife of Senate majority leader Mitch McConnell and a member of the last Bush Cabinet, for secretary of transportation; Steve Mnuchin, of Wall Street and the film-financing industry (hardly hotbeds of Trump supporters), for secretary of the Treasury; Marine General James Mattis for secretary of defense; primary opponent Dr. Ben Carson as secretary of Housing and Urban Development; environmental anti-alarmist Scott Pruitt for director of the Environmental Protection Agency; Exxon chief executive Rex W. Tillerson for secretary of state; former Texas governor Rick Perry for secretary of energy; Montana Congressman (and former Navy SEAL) Ryan Zinke for secretary of the interior; Linda McMahon, wife of Trump's old World Wrestling sidekick Vince McMahon, for head of the Small Business Administration; Marine General John Kelly for homeland security secretary; and Congressman Mick Mulvaney for director of management and budget.

In January, but before the inauguration, former Indiana senator Dan Coats was named director of the National Intelligence Agency; Congressman Mike Pompeo was chosen to head the CIA; Dr. David Shulkin was nominated to lead Veterans' Affairs, and former Georgia Governor Sonny Perdue was nominated as secretary of agriculture. All of these nominees were eventually confirmed, but McConnell wasn't hurrying and the Democrats were slowing the process unreasonably.

It was legislative guerrilla warfare already. DeVos, as a champion of charter schools and an enemy of the teachers' unions, was attacked by all Democrats and some Republicans. Sessions was fiercely attacked by the Democrats' Senate leader, Chuck Schumer, for allegedly being insufficiently sensitive to civil rights issues when Sessions had been a U.S. attorney in Alabama twenty-five years before. Schumer announced a policy of endless obstruction, and his party backed him. Vice President Pence had to cast the deciding vote in a 50-50 tie to secure the DeVos nomination and Sessions, despite many years in the Senate, got no Democratic votes.

"Never-Trump" Republicans and Democrats forming themselves into the loosely organized "Resistance" collaborated to try to prevent Trump's installation as president by instigating a rebellion among the electoral college electors. In an op-ed in the *Washington Post*, Harvard law professor Lawrence Lessig called on the Trump-pledged members of the Electoral College to break their pledges and deny Trump a majority, thus pushing the election to the House of Representatives. (The House had chosen the president three times before, selecting Thomas Jefferson over Aaron Burr in 1800; John Quincy Adams over Andrew Jackson in 1824; and Rutherford Hayes over Samuel Tilden in 1876; but this was an extraordinary proposal to make in 2017, though Trump would almost certainly have won such a referral.)

The following day, Jill Stein, candidate of the Green Party, having rummaged together the $5 million dollars necessary (it was widely suspected that a considerable part of it came from the Clinton campaign), funded the challenge of the election vote in Wisconsin. The Wisconsin recount was completed on December 13, and increased Trump's lead in that state by 131 votes.

The Democrats, meanwhile, took out television advertisements in an attempt to convince Trump's pledged electors that the republic needed them to desert Trump for Clinton (or perhaps Kasich). This was a manifestation of insanity, in terms of the ratio between cost and effectiveness. (An initial $500,000 was spent by a Democratic Party front called "Unite for America," which was composed largely of washed-up actors.[2]) Seven electoral college members did switch their votes, but five departed Hillary and only two quit Trump. The seven new choices made were: three for General Colin Powell, former secretary of state, and one each for Ohio Governor John Kasich, Senator Rand Paul of Kentucky, Senator Bernie Sanders of Vermont, and Faith Spotted Eagle of the Yankton Sioux. The Never-Trumpers and Resistance would prove as tenacious as they were numerous, but their opening gambits were desperate fiascos.

Before he had invited Tillerson to be secretary of state, Trump had an amiable meeting with former outspoken critic Mitt Romney, and there was allegedly some suggestion of Romney assuming that position. The cordiality between the two men continued after this. Trump had received congratulations from most world leaders, though very guardedly phrased in the case of German Chancellor Angela Merkel, who spoke anxiously of some of Trump's campaign confrontations being "difficult to bear." The German justice minister, Heiko Maas, said "The world won't end, but things will get more crazy." French president Francois Hollande, in the last few months of his term (with approval figures in single digits in most polls of the French electorate), histrionically announced that France "would need to be strong in the face of an upcoming period of uncertainty," and scaled the heights of French ponderousness: "What is at stake is peace, the fight against terrorism, the Middle East, and the preservation of the planet." The British, Canadian, and Australian leaders were correctly cordial, and some authoritarian leaders, especially China's Xi Jinping, Russia's Vladimir Putin, and Turkey's Recep Tayyip Erdogan, were more upbeat.

The media adhered to its now well-entrenched practice of magnifying anything they could present as a miscue by Trump as a luridly immense *faux pas* that would shake his credibility to its feeble foundations. Thus, when he telephoned the president of Taiwan, Tsai Ing-wen on December 3, the American media, which knows almost nothing about China, and has to consult specialists to explain anything beyond Chinese government press releases, concluded that Trump was guilty of a diplomatic blunder. It was soon clear that relations with China were good, and that the Taiwan call was not controversial, as relations with that country afforded the United States some leverage on the People's Republic.

As the interregnum between the election and the inauguration unfolded, Trump, often with Vice President–Elect Mike Pence in tow, pursued companies that had announced that they were going to close plants in the United States and relocate to countries where it was cheaper to do business. The Carrier Corporation, manufacturer of air conditioners, had made such an announcement about a plant in Indiana (where Pence was still acting governor) and Trump and Pence held a press conference on December 1 to announce that they would discourage Carrier from such a move, and eventually an arrangement was made, canceling the plant closure. Trump was very active in this area, and on December 6 was able to announce that Japanese businessman Masayoshi Son had pledged a $50 billion investment and the creation of fifty thousand new jobs in the United States. On the same day, Trump successfully demanded a serious reduction in the cost of a new Air Force One presidential aircraft. It briefly affected the Boeing stock price negatively. On December 14, almost as if he were already president, Trump met with Silicon Valley CEOs to discuss opportunities to increase domestic high-tech manufacturing and to create an environment for innovation in America. On December 28, Trump was able to announce that other corporations would be creating eight thousand new jobs.

There was a terrorist attack on the Berlin Christmas Market on December 19 that killed twelve and injured fifty-six. The terrorist, a failed Tunisian asylum-seeker, was killed in a police shoot-out in Milan a few days later. Trump called the terrorist outrage "an attack on all humanity" and when questioned about banning the entry into the United States of Muslims, Trump responded that he believed his plans were correct and would be made explicit soon after he was in office. Trump's domestic enemies, however, were already planning legal challenges to whatever he might impose, on grounds of unconstitutional discrimination against a religious group, which they attempted to prove by using Trump campaign rhetoric. This would not be the last lesson the incoming president would need to learn about the hazards of imprecise language leavened by "truthful hyperbole."

On December 23, Obama had his ambassador to the United Nations, Samantha Power, abstain from a United Nations security council vote on a resolution that demanded a halt to Israeli settlements in the so-called "occupied territories" (captured during the 1967 Six-Day War). The resolution further declared that Israeli possession of the Western Wall, the Hebrew University and Hadassah Hospital on Mount Scopus, and the Jewish Quarter of Jerusalem, was "a flagrant violation of international law." This abstention was a final act of frustration from Obama that he had made no progress in advancing peace in the Middle East in his eight years as president, a failure he blamed on Israeli intractability. Trump issued a statement advising Israel to "Stay strong. It will be different when we take office." He dismissed the United Nations as a social club and talking shop "for despots and human rights violators," of little use to anyone but those who profit from its corruption.

Donald and Melania received great applause from their fellow congregants at Bethesda-by-the-Sea Episcopal Church in Palm Beach, where they had been married almost thirteen years before, when they attended a Christmas Eve service there. As the New Year approached, Trump's opponents were resigned to his taking office, but not to providing the least measure of cooperation to enable him to be successful.

On January 8, the distinguished actress Meryl Streep gave the Golden Globe Awards night an anti-Trump tirade, with the usual insinuations that Trump was a racist and a sexist. Trump, inevitably, responded, saying that Streep was "a Hillary flunky who has lost big." This was fair enough, but he showed his somewhat churlish and even juvenile side by also calling her "one of the most overrated actresses in Hollywood." If he had said she was merely an actress, that would have been possibly effective as snobbery, but it was unwise and not well-received for him to imply that even as an actress she was not very talented. It was the wrong type of response from a person about to be inducted into the presidency of the United States. He could now, and needed now, to rise above most of this malice, which was usually completely uninformed, as Streep's allegations were. He would spend the next year struggling with a steep learning curve about how American presidents should behave and how to rely on the dignity lent by the office.

In the last ten days before he was inaugurated, the intensity of the fear, anger, and hostility of his enemies, who a year before had been doubling over laughing at the very mention of a Trump candidacy, became sharper and more destructive. The appointment of his son-in-law, Jared Kushner, as a senior advisor, was denounced by most of the media as rank nepotism, and Kushner was gratuitously portrayed as completely unqualified to do anything around the White House except empty waste baskets. Kushner proved to be smarter than his critics, and suggestions that such an appointment might be illegal were nonsense, as were suggestions that Kushner's wife, Ivanka Trump, not be allowed to act as an advisor to her father.

The biggest shoes dropped on January 10, when CNN breathlessly reported on a story that no respectable news site was willing to touch, until then, the so-called Steele dossier, compiled by a former British intelligence officer, but for parties that were not immediately identified and for motives that were not at first clear. The Steele dossier had been out on BuzzFeed, a pretty scurrilous and rabidly partisan website (it wouldn't accept advertising from Republicans) but serious journalists had ignored it because of its lurid and improbable nature. CNN, however, not only took the bait, but Wolf Blitzer ran about his "Situation Room" like Groucho Marx, bent forward in his hurry to get to his next graphic, and exclaiming ad nauseam about the enterprise that had been required to produce this triumph of investigative journalism. The bedraggled old greaser Carl Bernstein, co-author with Bob Woodward of the destruction of Richard Nixon, and always a questionable source of information, was disentombed from his dust-accumulating obscurity to declare this malicious drivel "very significant and potentially extremely damaging to the president-elect." His co-assailant Woodward rather more scrupulously called the dossier a "garbage document" and FBI director James Comey in due course called it "salacious and unverifiable."

Though responsible media had passed on this document for months, now that a semi-respectable organization had put it out, the rest of the media was happy to cite it as a CNN story without opining on how much credence should be attached to it. The most bizarre of the many fabrications in it was that Trump had organized for a group of prostitutes to urinate in a hotel bed in Moscow because the Obamas had once slept in it. This entered American presidential history as "the Golden Shower." In getting into this, the Democrats and their media allies took on much more than they had imagined. It eventually emerged that the dossier had been commissioned by Fusion GPS, a commercial and political espionage and "special service" company that generally works for the Democrats and had been extensively patronized by the Clintons. Further very damaging information about it came within a few months, but it was a very dubious source from the beginning. Trump coined the phrase "fake news" for documents such as this and denounced it in terms that, though vituperative, were for once, not excessive. It is hard, even for a close observer of the febrile political atmosphere of the time, to imagine what possessed anyone to touch this stink-bomb; the story behind it would soon become much more astonishing, and besmirch its sponsors and propagators.

Also on January 10, in words that would have extensive consequences, Senator Sessions, as attorney general-designate, told the Senate Judiciary Committee that he had had no contact with the Russians during the campaign. These words of denial would soon be altered and would ramify widely, if unfairly. Trump's enemies were already placing their bets on the Russian card for destroying his presidency, however wildly improbable that card was. Trump had finally been acknowledged as the winner of the election, but he had not won the normal deference that is given a new president. The war Trump had unleashed on the entire political establishment continued.

Congressman John Lewis of Georgia, a former civil rights activist, provided a brief glimpse of what was about to come. On January 14, Lewis said the election result was "illegitimate." Trump said Lewis should deal with his own congressional district, which Trump virtually described as a crime-infested rubble heap. A few days later, wildly irresponsible California congresswoman Maxine Waters called for Trump's impeachment, and under media questioning, said the cause for impeaching him would be turned up by the Russia investigation. For the next year (at least), she regaled the after-dinner circuit (and greatly supplemented her income) with the chant "Impeach 45." (Trump is the forty-fifth president when, as is the odd practice, Grover Cleveland's two non-consecutive terms are counted as two presidents.)

The less publicized toilers in the Democratic Washington boiler rooms were working feverishly on plans for a guerilla war to undermine, immobilize, and if possible, destroy his presidency. Donald Trump would be president at last, but of a severely divided country and of a fractured political system. He had the great office, but was surrounded by enemies, many of them in his own party. It was both great and tawdry drama, a mighty epic, many of whose protagonists were not very galvanizing personalities. The American people were both the prize and the prize-giver, and they prepared for an inauguration unlike any other. What Franklin D. Roosevelt called, in reference to his own first presidential inauguration, "a day of national consecration," was at hand, but it would be the starting pistol for a second, almost bloodless, American Civil War.

CHAPTER 10

President at Last

In his inaugural address, President Trump greeted four previous presidents behind him on the podium (Jimmy Carter, Bill Clinton, George W. Bush, and Barack Obama) and thanked the Obamas for their "gracious [and] magnificent" help throughout the transition. What followed was a rather strained proclamation of unprecedented change. "Today we are not merely transferring power from one administration to another, or from one party to another, but we are transferring power from Washington, D.C., and giving it back to you, the American people. For too long, a small group in the nation's capital has reaped the rewards of government while the people have borne the cost. Washington flourished but the people did not share in its wealth. Politicians prospered but the jobs left and the factories closed. The establishment protected itself but not the citizens of the country....January 20, 2017, will be remembered as the day the people became rulers of the country again." This was a rather stern reproof of his four predecessors sitting nearby, who had occupied the White House for twenty-eight years. It was not calculated to attract the accolades of the Congress, most of the members of which were also present and were among the accused. According to Hillary Clinton's memoir, which purported to explain why it had been Trump and not her addressing the crowd gathered on the National Mall, George W. Bush offered this blunt assessment of Trump's speech: "That was some weird shit."[1]

Returning to a more uncontroversial version of Trumpian Truthful Hyperbole, he said, to the country: "You came by the tens of millions to become part of a historic movement the likes of which the world has never seen before." He was referring to "Mothers and children trapped in poverty in our inner cities; rusted out factories scattered like tombstones across the landscape of our nation; an education system flush with cash, but which leaves our young and beautiful students deprived of knowledge; and the crime and drugs and gangs that have stolen too many lives and robbed our country of so much unrealized potential....We've made other countries rich while the wealth, strength, and confidence of our country has disappeared over the horizon. One by one, the factories shuttered and left our shores, with not even a thought about the millions upon millions of American workers left behind. The wealth of our middle class has been ripped from their homes and then redistributed across the entire world." This was essentially a campaign speech although the campaign had ended ten weeks before and the campaign before him now was to get the legislation to enact his proposals through a Congress that was only marginally different from the one that had co-authored the Dark Age of recent years he was, with a dosage of his notorious hyperbole, describing.

But, the president of just five minutes promised: "America will start winning again, winning like never before. We will bring back our jobs. We will bring back our borders. We will bring back our wealth. And we will bring back our dreams. We will build new roads, and highways, and bridges, and airports, and tunnels, and railways all across our wonderful nation. We will get our people off of welfare and back to work—rebuilding our country with American hands and American labor....We will be

protected by the great men and women of our military and law enforcement and, most importantly, we are protected by God." This was taking
a lot on himself, but "A new national pride will stir our souls, lift our
sights, and heal our divisions. It is time to remember that old wisdom
our soldiers never forget: that whether we are black or brown or white,
we all bleed the same red blood of patriots, we all enjoy the same glorious
freedoms, and we all salute the same glorious American flag. And
whether a child is born in the urban sprawl of Detroit or the windswept
plains of Nebraska, they look up at the same night sky, they fill their
heart with the same dreams, and they are infused with the breath of life
by the same mighty Creator. So to all Americans in every city, near and
far, small and large from mountain to mountain, and from ocean to
ocean, hear these words: You will never be ignored again. Your voice,
your hopes, and your dreams will define our American destiny. And your
courage and goodness and love will forever guide us along the way." He
closed with, "Together, we will make America strong again; we will
make America wealthy again; we will make America proud again; we
will make America safe again; and yes, together, we will make America
great again. Thank you, God bless you, and God bless America."

He could not possibly deliver quickly on such promises. The
response of his own party's congressional delegation was bound to be
muted and ambivalent, which would make any such jolting change as
he pledged especially difficult. He had not swept into office like Roosevelt in 1933 with an almost unlimited mandate for change from a
desperate country, or even like Reagan in 1981 with a clear enough
mandate to reduce taxes and increase defense spending. Trump had
never been too precise about how he was going to address the evils he
denounced, apart from stopping illegal immigration with stricter border
controls, including a wall, deporting some illegal immigrants already
in the country, renegotiating trade deals that generated large trade
deficits for the United States and eliminated American manufacturing
jobs, and taking a tougher line with North Korea and Iran.

The key to advancing his goals now was not continuing to lash the
remnants of the political establishment, who were digging in. The

Democrats, anti-Trump Republicans (who might well have included House Speaker Ryan and Senate leader McConnell), the national media, and the entire entertainment industry were still at war with Trump. The inauguration of the new president had not had a halcyon effect on American public and media opinion about him.

Speaking at CIA headquarters the next day, he betrayed the absurd hyper-sensitivity that sometimes accompanies Trump's rhinoceros-hide. He objected to public estimates that there were only 250,000 people at his inauguration and parade. (Given that 96 percent of the District of Columbia had voted against him, and that it was well-publicized that mobs of vandals would be protesting his inauguration, it was miraculous that he had any such large gathering of supporters.) But the president took it upon himself to tell the CIA personnel (who cannot possibly have had the slightest interest and must have been nonplussed that the subject was raised) that it was 1.5 million people who attended his inauguration. He had his press secretary, Sean Spicer, labor through his first press conference making and defending the proposition that the inauguration crowd the day before was "the largest audience to ever witness an inauguration, both in person and around the globe." Technically, this gave the president an escape hatch, as no one had any idea how many people around the world or even across the United States had witnessed it, but that had not been the source of the controversy, which was Trump's opponents scoffing at the physical turnout. This was what Kellyanne Conway had in mind the following day when she referred to "alternate facts." Estimates of the Trump crowd went as high as six hundred thousand—it was in any case a formidable turnout, but substantially less than Obama's at his first inauguration.

There had been some disorderly behavior around the parade the day before, but this was the merest foretaste of the large demonstration that took place in Washington and in other cities and countries while the president was addressing the Central Intelligence Agency. It was a cry of anguish and vengeance from a vintage coalition of the Left: Planned Parenthood, the Natural Resources Defense Council, AFL-CIO, Amnesty International, National Center for Lesbian Rights, National

Organization for Women, MoveOn.org, Human Rights Watch, the American Indian Movement, Greenpeace, and many others. Anti-abortion organizations that were otherwise supporters of the women's movement were at first admitted and then expelled from the coalition. Among the speakers to the four hundred fifty thousand or so marchers in Washington were the inevitable Gloria Steinem, Scarlett Johansson, the venerable Communist Angela Davis, Michael Moore, Cecile Richards, Ashley Judd, and Democratic senators Tammy Duckworth and Kamala Harris. There were 408 marches in the United States and 198 in eighty-four other countries, all ignited by Trump's election and coming to the aid of every conceivable leftist cause, with particular emphasis on hostility to white males. Among those who participated in these marches in various places were Gillian Anderson, Alec Baldwin, Drew Barrymore, Beyoncé, Cher, Jessica Chastain, Jamie Lee Curtis, Miley Cyrus, Fran Drescher, Jane Fonda, Ariana Grande, Chelsea Handler, Blake Lively, Madonna, Helen Mirren, Julia Roberts, Chris Rock, Barbra Streisand, Charlize Theron, and Emma Watson.

An additional feature of the marches were the Pussyhats—hundreds of thousands of pink knitted tuques with pointy ears like cats, to remind everyone of Trump's unfortunate comment from eleven years before. It was the usual unfocused, broad coalition of whiners and faddists interspersed with extremists and heavy-laden with Hollywood figures satisfied that their celebrity entitled them to contend for direction of the country, even one day after the inauguration of the person who won the election. The speeches, in Washington and as far afield as Perth, Australia, took their cue from Bruce Springsteen, who declared, "We are the new American Resistance." There was no violence, but it was a monumental tableau of the idiocy and pretention of America's over-indulged entertainment industry and the gullible naiveté of many foreign analogues. The conservative movement in the United States fairly vocally accused the marchers of being infested with Islamists and other anti-Semites, and of verging on anarchism in places. Various commentators said the marchers had a questionable right professing to represent democracy while protesting the installation of a democratically elected leader of the United States. President Trump wisely ignored the entire orgy of raging exhibitionism.

He was too busy perhaps working. He was a ball of fire from the opening bell of his inauguration and left no doubt of his intention to move as quickly as he could to advance the policies he had promised. In his first ten days in office, he withdrew the United States from the Trans-Pacific Partnership, which he promised throughout the campaign, claiming it would import unemployment to the United States. He ended the previous administration's policy of giving $600 million annually to assist abortions in foreign countries. He had a useful and cordial meeting with American labor leaders, who generally approved his pro-industrial employment policies, and many of whose workers had voted for Trump. He approved the Keystone XL and Dakota pipelines. He started strengthening security along the Mexican border, using unspent funds in the homeland security department, and blocked federal grants to sanctuary cities (which declared they would not enforce American laws against illegal migrants; this issue was shortly mired in the court system). He had a successful meeting with the new British prime minister, Theresa May, and said, "A strong and independent Britain is a blessing to the world."

More controversially, he claimed widespread voter fraud, with many jurisdictions allegedly permitting illegal migrants to vote. The charge could not really be judged as many states refused to cooperate in examining voter returns. Many in the media criticized Trump on the grounds that it was ridiculous for the winner of an election to charge voter fraud and demand an investigation (as if the president of the United States could not have an objective interest in fair elections) or on the grounds that investigations of voter fraud were implicitly racist, a covert way to purge Hispanic voters from the rolls (which was ludicrous).

On January 28, Trump issued an executive order temporarily banning the admission to the United States of travelers from Afghanistan, Iran, Iraq, Libya, Syria, and Yemen. They were all, apart from Iran, countries in some state of civil war. There were immediate disputes about the order's legality and the Democrats went judge-shopping among the West Coast left-wing benches to find a federal judge who would purport to block the imposition of the executive order. The previous administration's deputy attorney general, Sally Yates, declined to execute the president's order and was fired.

A Washington state judge did find fault with the order, and the Democrats undoubtedly hoped Trump would just ignore the ruling (as President Andrew Jackson had when he said of Chief Justice Marshall, "He has made his decision; now let him enforce it"). This would have enabled them to torque up talk of impeachment, which was already being bandied about by the Democrats, focusing now on Trump's alleged sinister relations with Russia, and dark claims that he had colluded with the Russian regime to sandbag the Clinton campaign through WikiLeaks and cyber-hacking and as yet unspecified skullduggery. Trump abided by the judge's order, and instead imposed his policy when travelers reached the United States (rather than forbidding them to come from their originating countries), and waited for the Supreme Court to rule on the dispute.

He nominated Judge Neil Gorsuch to fill the vacancy on the high court left by the death of Justice Antonin Scalia a year before. Gorsuch would be confirmed, shoring up the thin conservative majority at the Supreme Court, and thus saving conservative America from one of its worst nightmares—the possibility of a liberal court that would give a blank check to liberal judges, the bureaucracy, and Democratic presidents to override the legislative branch and effect any "progressive" measures they wished.

Riots and demonstrations erupted in many parts of the country, and a few places overseas, to protest Trump's travel and immigration policies. There were sit-ins and traffic blockages at airports that greatly inconvenienced the traveling public. The theme was that Trump was a racist, and that he was reversing the openness of America to the world that was one of the foundations of the country. Democratic Senate leader Chuck Schumer, choking back crocodile tears, called Trump's executive order "mean-spirited and un-American," claiming solidarity with the Statue of Liberty, which, Schumer claimed, was also weeping over the temporary ban.

On January 31, Trump extended Obama's LGBTQ workplace protection for employees of federal contractors. He issued a statement saying that he was "determined to protect the rights of all Americans, including the LGBTQ community...[and is] respectful and supportive of LGBTQ rights, just as he was throughout the election." He said he was "proud to have been the first ever GOP nominee to mention the LGBTQ community in his acceptance speech, pledging then to protect the community from violence and oppression."

Polls indicated the majority of Americans supported his crackdown on travelers from terrorism-sponsoring or -infested countries, and his LGBTQ order sharply undercut the pussyhatted caterwauling of the women's marchers. He was off to a predictably stormy, but not a bad, start.

In the first months of the new presidency, practically nothing was accepted as normal and unexceptionable, and as Schumer and his Democratic colleagues in the Senate were obstructing and delaying every Cabinet and senior departmental appointment that came before them, the Obama holdovers were making government as difficult as possible and leaking like waterfalls to the anti-Trump media, which was practically all of the media except for the *Wall Street Journal*, the *New York Post*, and Fox News. Like almost every controversy involving Trump, the partial travel ban receded from the distracted consciousness of the country after a few weeks, as the hyenas in the media were unable to sustain the story and moved on to other subjects in their litany of what Trump dismissed (often rightly) as "fake news."

On February 1, the contents of a rather heated telephone call with Australian prime minister Malcolm Turnbull were leaked, in which Trump became audibly irritated over Turnbull's insistence that he honor Obama's informal commitment to accept twelve hundred refugees from the Middle East who were being provisionally sheltered on the small Pacific island nation of Nauru. Australia was discouraging trans-Pacific people-smuggling by not admitting undocumented people and moving them off-shore where they could be assessed by immigration authorities. Turnbull's deal with Obama was that in exchange, Australia would accept some Central

Americans attempting illegal entry into the United States, and Turnbull emphasized to Trump that the United States did not have to accept any of the people on Nauru—immigration officials could screen them and reject them—but it would be up to the United States to maintain them where they were or move them elsewhere. The revelation of the transcript of the conversation, a disgraceful betrayal by disloyal White House insiders, made the two leaders appear to be engaged in a cynical game at the expense of the pathetic fugitives from the distressed Middle East. This wasn't an entirely fair impression and like all these incidents, it passed quickly.

Also on February 1, hoodlums in ninja costume smashed parts of buildings and set fires on the Berkeley Campus of the University of California in protest at the proposed address of controversial gay free speech firebrand Milo Yiannopoulos, invited by one of the campus clubs. Antifa, which took a lead role in this protest, and in violent opposition to Trump, was a ragtag group of militant anarchists, anti-capitalists, and neo-Marxists who purported to see fascism, by those with whom they disagreed, in the exercise of the first amendment rights to freedom of assembly and speech. It took an unconscionable time for leading Democrats to disavow this riff-raff.

More damaging was the *Washington Post*'s leak on February 9 that National Security Advisor General Michael Flynn had discussed with the Russian ambassador Sergey Kislyak the possibility that the Trump administration might reduce the sanctions President Obama had imposed on Russia for its alleged interference in the United States elections. Flynn had denied this, and the *Post* story indicated that there was—as Trump would soon claim, to fierce objections but subsequent partial vindication—some official surveillance of his campaign or transition team prior to his inauguration. The *Post* story revealed that former deputy attorney general Sally Yates had warned that Flynn could be vulnerable to blackmail, indicating questionable and quite possibly illegal official telephone intercepts on Trump campaign personnel, as well as illegal post-inauguration leaks of confidential information to the media.

Five days later (February 20), Flynn resigned, acknowledging that he had had some telephone discussions with the Russian ambassador, that the issue of the sanctions had arisen, and that in the "fast pace" of events, he had inadvertently misinformed the vice president–elect, who had accordingly assured the media that there had been no such discussions. In his statement, Flynn said that he had apologized to the president and vice president, and that his apology had been accepted. This turn of events was a legitimate embarrassment for the administration and was enthusiastically amplified by the political and media opposition to lend credence to the vague but constant allegations of a dishonest, possibly treasonous, and, implicitly, eminently impeachable relationship between the Trump campaign and the Russian government. General H. R. McMaster, a respected military intellectual, replaced Flynn at the National Security Council on February 20. The Flynn story would not go away soon or easily.

Another instant media addiction that lingers still, though Trump has taken precautions to reduce his vulnerability to it, has been the practice of seizing on the least ambiguity in Trump's remarks to misrepresent his comments as indicative of his ignorance or bigotry. His notorious imprecision with some facts as well as his infamous "truthful hyperbole," opened the door to this problem, and the media rushed through it.

On February 2, he said that he was very proud that there was now a museum on the National Mall in Washington for African American history (the Smithsonian Museum of African American History and Culture). "While listing prominent African Americans featured in the museum's exhibits, including Martin Luther King, Harriet Tubman, and Rosa Parks, Trump said of famous abolitionist Frederick Douglass that he is 'someone who has done an amazing job and is being recognized more and more.'"[2] CNN, the *Washington Post*, the *Atlantic*, and the full gamut of other leftist anti-Trump outlets gratuitously seized upon this as evidence that Trump had no idea who Douglass was. His knowledge of Douglass's career may not be extensive, but no such inference was justified, and the media's overzealous treatment of the story was compounded by its implication that such ignorance was further proof that Trump was a racist (a demonstrably false conclusion).

Similarly, when Trump said to the press during the visit to Washington of Israeli prime minister Benjamin Netanyahu on February 15 that he was looking at both one-state and two-state solutions to the Israel-Palestine conflict, the anti-Trump media raised the alarm, for no reason whatever, that he had abandoned the two-state option. On February 18, Trump spoke at one of his heavily attended rallies, in Florida, and listed places in Europe struggling to assimilate a large influx in refugees. In addition to mentioning Germany, Belgium, and France, he said, "You look at what's happening last night in Sweden…they took in large numbers [of refugees]; they're having problems like they never thought possible." Nothing noteworthy had happened in Sweden the night before and Swedes and Trump's domestic opponents became very exercised that he had invented a terrorist attack in Sweden. He eventually clarified that he misspoke and was referring to having seen a Fox News report the night before that represented Sweden as "the rape capital of Europe," because of the recent admission of three hundred fifty thousand Middle Eastern migrants. In their typical rush to rebuff the president, his opponents overplayed their hand, essentially painting Sweden as a perfect example of refugee integration. Two days later riots broke out in a predominantly immigrant-populated suburb of Stockholm. Trump avoided comment.

When Japanese prime minister Shinzo Abe arrived on February 10, the media fussed about the extended hand-shake they had (nineteen seconds; it is common practice to extend a handshake for a photo op). Constant camera shutters can be heard in the video during the handshake so it's reasonable to assume Trump was just posing.

That meeting, and the visit of Canadian prime minister Justin Trudeau three days later, as well as the Netanyahu meeting, were all very satisfactory. Trump and Trudeau set up a Canada–United States Council for Advancement of Women Entrepreneurs and Business Leaders, a little-noticed debunking of the canard about Trump's supposed misogyny.

With their customary priggishness and snobbery, the British, a wide swath of their opinion still irritated at being so thoroughly surpassed by the Americans in world influence, became spontaneously annoyed when their new prime minister, Theresa May, invited President Trump to make a state visit to the United Kingdom later in 2017. A petition signed by 1.8

million Britons asked that the visit be reduced to a simple intergovernmental visit, so as not to embarrass the queen. This was nonsense, as the president of the United States is a chief of state and cannot be, and would not consent to be treated as unworthy of meeting the British monarch. In the prevailing circumstances, as Britain began to negotiate its exit from the European Union, it was in no position to slap America in the face, though, unfortunately, Trump's domestic opponents were so pathological in their hatred for him that they would relish the office of president being dragged through the international mud as long as it looked bad for Trump. The issue was debated in Parliament on February 20, with the speaker of the House of Commons having pandered with silly and unjust remarks about Trump the notorious racist and misogynist, but the government dismissed the argument as contrary to the British national interest. The atmosphere was further soured by the endless and cheeky comments of the vain and belligerent leftist Muslim mayor of London, Sadiq Khan. Boris Johnson, Britain's redoubtable foreign minister, later said, in one of the finest uses of Twitter: "We will not allow US-UK relations to be endangered by some pompous, puffed-up popinjay in City Hall." It was agreed by May and Trump several months later at the G20 meeting in Hamburg that the president's visit would be deferred to 2018.

Trump's Cabinet secretaries generally performed admirably, but his lively and chaotic White House staff sometimes seemed composed mostly of members of a "floating crap game," as veteran journalist and fair-minded commentator Brit Hume noted. Nevertheless, if the new administration's progress was sometimes forward, sometimes sidewise, it took its dynamic lead from the top. Trump was nothing if not hardworking on both domestic issues and foreign affairs.

After Iran tested a long-range ballistic missile on February 3, Trump warned the country's Islamist regime that it was "playing with fire" and imposed new sanctions on it. Trump hosted German chancellor Angela Merkel on March 17, and they made progress on Germany (representing NATO's second greatest economy) raising its defense budget to better approximate its NATO commitments. There were problems on the climate side, however, as Merkel was obliged by domestic politics to pitch in with the greens.

Trump did what he could by executive authority alone. He rolled back Obama's "transgender" bathroom guidelines, leaving such matters to the states, on February 22. On March 6, Trump issued a new travel ban order that was less vulnerable legally than the first, though the legal issues around even the first were largely fraudulent. The president controls immigration policy and it is no business of federal or other judges, but Democrats and pro-Islam activist groups cited comments Trump had made in his campaign about temporarily banning entry by Muslims, a suggestion he had drastically revised, and which should have been irrelevant, in any event, to adjudging the executive order. His opponents wanted the courts to ignore the president's constitutional authority and instead impute to him a violation of religious liberty, which was nonsense, as foreign residents and citizens do not possess religious rights to enter the United States. An Obama law school classmate in Hawaii, whom Obama had appointed to the bench, purported to strike down the revised travel ban on March 16 as it progressed upwards in the court system. Trump eventually included non-Muslim countries (Venezuela and North Korea), and in late November 2017, the high court tentatively upheld Trump's last formulation of his executive order, deferring a decision on the main issue to its normal place on the court calendar.

On February 27, 2017, the House Intelligence chairman, Republican Congressman Devin Nunes of California, revealed that Congress had no evidence of collusion between Trump and the Russians. On March 4, the president, as was his custom at this point, announced via Twitter that his communications had been tapped at the Trump Tower, and accused his critics, with their endless speculation about Russian "collusion," of engaging in "McCarthyism." The anti-Trump media responded with its customary wave of incredulous disdain. Trump stuck to his allegation and advised critics to await events. On March 22, Nunes affirmed that some transition-era communications of the Trump campaign had been intercepted, putting a rod partially on the backs of the more hysterical anti-Trump media, who had been doing a native rain dance of derision over the Trump tweet of March 4. On April 6, Nunes would temporarily retire from direction of the Russian probe by his committee because of complaints that he had shown the president before he had shown his own committee colleagues some of the findings of the committee's investigation which confirmed Trump's wire-tapping claims. This required until December 8 to resolve, when Nunes was completely cleared by the ethics committee. It had been another partisan red herring.

The Russian question became cloudier when Attorney General Sessions on March 2 acknowledged that he had spoken casually with Russian officials at large receptions and during the campaign by telephone, that these facts had escaped his memory at his confirmation hearings, and that he had been advised by counsel that the telephone contacts need not be reported for his application for a security clearance. The meetings appeared to have been mere exchanges of pleasantries, but the *Washington Post* claimed that it had evidence that Sessions had discussed sanctions and campaign matters with the Russian ambassador during the campaign. Sessions denied this forcefully, and as any such information as the *Post* claimed to have would have been procured illegally, it is of doubtful veracity, especially as Sessions had no authority to speak for Trump during the campaign, and especially not with a foreign ambassador.

It was a very clumsy performance by Sessions and he announced his recusal on the whole Russian matter, leaving the president with no attorney general or deputy attorney general (as he had fired Sally Yates for refusing to carry out his immigration order) immediately involved in the Russian investigation. Trump had nominated Rod Rosenstein as deputy attorney general, but the Senate had not yet confirmed him (though it eventually did by a vote of ninety-four to six). In the meantime, he had a very politically meddlesome and suspect FBI director, James Comey, whose loyalty Trump had good reason to doubt. Trump was very litigious and legally experienced and he saw at once the problems of the position Sessions had created for him. He would tell the *New York Times* on July 19: "Sessions should have never recused himself, and if he was going to recuse himself, he should have told me before he took the job, and I would have picked somebody else." Trump told the *Times* nothing but the truth when he said of Sessions' conduct: "It's extremely unfair, and that's a mild word, to the president."

At this point there was the predictable overreaction to Trump's comments, with publicity-addicted posturers in the Congress even sponsoring legislation to protect the attorney general from being fired, as if it were not the express right of the president to fire whomever he wishes in the executive branch. In any event, Trump did not intend to fire Sessions, which would obviously have been unwise at this point, and Sessions soldiered on, giving a passable performance on June 13 when he appeared before the Senate Intelligence Committee and poured cold water on the Russian issue. The Russian collusion argument never had the appearance of anything but a desperately seized canard to harass and defame Trump and distract the new administration from putting its program through, while consoling a sulky Hillary Clinton over her defeat—and that remains the case at time of writing.

Meanwhile, Trump spoke well and was generously received when he addressed Congress for the first time on February 28. He stole the Democrats' clothes in many policy areas and went to considerable and somewhat eloquent lengths to destroy any suggestion that he was anything but a passionate opponent of racial or sex discrimination. The well-applauded appearance of his dazzlingly attractive wife and daughters and daughters-in-law in the gallery enabled the Trump family, in this unique setting, to appear unfazed and somewhat above the controversy that had swirled around them for many months.

On March 14, one of Trump's most rabid detractors, MSNBC's raucously opinionated Rachel Maddow, triumphantly announced that she had a copy of part of Trump's 1995 tax return. Democrats had been demanding sight of his returns, which Trump refused while they were still being audited and in dispute, and various media personnel had publicly asked for the leakage of them (incitement to criminal behavior, but this was now fairly routine among Trump's enemies). Maddow breathlessly plunged into her revelation on air without analyzing it very much and it showed that, contrary to *New York Times* and other claims that Trump had paid no taxes for decades, he had in fact in 1995 paid federal income tax of $38 million. The Democratic assertions for months, such as by Senator Chris Coons of Delaware, that his tax returns would validate the Russian charges, went mercifully quiet.

The press was also uncharacteristically quiet about one of the greatest achievements of the administration, which gained steam throughout his first months in office, as Trump began a massive rollback of red tape and regulations, which had an immediate and salutary effect on the health and well-being of American business. On March 28, 2017, Trump repealed Obama's global warming emissions reduction policies, as he considered these punitive to American business and consumers. This move was one that the media could not ignore, but could not praise either.

When Trump did, finally, win plaudits, it was for taking military action against Syria, something approved of by many Democrats and Never-Trump Republicans. On April 4, the embattled Russo-Iranian puppet-president of Syria, Bashar al-Assad, again used sarin gas on Syrian civilians, a specialty of his late father, and the sort of incident that violated Barack Obama's infamous "red line" and caused him to huff and puff and abdicate his role of commander-in-chief to Congress and then back down ignominiously, deferring to Russia. Trump ordered the firing of fifty-nine cruise missiles from an American warship against a Syrian airfield and gas storage complex two days later, after giving a brief warning to Russia which had personnel in the target area. The cruise missile attack took place while Trump was having dinner with Chinese president Xi Jinping at his Florida home, Mar-a-Lago. The Chinese leader was quite unruffled, as China has no dog in the Middle East hunt, and the visit seemed to go well. On April 13, Trump approved a military recommendation to drop a ten-ton bomb on an underground ISIS complex in Afghanistan, which destroyed the target and killed at least ninety-two ISIS terrorists.

All polls showed that approval of the president's performance, though lukewarm at about 40 percent, was twice that of Congress and three times that of the media. His dominance of social media (more than forty million followers of his Twitter accounts) and the talk radio world allowed Trump to offer his own alternative to the narrative of the *New York Times*. Rush Limbaugh, who is intelligently pro-Trump, has more than twice as many listeners as the *New York Times* has readers, and Rush, unlike the *Time*s, focuses almost exclusively on politics.

Three months into his presidency, Trump had already arrayed himself for battle against the establishment and achieved significant victories. But the struggle for mastery in Washington was just beginning.

CHAPTER 11

A Honeymoon of Hand-to-Hand Combat

It was now to be the hour of James Comey, though not in the manner that the tall publicity-seeking FBI director might have planned. On May 3 he testified before the House Judiciary Committee and said that the Bureau had not, in his time, been asked to stop or change the course of an investigation, though advice had sometimes been given, but not more than that. He laid great emphasis on the investigation of Russia's attempted interference in the 2016 election and said that "Russia is the greatest threat of any nation on earth." He said they would "do this again, because of the 2016 election, they know it worked." He did not expand on this, and did not claim that Russia had determined the result of the election. He said that Russia should be made to pay a price for its interference. These assertions were all far beyond his remit—it was not the business of the federal police director to pronounce on matters of geopolitical strategy. Even J. Edgar Hoover, who directed the FBI or its previous equivalent for forty-eight years, left such determinations to the eight presidents whom he serviced.

Six days later, Comey was fired by Trump, very unceremoniously, an event he only learned of by television, as he was out of Washington and the president's letter had been delivered to his Washington office, and given the identity of the sender, had not been opened. The FBI director was entitled to greater personal consideration. The White House initially stated that the firing was at the suggestion of the attorney general and his just-appointed deputy, Rod Rosenstein. Rosenstein had been critical, in a memo to Sessions, of Comey's conduct in the Clinton investigation. Comey had certainly been presumptuous and inconsistent, even unprofessional.

Trump let it be known in interviews that, apart from what Rosenstein and Sessions had to say about Comey, Trump was annoyed because although Comey had told him three times, as Comey subsequently confirmed, that he, the president, was not a suspect in the Russian investigation, Comey declined to make that point publicly. He was thus effectively facilitating the efforts of the Democrats to immobilize the president and compromise him internationally and feed the media smear machine by pretending that a Watergate-style evaporation of executive authority was underway. (Anti-Trump commentators were predictably eager to make comparisons with President Nixon's "Saturday Night Massacre"—his firing of the attorney general and the special prosecutor in 1973. These were completely incomparable events, but very few people now remembered Nixon's actions with any accuracy.)

Comey had asked to see Trump, had dinner with him on January 27, and made clear to the new president that he wished to remain as FBI director. Comey claims Trump asked him for loyalty and Comey, instead, promised honesty. Trump was irritated with Comey because he thought the FBI director should be doing more to apprehend and prosecute the leakers within the administration, all of the leaks being criminal offenses. On February 14, Trump allegedly told Comey that he hoped the FBI director would seek the imprisonment of reporters who were publishing classified information, which they knew to be illegal. In addition, he allegedly said that "I hope you can see your way clear to letting…[former National Security Advisor Michael] Flynn go." Comey wrote a memo of the conversation for his own files and later testified to Congress (June 8), that he took Trump's comments as an order to drop the Flynn investigation, though that does not accord with Trump's alleged words or his conduct, but he did not consider that Trump was attempting to obstruct the Russia investigation. Comey asked on March 4 that the Justice Department authorize him to deny publicly that the Obama administration had tapped Trump's telephones at Trump Tower, as Trump had alleged, but permission was denied. (And at time of writing it seems quite likely that Trump's allegation was accurate.)

As Comey acknowledged in his testimony to Congress on June 8, he leaked his memo of the February 14 meeting, whose contents Trump disputed, to the *New York Times*, shortly after he was fired and said his motive was to provoke the appointment of a special counsel. This was slightly incongruous, as he did not allege that he feared Trump was trying to shut down the Russian investigation and had confirmed that Trump was not a suspect. But the differences between Trump and Comey were numerous, going back to what Trump considered his effort to deliver the election to Clinton, and including Trump's belief that Comey was complicit in perpetuating the "made-up story" of Russian collusion by refusing to acknowledge publicly that Trump was not under investigation. Trump was also angry, with some reason, with Comey's failure to do anything about illegal leaks from Obama holdovers in the administration, his failure (as Trump saw it) to look seriously at the dubious antics of the Clinton Foundation, and his failure to acknowledge or prevent government surveillance of Trump Tower.

On May 12, Trump tweeted that Comey should hope that "there are no tapes of our conversations before he starts leaking to the press."[1] This was a bothersome comment, although Trump may believe that it obliged Comey to be careful in subsequent accounts of their conversations. On June 22, two weeks after Comey's congressional testimony, faced with a subpoena for production of such tapes, Trump tweeted that he had "no idea whether there are 'tapes' or recordings of my conversations with

James Comey, but I did not make, and do not have, any such recordings."[2] A tweeted response was a calculatedly cavalier slap in the face to the militant Democrats on the committee, who reacted rather petulantly. The pugnacious Adam Schiff, Democratic congressman from Hollywood (to whose rabidly partisan and usually foolish collective views he gave unceasing voice), demanded elaboration and said Trump's tweet had made things less and not more clear. Trump ignored Schiff, who was a constant television presence sanctimoniously implying the president was guilty of outrages almost every night, and Trump had his assistant press secretary say the president's tweet was "extremely clear."

On May 17, Trump met with two Russian diplomats and described Comey to them as a "nut job" and also mentioned that he had received intelligence that ISIS might try to smuggle bombs onto aircraft in laptops. This was all leaked by White House personnel to the press who then accused Trump of giving away Israeli intelligence. This backfired on the media, when it was pointed out that it ill-behooved the media to incite and publish leaks of confidential information while righteously accusing Trump of causing these indiscretions. Israeli prime minister Netanyahu dismissed suggestions that he had any concerns about what Trump told the Russians, and these complaints quickly vanished; in the Washington jargon of the times, it was another nothingburger.

Comey's predecessor at the FBI and long-time friend and sponsor, Robert Mueller, was appointed special counsel on May 17 by deputy attorney general Rosenstein, with authority to look into all aspects of the Russian question. He took over an investigation in progress, and there were triumphant rejoicings from Trump's enemies and groans from his supporters that this would be another endless warlock hunt such as Archibald Cox and Leon Jaworski conducted against Nixon, Lawrence Walsh against Reagan over the Iran-Contra nonsense, and Kenneth Starr conducted against President Clinton with an investigation that started with Whitewater and ended with a tawdry affair with an intern. There were not normal grounds to justify such a counsel at this time, and Sessions's recusal and the malleability of Rosenstein after only a few days in office left Trump rather isolated officially, and if

Rosenstein felt compelled to name a counsel, it should not have been someone so closely associated with Comey, whose own conduct was going to require explanation.

Mueller aggravated the controversy by recruiting a group of notorious Clintonites for his legal staff, which denied the appearance of an impartial inquiry and instead made it seem like an anti-Trump fishing expedition (which it almost certainly was), though Rosenstein publicly said that he would not authorize Mueller to go beyond the logical remit of his investigation.

President Trump left Washington on May 19 with his wife and an official entourage for his first foreign trip as president amid renewed hysteria and predictions of his impeachment. Nate Silver, ABC News political analyst, said the chances of impeachment were from 25 to 50 percent on May 22, though he offered no opinion on whether such a move would succeed. The firing of the FBI director and the appointment of a special counsel encouraged the media to run with its preferred narrative of a presidency in crisis, but there was no substance to any of it, just the writhings and thrashings of the endangered and half-decapitated Washington political establishment and its media, Wall Street, Hollywood, and Silicon Valley accomplices.

The president made a splash in foreign policy, first by meeting with Turkish president Recep Tayyip Erdogan on May 16 in the Oval Office, and then by traveling to Saudi Arabia, Israel, and Rome—an interesting and ground-breaking trip between the three Abrahamic religious centers—before appearing at NATO headquarters in Brussels to urge a better effort by the laggard allies to fulfill their duties and military pledges.

In Saudi Arabia, the Trump party was greeted with immense deference by the country's eighty-one-year-old monarch, King Salman, and Trump addressed a conference of the Arab states calling for a united effort against terrorism, and was well-received. The Arab world had not been charmed by Obama's overtures to Iran, and found his foreign policy tentative and ambivalent, confusing and worrisome. The Trumps were very generously received in Jerusalem, and the president and Israeli

Prime Minister Benjamin Netanyahu are old friends. Trump also met with the Palestinian leader Mahmoud Abbas, and professed cautious optimism about advancing a lasting peace between the Israelis and the Palestinians. His Middle East peace representative is his son-in-law Jared Kushner, a much-criticized arrangement, but as far as could be determined, the visit went off well at all levels.

The meeting in Rome with Pope Francis was cordial and seemed to rebuild the generally good relations between the White House and the Holy See that have existed at least since the time of Pope Pius XII and Franklin Roosevelt and certainly since the time of Pope John Paul II and President Ronald Reagan (who appointed the first American ambassador to the Holy See).

On this occasion, it came to light that Melania Trump is, in fact, an observant Roman Catholic. Her religion was revealed by the London *Daily Mail*, which was ironic, as it was from this newspaper that she had recently collected almost three million dollars in a libel settlement over the insinuation that she had, in effect, been a prostitute while modeling in New York. (She had the pope bless her rosary and inclined her head respectfully when shaking hands, but did not kiss the pope's ring, as the last Roman Catholic wife of an American president, Jacqueline Kennedy had done.)

The Meeting in Brussels was a little less convivial, but Trump certainly got his message across. He was emphatic about American faith in NATO, but because he did not specifically mention Clause 5, which states an attack on one member is an attack upon all, there were loud complaints among the domestic opposition commentators that he had undercut and conditionalized the whole alliance; once again, utter nonsense. (The following clause says that each country will decide for itself how to respond to an attack.) Even the press had a hard time denying that the president and his family represented the country with dignity and success, and a fine balance between the different religious forces with whose leaders he met.

He left Chancellor Merkel and some others with the distinct impression that he would act on his campaign promises not to ratify the Paris

Climate Accord, and he followed through on this on June 2, shortly after his return to Washington. There was the customary outcry of the fanatical climate lobby, claiming the end was nigh, but the president, environmental administrator Scott Pruitt, commerce secretary Wilbur Ross, and others all explained effectively that the United States was unequivocal in its fight against pollution and the spoliation of resources, but was not prepared to turn its pockets inside out to placate a large number of countries whose ecological performance had been a good deal less distinguished than that of the United States.

On May 22, while Trump was in the Middle East, there was an Islamist terrorist attack at a pop concert in the British city of Manchester, killing twenty-two people and injuring fifty-nine, many of them youngsters. On June 14, a far-left activist and Bernie Sanders supporter, James Hodgkinson, launched a terrorist attack on Republican congressmen at a baseball practice in northern Virginia, seriously wounding Republican House of Representatives whip Steve Scalise of Louisiana and several others. Hodgkinson was killed by capitol police and was the only fatality, but it shocked the political community. On May 30, comedienne Kathy Griffin conducted an imitation ISIS-style photo-shoot and sent around a picture of the blood-stained, apparently severed head of the president. This was too much even for his more strenuous enemies and she was roundly condemned as temporarily unhinged, as she oscillated between apologies, tearful lamentations that Trump had "ruined" her, and defiant statements that he was "picking on the wrong redhead" and all her life she had been hassled by "older white guys." Trump hadn't done anything to her, and when he commented on the incident he said, quite rightly, that Griffin "should be ashamed of herself," especially considering that he was the father of an eleven-year-old son who was "having a hard time with this." Melania issued a statement that called the photo "disturbing" and said it raised questions about Ms. Griffin's "mental health," a reasonable inference.

On June 15, CNN's mouthy White House reporter, Jim Acosta, announced that the president had not visited Congressman Scalise after he was shot. In fact, the president and Mrs. Trump did visit him as soon as he could receive visitors. Acosta's report was a complete fabrication, as was the media claim that Trump had moved a bust of Martin Luther King Jr. out of the Oval Office. He had left it in place, but brought back the bust of Winston Churchill that Obama had removed from the White House. There have been endless media efforts to portray Trump as a racist and sexist, sometimes subtly and often not. On June 26, three CNN journalists were forced to resign after confecting and issuing false stories on the Russia investigation. It was a war of attrition and the media shed more blood than the president in this battle, but they were dispensable and replaceable media picadors trying to wound and provoke the president. Some of the attacks on the president, like those of Mika Brzezinski and Joe Scarborough on MSNBC, seemed almost demented.

On June 20, there was a special election in Georgia's sixth congressional district to fill the vacancy created by the confirmation of the sitting member, Dr. Tom Price, as secretary of Health and Human Services. The national media billed the election as a referendum on Trump (such was their confidence that Trump would not pass such a test). More than $30 million poured in from outside the state to assist the Democratic candidate. But the Republican won easily enough, as Republicans did in other elections at that time, and Trump demonstrated again that those who voted for him remained solidly behind him. The sixth district special election was the most expensive election in the history of the House of Representatives.

David Gergen, knowledgeable former aide to Presidents Reagan and Clinton, but now reduced to the CNN Goebbelsesque party line, had said that "We're in impeachment territory now," but that the president had won a strong vote of confidence in the special election and "deserves to take a victory lap."

By this time, two on-running dramas absorbed American political attention, one foreign and one domestic. The foreign policy issue involved North Korea. Its communist dictator, Kim Jong-Un, threatened to attack the United States territory of Guam, said his country could strike the West Coast of the United States with nuclear weapons, and claimed to have developed a hydrogen bomb. As part of his continuing provocations in the region, he periodically fired missiles over the home islands of Japan. The Clinton administration had rewarded his father, Kim Jong Il, with more than four billion dollars to discontinue his nuclear program, and he took the money and accelerated the program. The George W. Bush and Obama administrations engaged in purposeful negotiations punctuated by righteous and even minatory noises, but North Korea continued to advance to the threshold of nuclear military capability.

It was now Trump's problem and North Korea either had to be accepted into the company of nuclear military powers or had to be discouraged from taking that step by more drastic diplomatic and economic measures than had been employed up to now, or prevented from doing so by preemptive military action. Trump, Vice President Pence, and Trump's secretaries of state and defense repeatedly stated that they would not tolerate North Korea's acquisition of deliverable nuclear warheads. Trump had told the Chinese president Xi Jinping, when they met in February, that the United States would prevent North Korea from achieving this capability, preferably with the collaboration of the Chinese, but if necessary unilaterally. He assured Jinping that the United States was not insisting on "regime change" in North Korea, and was not seeking a united Korean peninsula, which China opposed as it would soon be another economic powerhouse almost of the proportions of Japan. But he forcefully repeated that a nuclear military North Korea was a non-starter.

After a brief lapse, China, which had as much to fear from a nuclear North Korea as anyone, did finally turn the screws on exports and banking facilities and declared itself to be neutral in any conflict between North Korea and the United States. This was a good deal more cooperation than Beijing had furnished before, having spent decades nodding in agreement with the United States and Japan about North Korea, but impishly enabling its mischief. Though Trump's critics were almost predicting that he would provoke war with China, his achievement of the greatest diplomatic progress in the Far East since Nixon opened up relations with China has been almost unremarked.

As always in the United States, there was the peace party calling for accommodation at any price, led by the imperishable Jimmy Carter, who thought relations would improve if the United States withdrew its forces from South Korea, and volunteered at the age of ninety-two to go to Pyongyang as American ambassador. (He also volunteered, as someone who had voted for the socialist Bernie Sanders, that national press coverage of President Trump was very unfair and unbalanced, for which acknowledgement Trump publicly thanked him.)

Trump's enemies, of course, were not only in the media and the Democratic Party but among many members of his own party, especially those who craved media adulation. Senate foreign relations committee chairman Robert Corker, for instance, claimed to believe that Trump could be a dangerous warmonger. Even so, Trump seemed to have created a diplomatic climate for stern action against North Korea; and there was a unanimous United Nations Security Council vote for sanctions. That would certainly not in itself constrain Kim, but it was a harbinger of firming international opinion.

Inevitably, as time passed and the war of words escalated, and the United States deployed increased forces to the theater, allies, foreign and domestic, quaked audibly at the knees, but Trump led effectively and from early October, the public saber-rattling went quiet and there were hopes that China was giving Kim a tutorial on where this could lead. Trump deployed three full aircraft carrier task forces (the immense nuclear carriers *Nimitz*, *Theodore Roosevelt*, and *Ronald Reagan*), just off North Korea, a serious show of strength.

In domestic affairs, the drama of health care consumed the first eight months of the administration. The Republicans in opposition had voted seven times to repeal the Affordable Care Act, Obamacare, and been vetoed by President Obama. Now that there was a president who would sign the bill to repeal, it was more complicated. Trump, who had no background in the subject, took his Republican congressional colleagues seriously and assumed they knew what they were doing and meant what they said. Whatever the lack of rapport of many of them with him, they were presumably on the same side on this issue and Trump had been assured that his health and human services secretary, Tom Price, a doctor and a congressman, knew about health care and the state of congressional opinion. Price and Speaker Paul Ryan eventually produced a bill that rolled back the coercive aspects of Obamacare and ended the state monopolies of insurers. But it also rolled back Medicaid, which had millions of dependents and it effectively deprived a significant number of people of health insurance, while it would reduce premiums for many more and would save the federal government substantial amounts of expense over the next decade. The Democrats went at once to their default position of howling hysterically that the Republicans were pandering to the rich and greedy and throwing the disadvantaged off the train, and spent around twenty million dollars on a national advertising campaign whipping up opposition to Trumpcare, as it was instantly called, though Trump was at first only sketchily aware of the bill's contents.

The warning bells sounded when Ryan could not bring the bill to a vote. With tweaking and arm-twisting from the White House, it eased through and went to the Senate, but there it stopped. Health care was a shambles and would have to be addressed. On July 31, Trump had the Republican senators to lunch at the White House and told them they looked like "fools" for their failure to reform health care after they had shouted from the housetops for seven years that they would effect important changes.

In modified forms it came three times to the brink of adoption. In the end, the administration could only get forty-nine votes, as John McCain defected, apparently, out of personal animus to Trump, thinly veiled behind tired pieties about cross-aisle compromise; Rand Paul was a libertarian perfectionist, but could only get forty-five votes for his own bill, and Susan Collins of Maine voted against repeal because of issues proper to her state.

The congressional Republicans were collectively exposed as frauds, cowards who had masqueraded as repealers, but folded like a $3 suitcase when it was their turn to legislate. It was a painful experience for Trump, but the game wasn't over. (Secretary Price, having charged more than $400,000 in airplane charters, was disembarked by the president on September 29. His tenure was a disappointment. Alex Azar, former head of the large pharmaceutical company Eli Lilly, replaced him.)

President and Mrs. Trump and a large entourage arrived in Warsaw for a state visit to Poland on July 5. The following day, he was thunderously applauded by a large crowd that frequently broke into chants of "Donald Trump, Donald Trump" as he praised Polish courage and patriotism, and pledged complete solidarity with his hosts, promising to deploy an anti-missile defense to protect Poland (a promise Obama had rescinded) and urging Russia to cease its "destabilizing" agitations. This was all rapturously received and it at least shut up his domestic critics who had complained that he had not explicitly endorsed the concept of "an attack upon one is an attack upon all" in his visit to the NATO headquarters at Brussels the previous month. But they immediately opened fire on another front—that because his speech included a rousing defense of Western Civilization, he was a white nationalist and racist, the usual outrageous falsehoods from a media that could not even report rationally on a well-written, well-delivered, and well-received speech.

He attended the Three Seas Conference of a group of twelve East European states that bordered the Adriatic, Black, or Baltic Seas. He proceeded on to Hamburg and the G20 meetings, which included private side meetings with many of the more prominent leaders, including Russia's Vladimir Putin, China's Xi Jinping, Britain's Theresa May, Germany's Angela Merkel, Japan's Shinzo Abe, Indonesia's president Joko Widodo, and France's Emmanuel Macron. He promised Mrs. May a swift passage of a free trade agreement should she wish to make one with the United States after exiting the European Union.

On July 14, he was in France to meet with Macron and review the traditional, formidable military parade the French put on along Paris's Champs-Élysées on their national day, July 14. Chic and impeccable in Chanel and Dior couture, Melania Trump made an excellent impression; and Trump, whom the French, in their contrariness, had not greeted with as much pompous skepticism as the British and the Germans, was an exemplary visitor. Trump and Macron, populists with beguiling wives, seemed the only vital major western leaders, with Merkel and Theresa May struggling with minority governments, and Italy in its usual state of disarray. (Trump chivalrously complimented Mme. Macron on her exemplary condition—she is twenty-four years older than her husband—which was taken by the French as a gracious remark, but disparaged by Trump's desperate enemies in the American media as verging on harassment.)

The country to which the president returned had been riled again, this time by the *New York Times* publication on July 9 of the news that there had been a meeting between Jared Kushner, Donald Trump Jr., then–Trump campaign manager Paul Manafort, and Russian lawyer Natalia Veselnitskaya during the campaign. Veselnitskaya had purportedly, according to the contact person, dangled damaging information about Hillary Clinton in order to get an audience with Trump's people. The real purpose of the meeting was almost certainly to lobby for the repeal of the Magnitsky Act, a U.S. law which has been effectively used to target and sanction close Putin allies following the death in Russian custody of Magnitsky, a reformist auditor and lawyer who alleged Russian crimes. As part of his campaign against the act, Putin rather spitefully passed a bill in 2012 banning the adoption of Russian children by American parents—a subject that evidently came up during the meeting.

The president dictated a response from Air Force One dismissing the meeting as a discussion of the adoption of Russian children in the United States. The anti-Trumpers leapt to unwarranted conclusions with great speed, Hillary Clinton's vice presidential candidate, Tim Kaine, even suggesting the trio were guilty of "treason." Jared Kushner, who had an in-camera but much praised meeting with the House Intelligence Committee on July 24, was fully responsive to all questions, and completely debunked any thought of collusion in the election with the Russians in his observations. This proved, in the parlance of the time, to be yet another flavorless "nothingburger."

But there continued to be unprecedented leaks from the White House, including the contents of conversations with foreign leaders, and a good deal of semi-public back-biting among White House factions. On July 21, outspoken Long Island financier Anthony Scaramucci was announced as White House communications director, and Sean Spicer—an amiable, but not agile, and often accident-prone person—retired as press secretary. Scaramucci promised to put some order into the press function and to staunch the leaks, if need be by drastic measures. It was an auspicious start, but was blown up on July 28 by a catastrophic "off the record" interview with the *New Yorker*, one of the most Trump-hostile media outlets in the country, in which an apparently intoxicated Scaramucci, in the midst of the breakdown of his marriage when his wife was nine months pregnant, uttered a number of extreme and very vulgar reflections on Steve Bannon, Reince Priebus, and some of his other colleagues. His comments were so intemperate and ill-considered, the media reported them almost without speculating on Scaramucci's likely fate, waiting for the president's response.

The press feasted on this with bacchanalian glee, and Trump finally moved decisively to clean up the White House. On July 31, Scaramucci walked the plank after only sixteen days in the job and was replaced by yet another glamorous woman of the Trump entourage, Hope Hicks, the publicity-averse but media-effective twenty-nine-year-old former model. Sarah Huckabee Sanders (daughter of former governor of Arkansas and Republican presidential candidate, Mike Huckabee) replaced Sean Spicer as press secretary. On August 18, Steve Bannon, controversial campaign strategist, was eased out of the White House ("by mutual agreement") and returned to Breitbart, his enterprising but not always reliable news website; former party chairman Reince Priebus was moved out as chief of staff and replaced by homeland security secretary and four-star Marine general John Kelly. He ran a tight ship and the workplace atmosphere quickly improved and there was a steady decline in indiscretions.

In the midst of these tempestuous events, Trump announced that, henceforth, transgender applicants would not be allowed into the armed forces. The whole status of transgendered people had been allowed to assume proportions out of all relation to their numbers under Obama— the ultimate manifestation of the inanities of identity politics. Trump believed that endless pandering to demographic subdivisions of the population was fragmenting the country. Given concerns about morale, readiness, and medical costs associated with gender reassignment, the previous ban, he asserted, on transgender personnel, overridden by an

Obama executive order, should be reinstated. Yet another activist judge intent on superseding the roll of the Executive Branch, effectively making the commander-in-chief subordinate to the federal bench, banned the enforcement of Trump's order. After an initial appeal was unsuccessful Trump declined to take it to the Supreme Court.

On August 2, Trump announced his intention to reorient American immigration policy from giving priority to extended family reunification to a merit-based standard, where priority would be given to immigrants who would contribute well and quickly to American life. This was an emulation of the immigration policies of Canada and Australia, and while it raised Democratic hackles, it was well-received in the country. Needless to say, it was not well-received in the media, which went into collective hysterics about Trump's allegedly turning his back on the Statue of Liberty. The media was driven to even more ferocious animosity against the president after riots erupted in Charlottesville, Virginia, on August 12. What began initially as a peaceful protest by supporters of retaining a statue of General Robert E. Lee in the city's main square—joined, fatally, by a group of white nationalists, self-proclaimed Nazis, and the remnant of the Ku Klux Klan—degenerated into violence when it met even larger numbers of counter-protesters, made up of social justice groups but infested, just as fatally, by far-left radicals (broadly referred to as Antifa), many of whom arrived armed with batons and wearing their now-familiar ninja outfits, and evidently looking for a fight. The police effort to avoid violence was understaffed and sporadic, on orders, it later emerged, from the mayor, militant Democratic "Resistance" (to Trump) leader Michael Signer.

One person died when a white supremacist drove his car into a crowd of people, killing a young woman, Heather Heyer. The chief villains here, aside from the violent protesters themselves, were the mayor of Charlottesville and the governor of Virginia, former Democratic National chairman Terry McAuliffe (also a wild-eyed anti-Trumper), who had allowed the protests to escalate like this, either out of sheer negligence or in the cynical hope of reaping some political gain, as the media quickly laid the blame with President Trump.

Trump, in a series of statements, clearly condemned the violence and the extremists—and acknowledged that there were extremists on both sides. That was entirely true, but the national and international media professed to see in this moral equivalence between the two groups a comparative vindication of the Klan and the American Nazis. Numerous members of White House business and cultural advisory boards retired to protest Trump's apparent indifference to racism. As one analyst, Don Luskin, noted, in remarks that were quoted in the *Wall Street Journal*, such reactions, and especially the reaction of the media, amounted to "a clinical case of mass hysteria—and one of the strangest we've ever seen. It's not about the event itself. It's about President Donald Trump's reaction to the event....And it's not even about whether Trump is a racist. It is self-evident that he is not....His sin is that he has failed to express his outrage at the event in a particular way—or, more precisely, that he has expressed it in a way that doesn't kowtow to the identity politics lobby."[3]

Just so, and Trump, with almost stylish contemptuousness, folded the boards and said advisory boards never accomplish anything anyway. The racist charge was still imputed to the president at every opportunity, and that and the bunk about misogyny were still all the Democrats really had to fight with. But Trump's awareness by now of the disposition of the media to lever or fabricate anything into a club to beat him with, should have warned the president to choose his words more carefully.

Trump was constantly derided by the national media as suspect in his relations with Russia, and as a distracted president who was struggling against tightening inculpatory evidence. But there was never any corroborative evidence for any of the sinister allegations against him. CNN and MSNBC announcers periodically referred to the "drip, drip, drip" of the controversy—that was a better description of the commentators themselves—but there was no such momentum behind it; weeks went by without a damaging leak on the subject, other than to indicate improprieties by the Justice Department and the FBI.

Much of the rest of the summer after late July 2017, was taken up with arranging and distributing emergency assistance to hurricane victims in Texas, Florida, and Puerto Rico. The pettiness of much of the anti-Trump media was exposed by criticism of Melania Trump for boarding the official aircraft to go to Texas wearing high heels. She disembarked in running shoes to go with casual attire, suitable for visiting flood-damaged areas. Mrs. Trump has perfected the technique of rising above these tribulations with elegantly calculated disdain. (As in most good marriages, her husband could learn something from her.)

The administration was determined to avoid the public relations disaster that befell President George W. Bush over Hurricane Katrina in New Orleans in 2005. (President Bush arrived late, joked about his rowdy antics as a young man in New Orleans, congratulated the emergency director, and then departed when the city was in desperate straits, with a quarter of the police having defected and thugs and vandals and looters dominating sections of it for several days and snipers shooting at rescuers and aid distributors.)

The Houston area and the middle and west coast of Florida enjoyed better local government, were better prepared, and the federal government was ready with massive emergency relief, and the president and his wife visited as soon as they practically could and came through the natural disasters with flying colors. Puerto Rico was more of a challenge because of its insularity, comparatively primitive electric and transport systems, and the relative vulnerability of much residential construction on the Caribbean island. Desperate for her ffiteen minutes of fame, San Juan Mayor Carmen Yulín Cruz, had time to custom make a tee-shirt saying, "Help us, we are dying," before her interview with CNN's Anderson Cooper, blaming Trump for an inadequate federal government response. Geraldo Rivera, who interviewed her for Fox News, challenged her statement, saying he had been around the island and saw nobody dying. She responded, "Dying is a continuum," making her correct in that all people die, but it was a shabby performance, though much appreciated by the anti-Trump media, which was less impressed by the much more impressive governor of Puerto Rico, Ricardo Rosselló—who holds a Ph.D. in biomedical engineering and is a centrist liberal—who praised President Trump and the federal government for its relief efforts. Not to be left behind in the hair-trigger, blame-Trump sweepstakes, Senator Bernie Sanders cited the hurricanes as evidence of the dangers of climate change (as if there had not been hurricanes of equivalent force at least since the times of Columbus) and the treatment of the Puerto Ricans as illustrative of Trump's racism. The Trumps' visit to the island and the great relief effort mustered for it certainly debunked such asinine comments.

On August 23, Trump spoke to a large crowd in Phoenix for seventy-seven minutes. Outside, protestors hurled projectiles and had to be dispersed by police using tear gas. Trump, as he generally does at these political revival and inspiration sessions, excoriated his opponents and taunted his media enemies. He had made it clear, again, that he condemned racism in the Charlottesville controversy—as he had, but the antagonistic media had invested in the argument that he had not. Two days later, he pulled the media's tail by pardoning Sheriff Joe Arpaio, the eighty-five-year old former sheriff (for twenty-four years) of Maricopa County, Arizona, who had been convicted by federal prosecutors for criminal contempt of federal laws against racial profiling and for the illegal detention of illegal immigrants. The media, inevitably, took this as another indication of Trump's racism.

On August 30 in Springfield, Missouri, in the heart of Trump country and in between visiting hurricane sites, the president unveiled his tax reform plan and spoke for it in a series of meetings around the country through the late summer and autumn. The plan proposed a one-page tax return, the shrinkage of the escalating brackets to four levels of reduced taxation, a 20 percent corporate tax rate (down from 35), and the elimination of most deductions except charitable gifts and mortgage payments. State income taxes would not be deductible against federal tax, putting the pressure on New York, California, and Illinois, three states Trump lost by a total of seven million votes in 2016, which are all chronically strapped for cash and have raided the cookie jar of state income taxes at the federal government's expense. The incomes of the country's often over-endowed and educationally inadequate universities (which were almost uniformly leftist) would also be lightly taxed. It was a well-crafted Trump measure, and the Treasury secretary, Steven Mnuchin, had prepared his bill much more carefully than Tom Price had written up the Obamacare repeal and replace measure with Speaker Paul Ryan.

After seven months, the Republican leaders in the Congress were effectively acting as if they held the balance between the president and the congressional Democrats. They seemed to be waiting to see if this radically different but generally moderate (in policy terms) president would be taken down by the venomous Democratic crusade against him in the Russian collusion investigation and elsewhere. If not, and the president prevailed and seemed to be driving a bandwagon they should climb aboard, they would do so, even while holding their noses. Trump moved to break up this very tedious and irresponsible waiting game by having the Democratic congressional leaders, Senator Chuck Schumer and former House Speaker Nancy Pelosi, to the White House for dinner on September 13, including Chinese food for which Schumer, whom Trump worked with in New York for years, had a well-known fondness. They sat, purring like tabbies on the Oval Office sofa, and agreed to $15.25 billion dollars of hurricane relief for Texas and Florida, and to extend the raise in the debt ceiling for three months.

This sent a message to Senate majority leader Mitch McConnell and Speaker Paul Ryan. Trump effectively seized the balance of power for himself, and made it clear that he would deal with whichever party could bring him results. The congressional Republicans had already failed him on health care, and if he could cut deals with the Democrats that would pass, he would do so. The administration's olive branch to the Democrats was presaged by the decision of the attorney general (and presumably the president) not to indict former senior justice department official Lois Lerner for harassment of Republican Political Action Committees.

As the Mueller and other investigations chugged along, the media refused to recognize what was rapidly apparent—the Democrats had more legal problems than the Republicans. No one could now seriously believe that Trump had colluded with Russia in the election, trading promises of policy shifts favorable to Russia in exchange for cyber-leaks. It was a mad proposition and it became clear from the antics of the leaders of both parties in the Senate Intelligence committee that all they had as evidence was the discredited Steele dossier. Republicans wanted the FBI to explain its role in funding the Steele dossier and in conducting legally questionable surveillance (especially telephone intercepts) on the Trump campaign. They also wanted answers on whether the FBI was complicit in the illegal revelation to the media of the names of Trump campaign officials "unmasked" in intelligence reports. Obama's national security advisor, Susan Rice, and his ambassador to the United Nations, Samantha Power, appear to have been aggressively demanding publication of the names of Trump campaign officials in order to imply that their conduct had been improper or suspect.

It was now known that FBI director Comey had written a draft exoneration of Mrs. Clinton before she was even questioned by the FBI about her emails. He had been investigating both candidates in mid-campaign and had taken it unto himself to announce that Mrs. Clinton, despite her serious misjudgments and apparently dishonest replies to FBI questioners, should not be prosecuted, followed by the panicky interlude when the Bureau reviewed the new batch of emails discovered on the server of former congressman Anthony Weiner. Comey had already acknowledged that he told the president three times that he was not a suspect in the Russian collusion question. Trump was inaugurated four months after the FBI took over trying to chase down Steele's sources to get to the truth, so the continued exposure of Trump to the innuendos of the hostile media and the leprous uncooperativeness of the congressional Democrats as if he were in a legal purgatory were unjustified by the legal facts. Comey's frank assertion that he had leaked his own contested version of what had occurred about the investigation of General Flynn in his dinner conversation with the new president on January 27, was a damaging admission, though the media did not treat it so. It was a criminal act if the memo to himself is considered a government document, which is legally probable, as deputy attorney general Rod Rosenstein confirmed to Congress on December 13, 2017. Comey had unwittingly contributed to the gradual shift of the balance of legal forces in favor of the administration and against the Democrats, a gradual shift that included the increasing congressional attention finally being paid to the questionable activities of the Clinton Foundation, then–Secretary of State Hillary Clinton, and other members of the Obama administration, including, possibly, Robert Mueller who had been director of the FBI when Russia was permitted to buy 20 percent of America's uranium extraction capacity. The transaction required the approval of the Committee on Foreign Investment in the United States, which includes representatives from sixteen U.S. departments and agencies, including the secretary of state. By the time the Committee approved the Uranium One sale, the FBI had already gathered a huge amount of evidence of bribery and kickbacks against a top official at the American subsidiary of the Russian company that was buying Uranium One. This and other evidence, including large pledges to the Clinton Foundation by parties with an interest in Secretary Clinton's goodwill, did raise great suspicions, however much the media wanted to downplay it.

President Trump, meanwhile, had considerable success, domestically and internationally, with his forceful address to the United Nations General Assembly on September 19. He warned North Korea and its leader, whom he had nicknamed "Rocket man," of the dangers of proceeding with his military nuclear program; he denounced the impoverishment and usurpation of freedom in Venezuela; he called for reform of the United Nations; he defined his policy of "America First" as the simple pursuit of America's national interest; and he renewed America's pledge to oppose terrorism everywhere. The international soft Left was repelled but domestic opinion was quite positive. The speech was well-crafted and well-delivered. The following day he met again with the president of Egypt, Abdel Fattah el-Sisi, and indicated that he would lift the embargo on military aid imposed by President Obama, which he duly did.

The sanctimonious hypocrisy of Trump's Hollywood and media critics soon came to the forefront with the exposure of prominent movie producer, and Clinton fundraiser, Harvey Weinstein's alleged sexual assault and intimidation of actresses in large numbers and over decades, which caused him to be cast out of the City of Angels like Lucifer. Weinstein was lynched on the basis of a carefully assembled article in the *New*

York Times and a follow-up in the *New Yorker.* Apparently, his conduct had been notorious throughout the industry for many years, and he had banked on the assumption that his generous support of left-wing candidates and causes would insulate him from criticism, and that more donations and liberal professions would save him after he was exposed. The whole lurid story laid bare the preposterous presumption of the entertainment industry to lecture the American people on politics and morals. Hollywood is a moral and intellectual pigsty, an asylum for the stupid, the corrupt, and the vocally shallow, who possess Thespian aptitudes or a saleable appearance and manner.

On September 22, Trump denounced professional football players who kneeled during the playing of the national anthem before the games. This began with Colin Kaepernick, former quarterback of the San Francisco Forty-Niners, who remained seated during the national anthem in protest against what he considered the routine practice of white American police to shoot unarmed African Americans, preferably killing them, or, in his own words: "I am not going to stand up to show pride in a flag for a country that oppresses black people and people of color....There are bodies in the street and people getting paid leave and getting away with murder." The movement grew and in an address at Huntsville, Alabama, Trump threw into a stump speech for a senatorial primary candidate the opinion that players who did not stand for the anthem should be fired. (His words were: "fire the son of a bitch.") Liberal opinion was offended and so were almost all the football owners and many of their players. Trump said anyone could protest anything they wanted but that well-paid NFL players enjoying a short working season should not hijack the National Football League and offend the sensibilities of their fans by affronting the flag, the servicemen and women who stand behind it, the national anthem, and the country generally. The exchanges escalated and he called for a boycott of the NFL. Attendance fell 20 percent in the first week after Trump's statement, and by year-end, the NFL was suffering a serious desertion of fans (who lean conservative) and advertisers. It might have cast a damper over one of the nation's most popular sports, but the NFL's absurdly overpaid commissioner Roger Goodell; the grandstanding, unsympathetic, over-paid players; and the owners of the immensely over-valued teams were the real losers in public opinion.

Trump is so hyperactive that, apart from North Korea, no particular issue lingers long. He swiftly moved on to other subjects. On health care, he virtually eliminated Obamacare's advertising budget (which had been set up to encourage public participation) and announced on October 12 that he would stop supplementary payments to insurance companies, which were meant to compensate them for the unanticipated—by the Obama administration; they were predicted by everyone else—costs of Obamacare. The Democrats tried to whip up public lamentations about short-changing those of modest means, but as it was just a pay-off to insurance companies, and was unconstitutionally conceived and imposed, the general public dismissed the Democrats' hysteria.

On October 13, Trump declined to certify that Iran was in compliance with the six-power accord negotiated by the Obama administration. Trump recognized that the agreement, which governs fissile material, is unverifiable, and ignores both Iran's progress toward developing a nuclear warhead and its accelerating program to develop and manufacture sophisticated long-range missiles. Foreign policy hawks applauded Trump's realism, even as many on the Left booed Trump for lacking their sophisticated defeatism.

There were other signs that the febrile Trumpophobes were weakening, though like cornered animals their attacks became more vicious and irrational. The resistance to his tax moves was relatively temperate and usually confined to the inevitable mantra that it was just a payoff to the rich, demonstrably as false a claim as it was predictable. Senator Corker of Tennessee, chairman of the foreign relations committee, uttered a few asides and hesitant comments in late September and October to the effect that Trump was unstable and that Secretary of State Tillerson, Defense Secretary Mattis, and Trump's chief of staff, General Kelly, were very exasperated and had to work full-time to keep Trump from doing something dangerously wrong-headed or provocative. Corker and Trump had the usual war of words, and as Corker could not be reelected in Tennessee without Trump's endorsement, he said he would not run again. While Corker played coy with the media, which assumed his support for Trump's tax bill was in doubt, he eventually voted for it.

Another controversy erupted, when it was reported (from anonymous sources) that Secretary Tillerson had called Trump a "fucking moron," though Tillerson denied the report. (Had he really said that, it is unlikely he would have retained his post, or even wanted to keep it.) When asked by reporters, Tillerson, a southern gentleman, responded with "I'm not going to dignify that question," which the press, predictably, reported as confirmation of the rumor. Trump did unceremoniously fire Tillerson on March 23, 2018, speaking well of him but confirming their partial lack of rapport. Mike Pompeo, the CIA director, replaced him.

On October 30, Mueller indicted former Trump campaign manager Paul Manafort and his associate, Rick Gates, for financial offenses allegedly committed years before Manafort knew Trump, and on the insidious charge of "conspiracy against the United States." Mueller had organized a pre-dawn Gestapo or KGB-style raid on Manafort's home on July 26, with armed men barging into the bedroom where Mrs. Manafort was in her sleeping attire (as people frequently are when sleeping in their homes at night).[4]

The new cry after this excitement subsided was that the Twenty-Fifth Amendment (Section Four) could be applicable, by which the Cabinet could vote to remove Trump by reason of mental incompetence. This was as absurd an idea as the national publicity campaign to urge members of the Electoral College to repudiate their pledges to vote for Trump. It was the lowest depth yet plumbed by the Trumpohobes; the "Resistance" was verging on mental incapacity itself. The Twenty-Fifth Amendment was designed to deal with a severe medical failure, as in the case of President Wilson when he was incapacitated by a stroke, not with policy differences or illegalities. It was contemplated once, when President Reagan was shot, but he recovered so quickly there was no need for it. In other desperation moves, the anti-Trump forces unearthed the antiquarian and totally inapplicable Logan Act (1799), which prohibits unauthorized people from trying to conduct American foreign policy, and which they charged should be invoked against the then-president-elect Trump and his staff for meeting with foreign officials, as if this were not common, accepted diplomatic practice. And there were repeated fatuous murmurings about the president obstructing justice when he exercised his constitutional right as chief of the executive branch to fire the inept and universally distrusted (up until Trump fired him, where-upon he instantaneously metamorphosed into the patron saint of the Democrat Party) FBI director, James Comey.

Trump's enemies were grasping at straws.

CHAPTER 12

Gaining the Upper Hand

In late October, the greatest explosion yet in the whole Trump-Kremlin collusion controversy was detonated by the *Washington Post* from leaks that were sprung by the squeaking wheels of justice: the Clinton campaign and Democratic National Committee had taken over the Fusion GPS anti-Trump research originally commissioned by Trump's Never-Trump Republican opponents, after Trump clinched the Republican nomination, and ramped it up, approving and bankrolling the assembly of the Christopher Steele dossier to the extent of approximately ten million dollars. This financed a very scurrilous pastiche of what even Comey called "salacious and unverifiable" material, and Bob Woodward called "garbage."

The Mueller and congressional investigations appeared to be based on this nonsense (mere "campaign dirt" in political parlance), and congressional committees had issued subpoenas to the Justice Department and the FBI, requiring witnesses and evidence about their involvement in the Steele dossier. The subpoenas were ignored and there was soon agitation to cite the Department and Bureau for contempt of Congress. Trump was careful not to order Justice Department compliance with the subpoenas, issued by the Republican majorities, and be re-tarred with the frayed brush of obstruction, but he also did not try to discourage his congressional supporters from impugning the impartiality of the Mueller investigation, and the competence of the Justice Department and the FBI. On January 4, Rosenstein finally agreed to hand over documents congressional committees had subpoenaed (under threat of a contempt of Congress citation), and senators Chuck Grassley (Judiciary chairman) and Lindsey Graham asked the Justice Department for a criminal indictment of Christopher Steele. They alleged that Steele had lied in a civil trial in London or to the FBI and had feloniously shopped his dossier to the press while under obligation to the FBI. This was another startling turn of events.

The Senate intelligence committee leaders, Republican Richard Burr of North Carolina and Democrat Mark Warner of Virginia, acknowledged that they could go no further without Justice Department and FBI responses to their questions about the Steele dossier. This same Senator Warner had been proclaiming nine months before that there had been "upwards of a thousand paid internet trolls working out of a facility in Russia" generating fake news which was broadcast to Wisconsin, Michigan, and Pennsylvania. He implied that the Russians had delivered Wisconsin to Trump—again, a completely unsubstantiated charge, and even Comey had said that Russia's efforts had had not influenced the outcome of the election.

Hillary Clinton's woeful memoir on the election, *What Happened* (not a question), almost accuses Trump of treasonable collusion with the Russian government to defeat her, citing exclusively Steele dossier sources, never mentioning that her own campaign commissioned and paid for it (presumably with her knowledge given the scope, cost, and implications of the work). Thus, the source cited for her heinous accusation was her own slime-smearing operation, which she henceforth described as "campaign information." The *Washington Post*, having broken the story, acknowledged that the fact that the Clinton campaign had financed the Steele dossier provided Republicans with "a talking Point," but without admitting how grievously it compromised the whole Russian collusion issue,[1] especially as many of Steele's sources were themselves Russian, perhaps peddling official disinformation, which would lead an impartial observer to wonder who, in fact, was colluding with the Russians, if not the Clinton campaign.

Mueller's investigation had tried to maintain momentum by indicting General Michael Flynn, who on December 4 pleaded guilty to a single charge of lying to federal officials (something Comey said he thought Flynn had not done). As the charge of collusion collapsed— under the implications of the fact that Mueller was essentially investigating the incumbent president on the basis of slanders collected and paid for by the defeated presidential candidate—the hope flared up in the Resistance and what was left of the Never-Trumpers that Flynn might inculpate the president. This was unlikely, as a cooperative witness would have had to confess to participation in the principal alleged offense (Russian collusion), which Flynn did not do; Flynn was pleading guilty to what Trump had fired him for—lying about conversations with the Russians and specifically the Russian ambassador in Washington (who had since been recalled).

This appeared to be a mouse-trapping operation, as the Obama administration seemed to have relied also on the Steele dossier to obtain a Foreign Intelligence Surveillance Act warrant to intercept the Trump campaign and transition team telephone conversations. There is also the possibility that on the strength of this, various names of Trump campaign personnel were illegally "unmasked" and leaked to the media as well, from intercepted conversations with Russian diplomats (which would not, in themselves, need a FISA warrant, but the unmasking would). This would have been part of the departing administration's effort to inflate the Trump-Russian collusion case as high explosives on a short fuse to discommode the incoming administration. (There would be the added benefit of breathing fetid air into Hillary Clinton's limp argument that the Kremlin and Comey had cheated her out of the election.)

Just as the Steele dossier, apparently the entire basis for the Trump-Russia sham, was crumbling, a torrent of revelations about apparent conflicts of interest among what months earlier the media was referring to as Mueller's "dream team" was pouring into the public domain. Mueller removed senior intelligence officer Peter Strzok in July for texting thousands of anti-Trump messages to his girlfriend, who was also an FBI official on Mueller's team (Lisa Page). It soon emerged that the same Strzok had persuaded Comey in July to describe Hillary Clinton's conduct in the email affair as "extremely careless" rather than the criminal description "grossly negligent." This was also the same Strzok who had conducted the FBI interview of General Flynn.

Mueller had withheld the reason for removing Strzok from his investigation until his virulently anti-Trump texting with Ms. Page was leaked. The leaks were now flowing both ways as the balance of forces in Washington on the Russian collusion issue shifted toward the president and away from his accusers.

Within two days of the revelation of the Strzok affair, it emerged that a senior Justice official, Bruce Ohr, had been demoted for an improper contact with the Russians and with Christopher Steele. Then it emerged that his wife, Nellie Ohr, a Russian expert, had worked on the Steele dossier for Fusion GPS. There were also plausible but unconfirmed reports that another of Mueller's investigators had disposed of two large batches of emails for Mrs. Clinton in that matter, and that many of Mueller's people had been Hillary Clinton contributors. One of them had attended the Clinton election night celebration (that did not, in the event, have much to celebrate) and later sent an email to former deputy attorney general Sally Yates professing to be "so proud" of her for being fired for insubordination by the new president. There were endless rumors of further indiscretions. It could not have been more different from the previous special investigations of Presidents Nixon, Reagan, and Clinton. Under Trump, the investigators were now being swarmed by doubters. Congressional Republicans snapped and tore at the vulnerable facades of the Justice Department and FBI which had been highly politicized under the previous administration. The president said the FBI's reputation was "in tatters" (December 16). Justice and FBI witnesses were badly mauled before congressional committees, and the deputy director, Andrew McCabe, was implicated in anti-Trump activities in one of Strzok's text messages. McCabe's wife had been a Democratic state senate candidate in Virginia and had received $467,500 from a PAC controlled by Virginia governor and Clinton intimate Terry McAuliffe. Three months after his wife's failed election bid, Comey appointed McCabe deputy director of the FBI with oversight of the Clinton emails "matter." It was announced just before Christmas that McCabe would be retiring from the FBI in April, as soon as he was eligible for a full pension. But he abruptly departed on January 29 after the new FBI director, Christopher Wray, saw a memo about to be released by the Republican majority of the House Intelligence Committee condemning use of the Steele dossier to obtain a FISA warrant on minor Trump campaign advisor Carter Page.

Trump continued to cooperate with Mueller and gave the FBI graduating class and rank and file a stirring address of support that was strongly applauded, on December 15. Trump's tactics in supporting the institutions and their personnel while the attempted politicization of them was being steadily exposed, was sophisticated and effective. As it became clear the tide was finally turning, most Democratic politicians were now rather circumspect, except for the egregious Congressman Schiff, who produced his own memo that the Justice Department requested be withheld because of its revelations of classified information. The anti-Trump case was in full disintegration by early 2018. It was released, heavily redacted, on February 23, and attempted a radical change of narrative, denying that the Steele dossier played a role in obtaining the FISA warrant to conduct surveillance on junior Trump campaign official Carter Page. The counter-memo had serious credibility problems, as it cited the appearance of McCabe before the committee in which he testified under oath to the contrary. Trump's enemies on this issue were losing ground and squabbling between themselves.

In the special election to fill the Senate seat vacated by Attorney General Jeff Sessions, Trump parted ways with his former strategist

Steve Bannon, endorsing Luther Strange in the Republican primary. Bannon's candidate, Roy Moore, won the primary runoff and the media trumpeted it as a Trump loss. They adapted their tune, but not its theme, as the story developed. In early November, the hyperactive *Washington Post* opened another front, with the aid of militant feminist lawyer Gloria Allred, and unveiled complainant Leigh Corfman, who alleged that thirty-eight years before, when she was fourteen, Moore had fondled her over her clothing.

Allred, in a career of forty years of relentless controversy, had been involved in scores of sex-related cases, many of them frivolous and vexatious. Her targets included Donald Trump (very late and implausible), Arnold Schwarzenegger, Rush Limbaugh, Michael Jackson, Senator Robert Packwood, Anthony Weiner, Herman Cain, Bill Cosby, Tiger Woods, Meg Whitman (head of eBay), and Roman Polanski. Ms. Allred is something of an ultra-feminist Roy Cohn in drag.

Moore denied the allegations, but was a peculiar candidate regardless, having been twice elected and twice removed as chief justice of Alabama for an unauthorized construction of a large monument to the Ten Commandments within the courthouse, and later for refusing to accept constitutional approval of same-sex marriages. He had been a supporter of the absurd birther movement against President Obama, was a fundamentalist Christian, and was apt to wave a firearm around at election meetings to show his support for the Second Amendment. As it turned out Trump's political instincts were far better than Bannon's. Strange would have won the seat easily (it was a safe Republican seat) but Moore, dogged by endless unfolding controversy, lost by twenty thousand votes out of more than 1.2 million cast. Trump could do without the Moore stigma, but Republican control of the Senate, with elections looming in 2018, was very unstable.

By now, it was clear that the Democrats thought they had a new Waterloo for Trump, on the imperishable misogyny issue. But unfortunately for them a litany of prominent media and Hollywood personalities, most of them associated with the Left, were soon forced out of their careers on the basis of an avalanche of post-Weinstein sex-related grievances, and so were Democratic politicians. Democratic senator Al Franken of Minnesota, a former comedian, was accused, by a Republican talk show hostess and former prominent model, of lewd behavior when they were preparing for a USO tour in 2006 and had a somewhat corroborative photograph; this unleashed the customary sequels of other ostensible victims. Franken denied the subsequent claims and remembered the original one "differently." He put himself in the hands of the Senate ethics committee.

The twenty-seven-term dean of the House of Representatives, African American Democrat John Conyers, was also accused, and at first defended by former speaker Nancy Pelosi as "an icon." When the Democratic leadership assessed the potential of the Moore issue, and further complainants came forward against these and other politicians, they swiftly forced the retirement of Franken and Conyers. They went with docility, victims for the cause.

Overall, media claims that Trump was a boorish misogynist ricocheted around rather hollowly as, to their own collective embarrassment, it seemed as though Hollywood and the media itself harbored the greatest quantity of misogynists and sexual harassers in the country, as new allegedly guilty parties were revealed on a daily basis, including liberal news lions like Charlie Rose and Matt Lauer.

There were more scandals of a more political nature to come. Shortly after the revelation that the Clinton campaign and Democratic National Committee had taken over the Fusion GPS anti-Trump operation and engaged Christopher Steele, former Democratic chair Donna Brazile published a book claiming that Hillary Clinton and her campaign had strangled the Democratic National Committee financially and had rigged primaries against Senator Bernie Sanders (contrary to the Federal Election Campaign Act). It was Ms. Brazile, as WikiLeaks revealed just after the election, who had given Mrs. Clinton advance notice of questions, because, as she later explained, "I did not want Hillary to be blind-sided by questions." She appeared to be oblivious to the fact that a main purpose of such a debate is to test candidates' familiarity with issues.

Mrs. Clinton's denial of the Brazile primary-rigging charges was rather perfunctory, but Elizabeth Warren, the leftist Democratic Massachusetts senator, agreed that Mrs. Clinton had stolen the nomination from Sanders. A couple of days later, as the sexual harassment tide rose, New York Democratic senator Kirsten Gillibrand said President Bill Clinton should have resigned the presidency because of the sexual outrages he committed. This gave the Republicans—including President Trump, tweeting to his scores of millions of followers—and conservative talk show hosts, the opportunity to rake over the Democrats' earlier dismissal of complainants against Bill Clinton's conduct as "bimbos" and "trailer trash" and tools of a "vast right-wing conspiracy."

Trump claimed that Gillibrand in her previous campaigns had begged him for financial assistance and said she would "do anything" for it, which Senator Elizabeth Warren denounced as an attempt to "slut-shame" Gillibrand, which did not do Gillibrand any favors. Indeed, the whole delirious attempt to co-opt the post-Weinstein "me too" movement as a political weapon against Trump backfired nearly every day. Caitlin Flanagan wrote a piece in the *Atlantic* titled, "Reckoning with Bill Clinton's Sex Crimes," which reminded Democrats that they already had a lot to answer for when it came to sexual harassment. This cascade of revelations and the failure of Hillary Clinton's election memoir to be taken seriously as an explanation for her defeat, compromised the position of the Clintons in public esteem. Investigations of her emails and the Clinton Foundation resumed. The book was a toe-curling exercise in blaming everyone else for her electoral loss. Churlish denigrations of Trump and his supporters were scattered throughout the book. Her masquerade as a loving intellectual, every day a celebration of her idyllic and faithful Norman Rockwell, Pleasantville marriage to Bill, strained credibility, even among long-serving Clinton supporters.

At the same time, the Clintons and Obama were struggling in the quagmire of having commissioned the Steele dossier, foisting it on the FBI as Steele shopped it to the most scurrilous media sites, and then invoking it as if it were a serious work of independent sleuthing in accusing Trump of acts of treason. This and the unplumbed depths of the email and uranium controversies appeared likely, eventually, to "ooze out, sluggish and filthy."[2]

While the Democrats were engaged in unwitting acts of self-destruction, the president had a very successful trip in November to Japan, China, South Korea, Vietnam, and the Philippines. The Chinese president Xi Jinping publicly emphasized that China entirely shared American determination that North Korea not become a nuclear military power. Trump claimed progress on trade and monetary differences and picked up tangible investment pledges of $250 billion, and appeared to have reached a complete state of solidarity with Seoul and Tokyo opposite North Korea. Even the most demonically hostile elements of the anti-Trump media could find no fault with his performance and accomplishments (an unprecedented occurrence). Unable to find legitimate cause to criticize the president, CNN's coverage focused on how Trump allegedly overfed the koi fish at Akasaka palace during a photo-op with Japanese prime minister Shinzo Abe, though this turned out to be another instance of "fake news." CNN contradicted the president's medical report and spuriously alleged that he had heart disease.

On December 7, President Trump announced that the U.S. embassy in Israel would be moved to Jerusalem. There was the usual outcry from the Russians (out of sheer hypocrisy as they had made the same move in April 2017); China (which prefers Americans to be mired in Middle East disputes); Western Europe (which has never had any policy in the region except to await the American position and take a stand more favorable to the Arabs); and the Arab and other Muslim powers. The Czechs and Hungarians indicated that they might follow the Americans (as Guatemala did), and Canada and Australia and many other countries were very judicious, deferring statements of any sort. The anti-Israeli Left in America wrung its hands even more vigorously than usual. Rioting, however, was almost entirely confined to Gaza and the West Bank, and by the standards of the region was minor. The Israelis, whose competence at dispersing Palestinian mobs has been amply demonstrated, had no difficulty dealing with riots in Israel-occupied territory.

The whole alignment of forces had changed in the Middle East. Israel's formerly most ardent enemies aren't enemies: Iraq and Syria have disintegrated; Saudi Arabia and Egypt are now Israeli allies against Iran. The Arab governments had used the Palestinians to distract the Arab masses from the misgovernment they were inflicting on them. But in Iran, their ancient Persian foe, they have a real threat and not a mere pretext based on bigotry and political cynicism.

Saudi Arabia was in the midst of an extensive clean-up of its medieval regime by the thirty-two-year-old crown prince Mohammad bin Salman, the first Saudi leader not to be a son of King Ibn Saud, who died in 1953.[3] He perhaps recognized the obvious: the Palestinian leaders could have had a state at any time in the last thirty-five years if they had been prepared to acknowledge Israel's right to exist as a Jewish state, but they would then have led a very small country. The Palestinian leaders had rejected instant floods of foreign assistance and chose celebrity, personal enrichment, and violence; they had allowed the Palestinian people to be used as cannon fodder and now they were no longer useful to Saudi Arabia or Egypt as they were irrelevant to the fight against Iran. Israel posed no threat to Saudi Arabia or Egypt; Iran did.

Donald Trump, as was often the case, sliced through the paralysis and pusillanimity of those invested in the stalled status quo, including the State Department, and did what he had promised to do in announcing that the United States embassy would move to Jerusalem, something his six immediate predecessors had pledged to do and never did. The sanctimony of the British prime minister, Theresa May, in denouncing Trump's action as "unhelpful" was especially galling, given that Britain precipitated the entire problem by promising, in the Balfour declaration of 1917, to make Palestine a "homeland for the Jewish people" without compromising the rights of the Arabs. They sold the same real estate simultaneously to two rival occupants. (Not even Donald Trump in his flamboyant heyday as a Manhattan developer was accused of that.)

On December 21, the United Nations General Assembly voted 128 to nine, with thirty-five abstentions, that the United States had no right to move its embassy in Israel to Jerusalem. The American ambassador to the United Nations, former South Carolina governor Nikki Haley, who has been an impressive spokesperson in that impossible place, warned that the United States "would not continue to pay for the 'dubious privilege' of being disrespected while bankrolling the U.N." On Christmas Day a 25 percent reduction ($285 million) in the annual U.S. contribution to the UN was announced, and there were suggestions that there would be economic reprisals against individual member countries who voted against the United States. Ambassador Haley promised that the vote would be remembered when, "as often happens, American assistance" is solicited by member countries.

With heavy interventions from the White House, Trump's tax reductions and reforms inched through both Houses of Congress, were slightly modified, went to reconciliation, and were adopted. Corporate taxes were cut to 21 percent, most Americans were left off the federal income tax rolls, and more than 80 percent of those who remained would see their taxes reduced. Tax forms would be highly simplified, and American companies were given incentives to return up to three trillion dollars of overseas profits to the United States.

Trump was no less a political hard-baller than his Democratic enemies: the bill retained the provisions that over-spending states like California, New York, and Illinois would have very reduced deductibility of state and local taxes against federal taxes. Also retained by the final tax bill were modest taxes on the incomes of the vast endowments of America's private universities. Many leading figures in the administration consider a large number of American universities to be infestations of the American self-hating Left where underworked and often seditious and over-stuffed faculties churn out under-trained and misdirected graduates, on campuses that frequently discourage freedom of expression. Much of American (and Western) academia was dedicated to the propagation of what the eminent British writer Malcolm Muggeridge fifty years ago called "the great liberal death wish."

The tax bill also struck out the most offensive core of Obamacare, the coercive mandate that fined those who were not insured. With this, Trump would begin the disembowelment of that measure, with which

Obama had addicted much of the country to apparently free medical care while inciting skyrocketing premiums and the rupture of doctor-patient relations for millions of others. With Trump's massive deregulation, economic growth rhetoric, and gradually solidifying promise of tax cuts and reform, economic growth had reached 3 percent, and would have exceeded that without the devastating hurricanes in Texas and Florida, and would approach 4 percent in 2018 (more than double the Obama-era growth rate).

Eleven months into his term, the Dow-Jones Industrial Average had set a new all-time record on sixty-two different days, and it broke twenty-five thousand on January 4, 2018, and twenty-six thousand two weeks later. That indicator had risen since the election by more than 40 percent at the end of January, representing more than six trillion dollars. The Democrats were reduced to their customary railings about a free ride for the rich and their hypocrisy about tax cuts worsening the national debt. Having increased the national debt by $10 trillion (125 percent) under Obama's spendthrift administration, they complained of a projected additional increase, under Trump, as projected by the Congressional Budget Office, of $1.5 trillion in debt over ten years, which would occur only if economic growth were just 1.9 percent, an almost impossibly pessimistic scenario, especially given Trump's sterling record of economic growth during the first twelve months of his administration. The Congressional Budget Office has never predicted anything accurately since the Eisenhower era.

The tax bill wasn't popular at first, because of the class warfare obloquy the Democratic and media propaganda machine heaped upon it, but there was a growing realization of the bill's benefits for working-class Americans. Polls showed ever more support for the measure, especially as businesses shared their tax relief by rewarding workers with bonuses and raises. Former speaker Pelosi dismissed these bonuses and raises as "crumbs," but they went out to many millions of workers and only showed how out of touch Democrats were with what was once their working class base.

Trump's tax bill was, with the Johnson tax reform of 1965 (initiated by President Kennedy) and the Reagan tax reforms of 1981 and 1986, the most important tax bill in American history, and the greatest legislative accomplishment in more than twenty years. Many large companies announced large investments and employment projects in the United States, and the repatriation of immense amounts of accrued profit. Apple was the largest early benefactor, bringing back $350 billion and announcing plans to hire fifty thousand more Americans.

Just as the Republicans were congratulating themselves on their tax triumph, they also had reason to believe that the Democrats' Russian collusion story was turning into a game of Democratic Russian Roulette. The full array of Justice Department, special, and congressional investigations was only unearthing embarrassments of the Democrats. As 2018 dawned, the Democrats on the Senate intelligence committee were still calling for more witnesses and documents, though they had already collected nearly three hundred thousand documents, and reviewed more than five thousand pages of testimony taken in 164 hours of hearings from sixty-seven witnesses. None of it produced anything remotely justifying the entire immense wild goose chase they had launched. But the insufferable Senator Warner and his colleagues fervently wished that it continue even as all the evidence appeared to show that Democrats were guilty of hypocrisy, cynicism, hysteria, and perhaps even collusion themselves in promoting a document, the Steele dossier, chock-full of Russian disinformation.

At time of writing, the war continues, with the media and the Democrats more hostile and frenzied than ever. Al Hunt, a formerly rational *Wall Street Journal* writer, wrote for Bloomberg News on December 10 that Trump might, if accused of wrongdoing, whistle his followers out into the streets of America—the implication was that the sixty-three million people who voted for him would in large numbers respond to a call for civil insurrection from the great rabble-rouser. My dear and esteemed friend David Frum remarked on CNN on December 11 that the chief failing of the media in its coverage of Trump was its "overzealous ambition to be fair to the president." It is hard to foresee how normally reasonable people could be induced to return to their senses anytime soon, having taken such distant leave of them.

The *New York Times*, scrambling to find cover as the Democrats' collusion narrative caved in, conjured up the completely spurious theory that the collusion investigation began because of the drunken indiscretions made by a junior Trump campaign advisor (George Papadopoulos, who pleaded guilty to minor offenses) to the former leader of the opposition in Australia, Alexander Downer in London's Kensington Wine Bar. Papadopoulos's babblings were eventually reported to the State Department, but only after the FBI investigation had begun. The discomfort of the *Times* and less august members of the Resistance in wanting to assign blame for the failing Russian narrative can be gauged by the absurdity of this initiative.

The implausible Carl Bernstein hit the speaking and interview circuit yet again, on the theme of the "constitutional crisis" that might require the removal of the president under the Twenty-Fifth Amendment for mental incompetence and instability. It was like the *New York Times'* Thomas Friedman claiming that the Trump campaign's alleged (and utterly unproven) Russian collusion was equivalent to Pearl Harbor and the terrorist attacks of 9/11, and Nancy Pelosi calling Trump's tax bill "Armageddon" and "the worst legislative disaster in history."

On an even lower level of professionalism and believability was a book by one of the Western world's most malicious and tedious gossips and one of the sleaziest published authors in American history, Michael Wolff (whom the author has encountered). Wolff purported to quote former White House strategist Steve Bannon accusing Donald Trump Jr. of "treason" in the collusion affair. Bannon denied this but the formerly Bannon-hating anti-Trump media briefly cited him respectfully; and if Bannon had spoken to Wolff in this way, out of hatred for certain factions in the White House, it was a suicide move that made one doubt why Trump had retained him in the first place. Trump tweeted that when Bannon "lost his job, he also lost his mind." The night of the publication of excerpts from the book, January 3, Bannon was on the air proclaiming that Trump was "a great man" whom he still supported. On CNN, correspondent Brian Stelter conceded Wolff's book was "sloppy" with errors, but claimed that "many Trump experts say the book 'rings true' overall." In fact, *Fire and Fury* made the Steele dossier seem like Revelation in its moral authority; to anyone who knew Trump, as this author does, it read like a fabricated, confessedly part-fiction, smear job from A to Z.

On January 17, 2018, Trump announced his awards of the most "corrupt and dishonest" political journalists. Paul Krugman, of the *New York Times*, won with his election night prediction that the stock markets would "never recover" from Trump's victory. Among respectable commentators in the press, however, there was a discernible shift away from lunacy. The *Wall Street Journal* seemed dedicated to common sense, and many of Trump's more measured opponents in the *New York Times* or at *National Review* now seemed more interested in setting up a loyal opposition than in reflexive hysteria.

In part this was because such hysteria could not be squared with the facts. Trump completely debunked the argument about his mental competence and stability with a deft, fifty-five-minute, televised White House discussion with the bipartisan congressional leadership about immigration, on January 9. But even this blew up when Senator Dick Durbin a few days later released the claim that Trump had asked why the United States had to accept so many immigrants from "s--thole countries" which was apparently at least a slight misquotation, but it enabled the president's enemies to accuse him of racism, rather than to focus on the president's point, which was that the United States should have a merit-based immigration system that gave preference to immigrants with skills rather than providing a giant welfare state for the world's poor. But whatever harsh language Trump might have used it was as nothing to the sort of language routinely used by Presidents Truman, Johnson, and Nixon (or even Dick Durbin who had once called American troops "Nazis"); and the whole issue was nonsense, which blew over, despite a media frenzy, because Trump's question was likely one held by a majority of Americans as well. It certainly had no perceptible impact on the polls when the government partially shut down on January 20 because of the Democrats' insistence that they would not vote for a stop-gap funding measure unless Congress also voted for the naturalization of eight hundred thousand children brought into the United States by their parents illegally. The shut-down fizzled after one business day, again indicative of how the balance of power in Washington was shifting.

In February, Robert Mueller indicted thirteen Russians, who cannot be extradited, for "conspiring to defraud the United States," by improperly advertising in American social media before and in the election campaign, decrying various conditions of American life and supporting Trump, Sanders, and Green candidate Jill Stein. It was an insignificant, ineffectual bipartisan intervention and the case will never be tried. Not even the Left was excited.

It came to light that the Clinton campaign had been feeding misinformation directly to Steele, and that Senator Warner of Virginia, one of the leaders of the spurious collusion narrative, had been attempting, "without leaving a paper trail," to deal directly with Steele. There were widespread calls for indictments of Comey and McCabe, and even Hillary Clinton. At last, the dangers of the criminalization of policy differences were being exposed. As the long effort to quarantine Trump failed, the Democratic congressional leadership showed signs of cooperating with the administration, and joined in a spending-cap agreement that put off the necessity of hand-to-mouth continuing spending resolutions for over a year. The pretense that Trump was a freakish president who should be impeached on general principle and prevented from governing effectively stopped. He was not a president like the others, but he was the president.

His reflexive denigrators were imperishable but he was unstoppable, and he was a moving target for his enemies. On February 14, an apparently deranged youth killed seventeen people at a high school in Parkland Florida, and Trump called for training and arming some teachers and parted company with the National Rifle Association by proposing curbs of public ownership of automatic weapons. In early March he unveiled proposals for new tariffs on steel and aluminum. On both these issues, as with admission of children who had been brought illegally into the

United States, he had more support from Democrats than Republicans. And he confounded those who had accused him of potentially blundering into war in Korea on March 8, by agreeing to meet with Kim Jong-Un with the goal of military denuclearization of the whole Korean peninsula. The combination of U.S. military force and sanctions and Chinese pressures had finally induced a change, and a compromise slightly like that of the Cuban missile crisis of 1962 seemed likely. No one could accuse Trump of being ineffective. The Republican majority on the House Intelligence Committee closed the committee's Russian collusion investigation on March 12, over Democratic protests, and declared that there was no evidence of collusion with Russians by either party in the 2016 election, though the Russians had spent a million dollars a month on social media lamenting the conditions of America and supporting Sanders and Stein (Green), and Trump. The committee majority did not consider that the Russian intervention had influenced the result. The whole Russia distraction was finally fading.

Nothing was easy and every week was a struggle, but Donald Trump was gradually taking hold of the vast apparatus of the U.S. government. He appeared to be slowly winning his tumultuous crusade against political correctness and systematic defeatism in foreign and domestic policy that had afflicted the U.S. government in all branches and both parties, and had enervated the spirit of the American people. His successful economic record could not be denied. He had made great progress in stopping illegal immigration. He had rolled back unsuccessful trade deals and rejected self-punitive climate change policy initiatives. On the issues of taxes, education reform, energy production, and health care, he had made significant advances. There was progress too in Korea, the Middle East, and Ukraine (where on December 24 Trump announced he would give Ukraine anti-tank weapons to deal with Russian incursions into eastern Ukraine). No one promised, or expected, quick makeovers in these very difficult theaters, but there appeared to be more hope to advance American interests in the world under Donald Trump than there had been under eight years of President Obama, and the sixteen previous years under Presidents George W. Bush and Bill Clinton.

Those who oppose Trump generally do not understand how desperate and disgusted almost half of Americans are at the most inept twenty-year streak of presidential misgovernment in American history that preceded the 2016 election. These decades of fruitless war, bone-cracking recession, humanitarian disasters, collapsing alliances, oceanic deficits, and the erosion of economic growth and private sector industrial investment to a third or a quarter of levels under Ronald Reagan, could rattle any American's patriotic self-confidence. Trump is a throwback to Reagan in that he rejects the chic defeatism of the establishment; and despite all the media and Democratic Party and Never-Trump calumny of him, his political program is essentially conventional, moderate, conservative wisdom lifted in large part from the policy recommendations of thoroughly respectable conservative think tanks such as the Heritage Foundation. Trump speaks to Americans fearful of decline. He wants, as his slogan says, to make America great again.

To those unaffected by the decline of America, that decline was invisible; to those who were affected by it, it is a challenge and a constant fear for their own welfare and national pride. The Democrats have had no policy for some years except to denigrate their opponents, and try to bribe and anesthetize a comatose lumpenproletariat addicted to state benefit. Their nomination of Hillary Clinton showed that they did not realize how many Americans rejected this vision of America.

The great majority of anti-Trump activity in the first year of his administration was devoted to the propagation of falsehoods, which were then justified by the selective and intentional misinterpretation of Trump's careless and ambiguous statements. Distaste for Trump's straight-shooting and sometimes vulgar style caused otherwise intelligent people to withhold any benefit of the doubt, and pathologically to interpret anything he said or did in the worst possible light. He is not, in fact, a racist, sexist, warmonger, hothead, promoter of violence, or a foreign or domestic economic warrior. No opposition can continue on this name-calling basis alone for much longer than this one has.

Every two weeks in the first year of his term a new alarm was raised, and all quickly fell silent. In a calmer atmosphere, the faddish frenzies will become rarer and shorter. For two weeks in August, Confederate statues were being taken down all over the South, but now such iconoclasm happens only intermittently; the abrupt termination of famous careers for alleged sexual liberties that once happened on a daily basis has become much less frequent. Trump's opponents are tenacious but unimaginative and they have yet to seem to prepare for the possibility, now more of a likelihood, that he might be a durable and effective president.

The Democrats committed all their energy to proving their assumed self-evident proposition that Trump could not win, then that his victory could be undone, and then that it could be vitiated by scorched-earth obstruction, or destroyed completely by investigations and indictments. Now that Trump has reduced most peoples' tax burden; relieved the fear that recession and unemployment are just around the corner (in fact provided a booming economy); and adopted a foreign policy of prudent and effective realism that has smashed and scattered ISIS, persuaded China to cooperate against North Korea's nuclear program, and defended American interests; Americans will likely and rightly judge him a success, despite his lapses of suavity. He has been chronically underestimated, as a nonstarter for the Republican nomination until he clinched it; unelectable until he was elected; and likely to be impeached until the investigations faded and his accusers were engulfed in suspicion.

Trump is unpredictable and somewhat erratic, and his stridency and ill-tempered outbursts are not what Americans expect of their presidents. But there is nothing unconstitutional, or even irrational about his use of social media and his aggressive tendency to counterattack (sometimes preemptively). This has been his only available method of surmounting dishonestly partisan and hostile media. The presidency is what its occupants make of it. No president smiled much or took to the airwaves or used airplanes or held frequent news conferences before Franklin D. Roosevelt. Some of Trump's techniques may be emulated by successors. If his policies succeed, so will he. And much more of his histrionics are just tactical than his hard-core critics imagine.

Donald Trump is not a blundering reactionary, but a battle-hardened veteran of very difficult businesses full of unethical people (and he is no

Eagle Scout himself). He is a very tough and an almost demiurgically energetic man. His personality is so startling and at times garish that there is a large section of the population that will not warm to him. But if his persistence brings continued success, he will accede to the support of the majority.

It was always the case that, in making billions of dollars, surmounting an acute financial crisis, being a great television star instantly and for fifteen years, revolutionizing the nature and potential for celebrity, and seizing control of a great political party in his first real try at politics, Donald Trump accomplished more before he was president than had any prior president of the United States except Washington, Jefferson, Madison, Grant, and Eisenhower. His exterior is uneven, but his history is one of astounding accomplishment.

The strange mélange of Donald Trump's virtues and weaknesses is unique in U.S. presidents. He genuinely loves the American people, but he has not always been above trying to pedal them his version of snake oil. He is contemptuous of most of the American financial and social elites as unmeritocratic snobs, who abuse their positions, misgovern the country, and bilk the people. He admires strength and respects earned success in every field.

Trump has promoted Americanism over the atomization of identity politics. His pursuit of America's national interest—with no evangelical or Wilsonian notions of purifying other countries—has been successful to date. His unquenchable energy, gifts as a popular tribune, sheer entertainment talent, and raw toughness have served him well.

Trump has learned something about how to gain and hold the respect that is naturally available to the chief of state, and the country has somewhat got used to him. There are markedly fewer malapropisms, there have been no bungled foreign initiatives, fewer indiscretions, his economic program is working, and his enemies are largely a tired coalition of character assassins and hacks uttering antique class-war claptrap on autocue, or affecting a false and complacent superiority.

On the subject of Donald Trump, righteousness can be overdone, and often is; he has, as has been recounted, his inelegant aspects. But

Benjamin Franklin's role in persuading Britain to expel France from Canada and fifteen years later in persuading France to help expel Britain from America was the ultimate demonstration of the art of the deal. Some of Jefferson's more florid passages in the Declaration of Independence are among history's greatest expositions of truthful hyperbole. In international relations, Richard Nixon was a chess player and Ronald Reagan a poker player, and both were very successful. Trump seems more of a pool shark, but it seems likely he will do well too. Trump isn't very reminiscent of Franklin or Jefferson or FDR or Nixon or Reagan; but he is a man of his times, and his time has come.

With President Trump, no setback is admitted or accepted; for him, rebuffs are really victories, disguised victories, moral victories, or the preludes to victories. Hyperbole, truthful and otherwise, is his common parlance. He speaks for the people, he has been a very successful man, and he has repeatedly outwitted his opponents, which is why he is attacked with such snobbery, envy, and spitefulness. But America is reversing its decline and wrenching itself loose from the habits of lassitude, elitist decay, appeasement of foreign enemies, and domestic inertia. His record is impressive; his foibles are not durably relevant.

Whatever happens, Donald Trump will be one of the most vividly remembered presidents and characters of American history. Difficult though it may be to believe at times, the office of the presidency, in that astonishing, ineluctable, and fateful American way, may have sought the necessary man again.

Acknowledgments

Heartfelt thanks to my wife, Barbara, for her patience, even as she writes a longer and more exacting book herself; to our shared executive assistant, Danella Connors, for her inspiring thoroughness and invaluable help in anything requiring organization and technology; and to my son James for his selfless assistance in research, editorial advice, and always good-humored tutorials in technical areas. And thanks to Nancy Feuerborn and Harry Crocker of Regnery for their unfailing cooperation. Finally, I wish also to thank Rhona Graff of the Trump Organization, for her many kindnesses and courtesies over the years when she was the conduit between Mr. Trump and myself.

Conrad Black
Toronto, February 2018

Notes

Chapter One: The Trumps in America

1. Gwenda Blair, *Donald Trump: The Candidate* (New York: Simon & Schuster, 2015), x.
2. Ibid., 4.
3. Ibid., 14.
4. Michael Kranish and Marc Fisher, *Trump Revealed* (New York: Scribner, 2016), 83.
5. Frequently quoted and confirmed personally to the author by Donald Trump.
6. Donald Trump, *Time to Get Tough* (Washington, DC: Regnery Publishing, 2011), 8.
7. Kranish and Fisher, *Trump Revealed*, 91.
8. Blair, *Donald Trump: The Candidate*, 93.
9. John R. O'Donnell with James Rutherford, *Trumped! The Inside Story of the Real Donald Trump—His Cunning Rise and Spectacular Fall* (New York: Simon & Schuster, 1991), 73–74.
10. Kranish and Fisher, *Trump Revealed*, 137.
11. Ibid., 137 et seq.
12. Blair, *Donald Trump: The Candidate*.
13. Ibid., 139.

Chapter Two: Donald Trump's Financial Crisis and Recovery

1. Kranish and Fisher, *Trump Revealed*, 143.
2. Ibid., 182.
3. Ibid., 165.
4. Ibid., 192.
5. Ibid.
6. Ibid., 197.

Chapter Three: Politics Beckons

1. Kranish and Fisher, *Trump Revealed*, 285.
2. Ibid., 272.
3. Ibid., 286.
4. Ibid., 218.

5. Ibid., 215.
6. Ibid.

Chapter Four: Rebranding for Profit and Elections

1. Kranish and Fisher, *Trump Revealed*, 225.
2. Ibid., 226.
3. Ibid., 237.
4. A typical example of Donald Trump's loyalty to friends was in February 2018, when the veteran vocalist Vic Damone, a neighbor in Palm Beach, was dying. On learning of this from a message from another neighbor though he was overseas, the president telephoned Damone directly in his hospital room, just ten minutes later and greatly cheered the singer's last days.

Chapter Five: Preparing to Seek the Grand Prize

1. Kranish and Fisher, *Trump Revealed*, 289.
2. Ibid., 290.
3. Ibid., 309.
4. Ibid., 312.

Chapter Seven: The Republican Nominee

1. Kranish and Fisher, *Trump Revealed*, 289.
2. Ibid., 338–39.
3. Ibid., 345.
4. David E. Sanger and Maggie Haberman, "50 G.O.P Officials Warn Donald Trump Would Put Nation's Security 'at Risk,'" *New York Times*, August 8, 2016.
5. Sanger and Haberman, "50 G.O.P. Officals."

Chapter Eight: Race to the Wire

1. Nick Corasaniti and Maggie Haberman, "Donald Trump Suggests 'Second Amendment People' Could Act Against Hillary Clinton," *New York Times*, August 9, 2016.
2. Angie Drobnic Holan and Linda Qiu, "2015 Lie of the Year: The Campaign Misstatements of Donald Trump," PolitiFact, December 21, 2015.
3. Though posthumous and unsought, the universal triumph of the Hitler brand for brutal authoritarianism, has been remarkable, due to the constant invocation of him by the Left against any opponent politically to the right of Che Guevara.
4. Ben Wolfgang, *Washington Times*, August 8, 2016.
5. Lisa Lerer and Julie Price, Associated Press, August 20, 2016.

Chapter Nine: President-Elect

1. Hillary Clinton, *What Happened* (New York: Simon & Schuster, 2017), 90.

2. Included in this group were Martin Sheen, Debra Messing, James Cromwell, B. D. Wong, Noah Wyle, Freda Payne, Bob Odenkirk, J. Smith-Cameron, Michael Urie, Moby, Mike Farrell, Richard Schiff, Christine Lahti, Steven Pasquale, Dominique Fumusa, Emily Tyra, Tanya Balsam.

Chapter Ten: President at Last

1. Clinton, *What Happened*, 11.
2. CNN, "Trump: Frederick Douglass 'Is Being Recognized More and More,'" February 2, 2017.

Chapter Eleven: A Honeymoon of Hand-to-Hand Combat

1. Donald J. Trump, @realDonaldTrump, Twitter, March 12, 2017, https://twitter.com.realdonaldtrump/status/863007411132649473?lang=en.
2. Donald J. Trump, @realDonaldTrump, Twitter, June 22, 2017, https://twitter.com.realdonaldtrump/status/877932956458795008?lang=en.
3. James Freeman, "Trump, Pershing and Persuasion," *Wall Street Journal*, August 18, 2017, https://www.wsj.com/articles/trump-pershing-and-persuasion-1503091778.
4. Mueller also unsealed a guilty plea from George Papadopoulos, involving trivial offenses.

Chapter Twelve: Gaining the Upper Hand

1. Clinton Campaign-DNC Paid for Research That Led to the Russia Dossier," *Washington Post*, October 24, 2017; Erin Burnett and David Chalian, Out Front with Erin Burnett, October 24, 2017.
2. James Joyce, *A Portrait of the Artist as a Young Man*, the confession of Stephen Dedalus in all editions.
3. In mid-December, the Saudi crown prince bought a portrait of Jesus Christ by Leonardo da Vinci for $450 million, the highest price ever paid for a work of art. The symbolism may be interesting.

Index

A

ABC News, 43, 103, 171
Abe, Shinzo, 159, 178, 201
Abedin, Huma, 93, 130
Acosta, Jim, 173–74
Adams, John, 64, 74, 137
Adams, John Quincy, 64, 74, 137, 142
Adelman, Ken, 107
Affordable Care Act, xiv, 61, 140, 176–77, 185, 189, 203
al-Assad, Bashar, 164
All in the Family, 76
Allred, Gloria, 198
American Idol, 44
America We Deserve, The, 42
Anderson, Gilllian, 153
André the Giant, 53
Apprentice, The, 43–44, 49, 54, 68, 70
Arpaio, Joe, 75, 184
Art of the Deal, The, 19
Atlantic, the, 158, 200
Atlantic City, NJ, 13–18, 23–25, 27, 29, 33, 53, 65
Azar, Alex, 177

B

Baier, Bret, 76
Baldwin, Alec, 153
Bannon, Steve, 97–98, 140, 180, 198, 206
Barnum, P. T., xii, 48
Barrymore, Drew, 153

Batra, Adrienne, 130
Beame, Abraham, 7, 10
Benanav, Jonathan, 23
Bernstein, Carl, 146, 206
Bessette, Carolyn, 41
Beyoncé, 100, 153
Biden, Joe, 101
Blair, Gwenda, 20
Blitzer, Wolf, 132–33, 146
Bloomberg, Michael, 42, 104
Bloomberg News, 205
Bollenbach, Steve, 30
Boot, Max, 107
Bork, Ellen, 107
Bradley, Bill, 42
Brazile, Donna, 125, 199–200
Breitbart, 97, 280
Bremer, Paul, 59
Brooks, David, 99
Bruni, Carla, 19
Bryan, William Jennings, 79
Brzezinski, Mika, 174
Burnett, Mark, 42–43
Burr, Aaron, 1–2, 142
Burr, Richard, 194
Bush, Billy, 120–23
Bush, George H. W., 19, 38–40, 74, 85, 91
Bush, George W., 40, 42, 44, 59–60, 62–63–64, 70, 91, 99, 101–2, 106, 149–50, 175, 183, 209

Bush, Jeb, 71–72, 79, 81–86, 91, 104, 124

C
Cain, Herman, 198
Camacho, Héctor "Macho Man," 23
Canada, 9, 70, 131–32, 159, 181, 201, 213
Carey, Hugh, 7
Carson, Ben, 79, 82, 85, 141
Carson, Johnny, 14
Carter, Jimmy, 7, 38, 40, 64, 149, 175
Casablanca, 121
CBS, 43, 139–40
Chao, Elaine, 141
Chase Manhattan Bank, 11, 27, 32
Chastain, Jessica, 153
Chávez, Hugo, 119
Cher, 18, 153
Chicago Sun-Times, the, 55
China, 143, 164, 175–78, 201, 211
Christ, Elizabeth, 4
Christie, Chris, 79, 82–83, 85–86, 94–95
Churchill, Winston, xv, 174
CIA, 141, 152, 190
Cleveland, Grover, 64, 104, 148
Clinton, Bill, 38–41, 62, 74, 93, 101, 105, 111, 121–22, 132, 149, 170, 174, 200, 209
Clinton, DeWitt, 104
Clinton, Hillary, xiii, 3, 25, 44, 60, 69, 71, 81, 86, 88–90, 93–102, 104–7, 109–12, 114–27, 129–37, 139, 150, 163, 168–69, 179, 186–87, 194–97, 199–200, 208, 210
Clinton Foundation, 111, 123, 169, 187, 200
Clooney, George, 100
CNN, 94, 105, 118, 131–132, 138, 146–47, 158, 173–74, 182–83, 201, 205, 207
Coats, Dan, 141

Cohen, Eliot, 107
Cohn, Roy, 6, 10, 14, 198
Collins, Susan, 177
Comedy Central, 54
Comey, James B., 93–94, 129–30, 146, 162, 167–71, 186, 191, 193–97, 208
Commentary, 99
Commodore Hotel, 8–9, 11, 32
Conway, Kellyanne, 97–98, 115, 124, 152
Conyers, John, 199
Cooney, Gary, 18
Coons, Chris, 164
Cooper, Anderson, 183
Corfman, Leigh, 198
Corker, Robert, 176, 189–90
Cosby, Bill, 198
Coulter, Ann, 83, 124
Cox, Archibald, 170
Crosby, James, 16
Cruz, Carmen Yulín, 183
Cruz, Ted, xi, 3, 79, 81–83, 85–89, 96, 124
Curiel, Gonzalo, 105
Curtis, Jamie Lee, 153
Cyrus, Miley, 153

D
Daily Mail, the, 56, 172
Davis, Angela, 153
de Blasio, Bill, 118
Delingpole, James, 98
Deng Xiaoping, 114
DeVos, Betsy, 141–42
Diana (princess), 19, 26
Dinkins, David, 31
Dole, Robert, 92
Donnelly, Tom, 107
Doonesbury, 13
Douglass, Frederick, 158
Dowd, James, 44
Downer, Alexander, 206

Drescher, Fran, 153
Drumpf, Friedrich, 4
Duckworth, Tammy, 153
Durbin, Dick, 207

E
Economist, the, 138
Electra, Carmen, 26
el-Sisi, Abdel Fattah, 117–18, 187
Erdogan, Recep Tayyip, 114, 143, 171
Etess, Mark, 23

F
Fahrenthold, David, 67
Farage, Nigel, 115
FBI, 93–94, 129–30, 146, 162, 167–
    68, 170–71, 182, 186–87, 191,
    193–94, 196–97, 200, 206
Ferguson, Niall, 107
Ferrer, Fernando, 42
Fiorina, Carly, 88
Fire and Fury, 207
Fisher, Marc, 95
Florida, xiv, 10, 15, 71, 79, 87, 92, 98,
    116, 133, 159, 164, 182–83, 185,
    204, 208
Flynn, Michael, 157–58, 169, 186,
    195–96
Fonda, Jane, 153
Forbes Magazine, 15, 35
Fox News, 44, 76–77, 125, 156, 159,
    183
Francis (pope), 172
Franken, Al, 199
Friedman, Thomas, 109, 206
Frum, David, 99, 205
Fusion GPS, 147, 193, 196, 199

G
Gates, Rick, 190
Gergen, David, 174
Gibbon, Edward, xv

Gillibrand, Kirsten, 200
Gingrich, Callista, 94
Gingrich, Newt, 68, 83, 94
Giuliani, Rudolph W., 40, 95, 104
Giustra, Frank, 111
Goldwater, Barry, 68, 83, 113
Goodell, Roger, 188
Gore, Al, 40, 42
Gorsuch, Neil, 155
GQ, 56
Graham, Lindsey, 78, 84, 92, 107, 117,
    194
Grande, Ariana, 153
Grassley, Chuck, 194
Green, Mark, 42
Griffin, Kathy, 173
Griffin, Merv, 16, 18

H
Haley, Nikki, 85, 141, 203
Hamilton, 1, 140
Handler, Chelsea, 153
Harris, Kamala, 153
Hayes, Rutherford, 64, 142
Heyer, Heather, 181
Hicks, Hope, 83, 180
Hillary the Horrible, 95
Hitler, Adolf, 119
Hogan, Hulk, 53
Holiday Inn, 14–15
Hollande, Francois, 143
Holt, Lester, 118
Hoover, J. Edgar, 167
Huckabee, Mike, 75, 79, 86, 180
Huffington Post, the, 130
Hume, Brit, 160
Humphrey, Hubert, 104
Hunt, Al, 205
Hyde, Stephen, 16, 23

I
Icahn, Carl, 33, 65–66

Iraq War, 59–60, 107

J

Jackson, Andrew, 137, 142, 155
Jackson, Michael, 14, 24, 198
Jaworski, Leon, 170
Jefferson, Thomas, 1, 142, 212–13
Johansson, Scarlett, 153
John, Elton, 19
John Paul II (pope), 172
Johnson, Boris, 160
Johnson, Gary, 134
Johnson, Lyndon B., 31, 38, 68, 83,
    113, 121, 205, 207
Judd, Ashely, 153

K

Kaepernick, Colin, 188
Kagan, Robert, 107
Kaine, Tim, 101, 140, 179
Kalikow, Peter, 18
Kardashian, Kim, 26
Kasich, John, 83, 85–89, 91, 94, 106,
    121, 133, 142–43
Kelly, John, 141, 180, 189
Kelly, Megyn, 76
Kennedy, Jackie, 57, 172
Kennedy, John F., 39, 83, 121, 205
Kennedy, John F., Jr., 41
Kerouac, Jack, 100
Khan, Ghazala, 102–3
Khan, Humayun, 102–3
Khan, Khizr, 102–3
Khan, Sadiq, 160
Khashoggi, Adnan, 13, 34
Kim Jong Il, 175
Kim Jong-Un, 114, 174, 176, 209
King, Don, 57
King, Larry, 40–41
King, Martin Luther, Jr., 158, 174
Kislyak, Sergey, 157
Klein, Calvin, 19

Knauss, Melania, 26, 41, 56
Koch, Ed, 17–18, 20, 30–31
Kranish, Michael, 95
Kristol, Bill, 100
Krugman, Paul, 207
Ku Klux Klan, 105, 187
Kushner, Jared, 146, 172, 179

L

Larry King Live, 20
Lashley, Bobby, 53
Las Vegas Review-Journal, the, 126
Lauer, Matt, 199
Lee, Robert E., 181
Lessig, Lawrence, 142
Lewandowski, Corey, 69, 75, 83, 91
Lewinsky, Monica, 41
Lewis, John, 147
Lilly, Eli, 177
Limbaugh, Rush, 83, 165, 198
Lively, Blake, 153
Los Angeles Times, the, 115
Lundestad, Geir, 63
Luntz, Frank, 75
Luskin, Don, 182
Lynch, Loretta, 93–94, 187

M

Maas, Heiko, 143
Machado, Alicia, 25, 119
Macron, Emmanuel, 178
Maddow, Rachel, 163
Madonna, 19, 127, 139, 153
Magnitsky, Sergei, 179
Manafort, Paul, 91, 97, 179, 190
Maples, Marla, 16, 56
Mar-a-Lago, 15, 19, 57, 66, 164
Marx, Groucho, 146
Mattis, James, 141, 189
May, Theresa, 154, 159–60, 178, 202
McAuliffe, Terry, 181, 197
McCabe, Andrew, 197, 208

McCain, John, xiii–xiv, 40, 42, 60, 62, 75, 117, 121, 177
McCarthy, Joseph R., 6, 92
McConnell, Mitch, 84, 92, 141, 152, 185
McLeod, Mary, 4
McMahon, Linda, 141
McMahon, Vince, 53, 141
McMaster, H. R., 158
McMullin, Evan, 106, 134
Meet the Press, 41
Merkel, Angela, 143, 160–61, 172, 178
Michigan, xii, 42, 116, 133, 135, 194
Middle East, the, 63, 143, 145, 156–57, 159, 164, 172–73, 201–2, 209
Midelfart, Celina, 56
Mills, Cheryl, 93
Mirren, Helen, 153
Miss Universe, 25, 43, 119
Miss USA, 25, 43
Mnuchin, Steve, 141, 184
Mondale, Walter, 106
Monroe, Marilyn, 16
Moore, Michael, 115, 153
Moore, Roy, 198–99
MSNBC, 119, 138, 163, 174, 182
Mueller, Robert, xv, 170–71, 185, 187, 190, 193–97, 208
Muggeridge, Malcolm, 203
Mukasey, Michael, 107
Mulvaney, Mick, 141
Murdoch, Rupert, 6, 125

N

Nader, Ralph, xiii
National Enquirer, the, 69, 126
National Review, 99, 207
National Rifle Association, 95, 109, 208
Negroponte, John, 107
Netanyahu, Benjamin, 158–59, 170, 172

Never-Trumpers, 76, 88–89, 143, 195
New York Daily News, the, 18
New Yorker, the, 131, 180, 188
New York Magazine, 19
New York Post, the, 18, 67, 156
New York Times, the, 11, 13, 20, 42, 71, 84, 106, 110, 130, 138–39, 141, 162–63, 165, 169, 179, 206–7
NFL, 14, 188
Nixon, Richard, 1–2, 6–7, 39, 75, 83, 89, 95, 146, 168, 170, 175, 196, 207, 213
North Korea, 64, 151, 161,174–76, 187, 189, 201, 211
Nunes, Devin, 161–62

O

Obama, Barack, xiii–xiv, 3, 44–45, 60–65, 69–70, 76, 80–82, 89, 92, 94–95, 99, 101–2, 104–6, 110, 114, 117, 131, 136–37, 139–40, 145, 147, 149, 152, 156–57, 161, 164, 169, 171, 174–78, 180–81, 185–87, 189, 195, 198, 200, 203–4, 209
Obama, Michelle, 94, 101
Obamacare. *See* Affordable Care Act
O'Donnell, Jack, 24, 29
O'Donnell, Rosie, 76
Ohio, xii, 83, 86–87, 91, 106, 116, 121, 133, 143
Ohr, Bruce, 196
Ohr, Nellie, 196
On the Road, 100
Oprah Winfrey, 20
Ornstein, Norman, 113
Oswald, Lee Harvey, 79

P

Packwood, Robert, 198
Page, Carter, 197
Page, Lisa, 196
Papadopoulos, George, 206

Parks, Rosa, 158
Paul, Rand, 86, 143, 177
Pazienza, Vinny, 23
Peale, Norman Vincent, 10, 14, 38, 40, 110, 164, 177
Pelosi, Nancy, 185, 199, 204, 206
Pena Nieto, Enrique, 115
Pence, Mike, 94, 122–24, 140, 142, 144, 175
Pennsylvania, xiv, 5, 89, 98, 116, 121, 133, 135, 194
Perdue, Sonny, 141
Perot, Ross, xiii, 38–40
Perry, Rick, 79–80, 92, 141
Pershing, John J., 84
Pipes, Daniel, 107
Pius XII (pope), 172
Podesta, John, 134
Polanski, Roman, 198
Pompeo, Mike, 141, 190
Post, Marjorie Merriweather, 15
Powell, Colin, 143
Power, Samantha, 145, 186
Prejean, Carrie, 25
Price, Tom, 141, 174, 176–77, 185
Priebus, Reince, 73, 110–11, 120, 140, 180
Pruitt, Scott, 141, 173
Putin, Vladimir, 114, 143, 178–79

R

Rabin, Yitzhak, 110
Rahn, Will, 139
Reagan, Ronald, 1, 3, 6, 17, 20, 27, 37–40, 61, 63, 79, 83, 85–86, 89, 100, 106, 125, 131, 133, 151, 170, 172, 174, 176, 190, 196, 205, 210, 213
Redford, Robert, 13
Remnick, David, 131
Ribble, Reid, 110
Rice, Condoleezza, 121

Rice, Susan, 186
Richards, Cecile, 153
Rigell, Scott, 110
Rivera, Geraldo, 183
Roberts, Julia, 153
Robertson, Lloyd, 132, 134
Rock, Chris, 153
Rockefeller, David, 53
Rockefeller, Nelson, 7, 68
Romney, Mitt, xiv, 60–61, 68, 91, 96, 120, 143
Roosevelt, Franklin D., 38, 74, 98, 132, 148, 151, 172, 211
Roosevelt, Theodore, 74, 79, 176
Rose, Charlie, 199
Rosenstein, Rod, 162, 168, 170–71, 186, 194
Ross, Wilbur, 173
Rosselló, Ricardo, 183
Rove, Karl, 106
Rubio, Marco, 79, 81–83, 85–87, 124
Rumsfeld, Donald, 59
Russert, Tim, 41
Russia, 97, 101, 105, 111, 114, 127, 143, 147–48, 155, 157–58, 161–64, 167–70, 174, 178–79, 182, 185–87, 194–96, 201, 205–6, 208–9

S

Saddam Hussein, 84, 114–15
Saltzman, Chip, 75
Samuelson, Heather, 93
Sanders, Bernie, 3, 86, 88–89, 95, 100, 104, 125, 136, 143, 173, 176, 184, 199–200, 208–9
Sanders, Sarah Huckabee, 180
Saturday Night Live, 54
Scalia, Antonin, 106, 155
Scalise, Steve, 173
Scaramucci, Anthony, 179–80
Scarborough, Joe, 174
Schiff, Adam, 170, 197

Schneiderman, Eric, 49

Schultz, Wasserman, 100

Schumer, Chuck, 142, 155–56, 185

Schwartz, Tony, 19

Schwarzenegger, Arnold, 198

Sessions, Jeff, 92, 141–42, 147, 162–
63, 168, 170, 197

Sex and the City, 54

Shelton, Kathy, 122

Shulkin, David, 141

Shultz, George, 20

Signer, Michael, 181

Silver, Nate, 171

Simpson, O. J., 19

Sinatra, Frank, 19

60 Minutes, 140

Slim, Carlos, 71, 139

Smith, Alfred E., 132

Smith, Liz, 18

Son, Masayoshi, 144

Spellman, Francis J., 6

Spicer, Sean, 152, 179–80

Spielberg, Steven, 14

Spinks, Michael, 18, 25

Spitzer, Eliot, 60–61

Spotted Eagle, Faith, 143

Springsteen, Bruce, 153

Starr, Kenneth, 170

Steele, Christopher, 146, 186, 193–97,
199–200, 205, 207–8

Stein, Jill, 134, 142, 208–9

Steinem, Gloria, 153

Stelter, Brian, 207

Stephanopoulos, George, 103

Stephens, Bret, 99

Stern, Howard, 19, 25–26, 56, 59

Steyn, Mark, 78

Stone, Roger, 41

Stornoway Gazette, 41

Strange, Luther, 198

Streep, Meryl, 100, 145

Streisand, Barbra, 116, 153

Strzok, Peter, 93, 196–97

Swid, Stephen, 31–32

T

tax reform, xiv, 42, 184, 205

Theron, Charlize, 153

Thiel, Peter, 97

Tilden, Samuel, 142

Tillerson, Rex W., 141, 143, 189–90

Toronto Sun, the, 130

Trudeau, Garry, 13

Trudeau, Justin, 159

Trump, Barron, 57

Trump, Donald, Jr., 10–11

Trump, Eric, 10

Trump, Ivanka, 10, 25, 117, 146

Trump, Mary MacLeod, 41

Trump Plaza, 12, 14–15, 23–25, 65

Trump Princess, 13, 27, 30, 34

Trump Taj Mahal, 16–17, 23–24, 27,
32–35, 65

Trump Tower, 10–13, 20, 43, 48, 66–67,
69, 74, 93, 105, 134, 161, 169

Tubman, Harriet, 158

Turnbull, Malcolm, 156–57

Tyson, Mike, 18, 25

U

Umaga the Samoan Bulldozer, 53

USA Today, 126

V

Vanderbilt, Cornelius, 8

Ventura, Jesse, 42

Veselnitskaya, Natalia, 179

W

Walker, Scott, 79–80, 86

Wallace, George C., 90

Wall Street Journal, the, 50, 125, 140,
156, 182, 205, 207

Walsh, Lawrence, 170

Warner, Mark, 194, 205, 208
Warren, Elizabeth, 200
Washington, George, 2
Washington Post, the, 95, 120, 138,
    142, 157–58, 162, 193–94, 198
Washington Times, the, 126
Waters, Maxine, 147
Watson, Emma, 153
Weekly Standard, the, 99–100
Weil Gotshal, 27, 30
Weinberg, Caspar, 20
Weiner, Anthony, 130, 186, 198
Weinstein, Harvey, 187, 198, 200
Westpride, 31–32
What Happened, 194
White House, the, xii, 1, 39, 41, 57,
    89–90, 97, 121–22, 124, 132, 139–
    40, 146, 150, 157, 160, 168, 170,
    172–74, 177, 179–80, 182, 185,
    203, 206–7
Whitman, Meg, 198
Widodo, Joko, 178
WikiLeaks, 100, 114, 119, 121, 125,
    155, 199
Will, George, 99
Williams, Serena, 67
Willkie, Wendell L., 98
Winfrey, Oprah, 19–20, 40
Winklmayr, Ivana Zelnickova, 9–11,
    16, 18–19, 26
Wisconsin, xii, 25, 73, 80, 87, 116,
    120, 133–34, 136, 142, 194
Wolff, Michael, 206–7
Woods, Tiger, 198
Woodward, Bob, ix, 146, 193
Wray, Christopher, 197

X
Xi Jinping, 143, 164, 175, 178, 201

Y
Yanukovych, Viktor, 97

Yates, Sally, 94, 155, 157, 162, 196
Yiannopoulos, Milo, 157
Young, Melissa, 25

Z
Zakaria, Fareed, 131
Zinke, Ryan, 141
Zoellick, Robert, 107